The end of medicine as we know it -
and why your health has a future

Harald H. H. W. Schmidt

The end of medicine as we know it - and why your health has a future

 Springer

Harald H. H. W. Schmidt
Aachen, Germany

ISBN 978-3-030-95295-2   ISBN 978-3-030-95293-8   (eBook)
https://doi.org/10.1007/978-3-030-95293-8

For Beate

Prologue: Many Questions, No Answers

Max has elevated blood pressure. This was discovered by his family doctor during a routine check. Max is prescribed a blood pressure medication, takes it relatively regularly, and the values normalize. 130/80. All good? Not at all, because many questions remain unanswered.

Why did his family doctor prescribe Max a medication in the first place? Well, elevated blood pressure correlates with the occurrence of heart attack or stroke. These and other possible complications from elevated blood pressure should be avoided.

But his family doctor cannot tell him with certainty whether he needs his blood pressure medication or he will benefit from it. The doctor has clinical studies in mind that were carried out with various blood pressure medications showing a reduction in heart attacks or strokes. However, on critical examination, it is noticeable that only a small percentage of patients with elevated blood pressure are at risk to experience a heart attack or stroke. Disappointingly, perfectly lowering the blood pressure in those patients at risk will prevent only a small percentage of these heart attacks or strokes. Most will still experience their heart attack or stroke. That is, most patients have elevated blood pressure but are at no risk and for most patients who were at risk their blood pressure medication ultimately failed to protect them.

However, the Max's GP can by no means advise him to discontinue taking his blood pressure medication because there is no better alternative. Not prescribing anything would put Max at risk that he might be the luckiest one who would have had a heart attack or stroke and could have prevented it by taking his blood pressure medication. So, Max and all other patients of Max's GP get their blood pressure medication prescribed and take it, chronically.

But the doctor has a much bigger problem: only in about 5% of all patients with high blood pressure can a cause for this be found. These include patients in whom one of the blood vessels that supply the kidney with blood is narrowed, causing the kidney to release hormones that lead to an increase in blood pressure.

With Max it is different. Apart from the fact that the blood pressure is elevated, no other diagnosis can be made and the indication for the prescription of the blood pressure medication remains solely the blood pressure itself. Max is no exception. On the contrary, he belongs to the large mass of other patients with elevated blood pressure, approximately 90–95%, for whom the diagnosis is the same as for Max: primary hypertension. This sounds quite scientific, but in normal language means nothing else but, "You have elevated blood pressure, but we don't know why". This explains things. If the actual cause of the elevated blood pressure (and the risk for stroke and heart attack) is not known, the only remaining treatment option is to prescribe drugs that dilate blood vessels, i.e. make the symptom disappear without curing (or even knowing) the cause.

So, in accordance with therapeutic guidelines, the family doctor continues to prescribe Max his blood pressure medication on a regular basis, which is legally, professionally, and ethically fully correct. Over the years, as a chronic hypertension patient, Max puts on some love handles, doesn't exercise much, and his blood pressure rises again, despite being compliant in taking his drugs. The doctor prescribes him thus a second blood pressure medication and eventually a third and, finally, his blood pressure drops again. Good? One of the drugs is suspected of causing white skin cancer, another causes Max to have erectile dysfunction for the first time in his life. So, his doctor finally exchanges both new drugs for two others. While Max is annoyed by all these pills, he also realizes that he is now truly chronically ill and a high-risk patient. He would so much like his high blood pressure problem to disappear, to be literally cured of it, but that doesn't seem to be possible. So, he hopes that he will at least be spared a heart attack or stroke.

There doesn't seem to be any alternative, another doctor whom Max asked for a second opinion recommends the same, and two of his friends have the same problem, they also take blood pressure medication permanently. I guess there's nothing Max can do, or can he?

Acknowledgements

Thank you …

… to the many medical and scientific colleagues who, through their feedback and insights, made it possible for me to gradually develop this comprehensive analysis of the current crisis of Medicine and the proposed solution by Systems Medicine, to my native speaker friend and colleague professor Rob Moulds from my former home, Melbourne, who polished and edited the text, and from Springer Nature to Susanne Dathe, who immediately believed in the success of the book and brought it to completion.

Contents

Part I

Crisis, What Crisis...?

1

Too Late

Dear reader, I am delighted that you are taking the time to join me on a journey. I promise you it will be worth it. It's about medicine and health, but it's about much more than that. It's about the world's next great social and economic revolution, which we are now at the beginning of. And that revolution has even begun is directly relevant to you. Big words, you may be thinking. What can be meant by them?

I am concerned with something of the dimension observed by the Russian economist Nikolai Dimitrijevic Kondratieff in the best-known theory on business cycles with the so-called Kondratieff waves. Historical phases of growth and development in our society since the eighteenth century can often be explained by key technologies and crises that made them necessary. Great inventions change the world: the wheel, the steam engine, the light bulb, and the Internet. What would our lives be like without them? Great inventions take time; sometimes only a massive crisis spurs the introduction of an innovation. But after that, everything is different.

This was the case, for example, with the first Kondratieff wave, the invention of the steam engine. What followed was the so-called industrial revolution with the construction of huge factories. A new age was dawning.

However, this was also the end of the only form of commercial shipping up to then, namely, that with sailing ships. Steam navigation was faster. The introduction of machine labour at sea also meant such a great long-term increase in efficiency that it enabled the expansion of the shipping business. Its expansion by English, Bremen, Dutch, and Belgian shipping companies eventually made sailing ships no longer competitive.

H. H. H. W. Schmidt, *The end of medicine as we know it - and why your health has a future*, https://doi.org/10.1007/978-3-030-95293-8_1

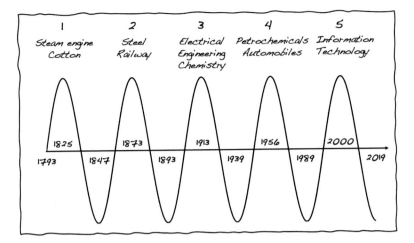

Fig. 1.1 The five Kondratieff waves of socio-economic revolutions through innovations that have had a lasting impact on our society. Typically, at intervals of about two generations and always following a severe crisis. What will the sixth wave be?

But the supporters of sailing did not give in so easily. Concepts that people thought would last forever are not so easily displaced. Just as in the twentieth century, some held the view that no private household needed a computer and that the Internet would remain an episode or at best a secondary tool for the analogue world. The physicist Max Planck wrote in his scientific autobiography that "A new scientific truth does not triumph by convincing its opponents and making them see the light, but rather because its opponents eventually die, and a new generation grows up that is familiar with it". In the same way, supporters of the sailing ship doubted for a long time that the sailing ship was of yesterday (Fig. 1.1).[1]

Similarly epochal were the three other socio-economic revolutions that Kondratieff himself still defined: the introduction of steel production and railways, then electrical engineering and chemistry, and finally the automobile and atomic power. Even the invention of the incandescent lamp was not a gradual development of a candle but something completely new. Candle lighting was henceforth only decoration, nostalgia.

And since then? The fifth wave? While no longer defined by Kondratieff himself, I think you'll agree that the last major revolution of this kind we

---

[1] Merkel C (2004) The industrialization of merchant shipping in the second half of the 19th century. The example of the "Hamburg-Amerikanische Packetfahrt-Aktiengesellschaft" (HAPAG), Helmut Schmidt University University of the Federal Armed Forces, Hamburg, https://edoc.sub.uni-hamburg.de//hsu/volltexte/2018/3203/pdf/Merkel_Christoph_Die_Industrialisierung_der_Handelsschifffahrt_in_der_zweiten_Haelfte_des_19._Jahrhunderts._Das_Beispiel_der_HAPAG.pdf

experienced was the introduction of information technology: computers, the Internet, and the smartphone. This was made possible by the rapid rate at which microprocessors became faster and smaller. But now we are at the end of that revolution. With Google, Amazon, Apple, and others, seven out of ten of the world's most valuable companies are now no longer linear industries that develop, produce, and distribute a product around the world but so-called platforms that can do basically anything. I'll come back to that later.

Now what? If you hadn't already read the title of the book, you might think: Industry 4.0, renewable energies, and climate catastrophe mark the further waves. But in my opinion, these keywords do not stand for the next big revolution. Industry 4.0 is a modest innovation, mostly doing the same thing as before, only more digitally. Renewable energies and the techniques for them to mitigate climate catastrophe have long been available in principle. They just must be used; the rest is management.

I would not have written this book, nor completely turned my entire scientific work around, if I were not convinced that the sixth Kondratieff wave will be a complete redefinition of health, disease, prevention, treatment, and healing and will do so in a maximally democratic, cost-saving way; this also means that the new medicine that thus emerges will not be a luxury medicine of the rich industrial nations and their citizens but can benefit all people.

But as with all Kondratieff waves, all this will not happen just because new technologies are available but because the enormous crisis of current medicine and our healthcare system will leave us no other choice. There will also be great resistance to overcome, just as Max Planck described. You may now ask, "Crisis? What crisis?" Read on.

Crisis, What Crisis?

My book initially consists of two parts, a negative description of the present and a positive prediction of the future. So, at the beginning, it is about the negative, the crisis, which first creates the pressure to act, in order to then bring about the radical change in medicine in the future. Does the second part contain pure dreams of the future? No. Because fortunately we are already at the beginning of the revolutionary further or new development of medicine, so that I can show you many examples of how the current weaknesses and errors can be corrected. In order not to give you the feeling that you have only read a foretaste of a wonderful but still distant future of medicine, a small third part follows at the end with concrete tips that you can already use or apply to take advantage of the innovations already available, because the future has already begun.

In the first part, I will show you that up to now almost no disease is understood regarding its causes. Therefore, early diagnoses are out of the question, but we wait or are surprised by the first symptoms. After that, as a rule, only a treatment of the symptoms remains, which, since we do not know the causes of the disease, is imprecise and usually must be carried out chronically. Cure is impossible. Or do you think that the medicine you are chronically prescribed and take will give you an advantage? You will be surprised: In most cases, it does not. You may even only feel the side effects.

The increase in life expectancy and quality of life has been stagnating for many years, even though we are pumping more and more money into our healthcare system, partly through the wrong incentives. Both research and the pharmaceutical industry, once known as Big Pharma—when some of them were still among the ten largest companies in the world—are stagnating. More than half of published biomedical research turns out afterwards not to be reproducible and serves only to enable research careers. The pharmaceutical industry is currently running into the wall; it will disappear in its current form within the next 10 years. The approach of starting early with prevention instead of taking drugs late in the course of a disease remains largely unused, although a large proportion of all chronic diseases could be prevented or at least favourably influenced by healthier lifestyles and environmental factors. One cause is certainly the lack of knowledge about the simplest components of a healthy lifestyle. A lack of education costs 8 years of life; if you are also male, your life expectancy is reduced by another 7 years. And the scary thing is that the two add up. Uneducated men live 15 years shorter than educated women. So, do you agree with me that we have a crisis?

Before I go into detail with you, I would like to make one comment beforehand that is very close to my heart. I will make a lot of criticisms below, and I will back them up, but please do not take this as a blanket condemnation of all doctors, scientists, and industry researchers. Most doctors, except for a few black sheep, want solely and absolutely the best for their patients and do the humanly possible to do so. But they can only do what is medically possible at all. If the diagnoses and possible therapies are as imprecise as they are, even the most dedicated doctor cannot change this. The pharmaceutical industry, too, can only develop precise drugs if there are precise disease definitions. If the research business runs the way it does, then an individual scientist cannot change it so easily without falling out of the system—and certainly not a young up-and-coming scientist.

What I will have no sympathy for, however, is as follows: If, after (!) reading this book, those who can make important decisions in biomedical research, at universities and in the health system—and I will name horses and riders—still claim afterwards that we can continue as before, then they are acting against their better judgement. I would therefore like to make a significant difference in the healthcare system and in biomedical research or to give it a lasting impetus. Let us therefore go into the details.

We Have a Disease System

If we are honest, we do not currently have a health system but a disease system. The insurance case usually only occurs when symptoms appear, and a disease exists. These are then treated, usually chronically.

It is usually the case that suddenly—as described in the prologue—a measured value that the doctor routinely determines is no longer within the normal range, and this several times. For example, an elevated blood pressure is measured, or cholesterol levels are elevated, or blood sugar is elevated. Until now, the patient has felt nothing, has felt perfectly healthy, and now this. He would still feel healthy if the doctor did not tell him that he was now a patient.

However, it can also be that you suddenly notice symptoms in yourself out of complete health or have the first complaints, for example, sudden heart pain during exertion. Or you notice that you can no longer breathe so well, for example, in spring when the pollen count is high or in the cold. Or jogging or even climbing stairs doesn't go so well anymore, and you must slow down or take a break more and more often. Or your shoulder, hip, or knee hurts more and more often.

So, what's the diagnosis? Usually the same as the symptoms: If blood pressure is elevated, then the diagnosis is hypertension, or in Latin, but not more accurately, primary hypertension; if cholesterol is elevated, then the diagnosis is hypercholesterolemia, which means nothing more than the cholesterol in your blood is elevated, only in Latin. Or if you get out of breath quickly because your heart is weaker, then the diagnosis is heart failure, which means nothing more than your heart is not functioning well. Or if you have trouble breathing even at rest because your airways are constricted, then the diagnosis may be bronchial asthma, which means nothing more than those bronchial tubes are constricted and you have trouble breathing—but you already knew that.

I like to use the car as a figurative comparison. That's partly because we Germans—especially us men—look after our cars so lovingly and take them in for maintenance more often than we do ourselves, but we hardly ever take ourselves for a "check-up". So, imagine you take your car to the garage because the headlights have failed for the third time in the past few months. After a thorough inspection of the car, the workshop foreman diagnoses a chronic headlight defect. You look puzzled and ask whether the diagnosis could be made a little more precisely, because you already know that the headlights are always broken. You don't need to come to the workshop for that. What you're interested in is why it happens all the time, what's behind it, and what you can do to stop it from happening. The actual cause of defective headlights could, if it remains undetected in the long term, perhaps cause much greater damage: You'll be stuck on the motorway with your car at some point because perhaps the whole electrical system has failed, the alternator is damaged, or the battery was too old. In any case, as a car owner, you wouldn't let up, and if the garage sticks to its terse diagnosis, you'd probably change garages soon and tell your acquaintances: "Well, you can't go there anymore. They have no idea. I can do what they can do. You don't need a garage for that."

Well, but with ourselves, with our own body, we accept that we are not told the cause or that the physical symptom becomes the diagnosis of the disease. Therefore, only the symptom can be treated. And since the cause is not treated, the symptoms keep coming back and must be treated again. In this way, we become chronically ill and have a chronic disease. These include, for example, cardiovascular disease, cancer, and chronic lung disease. These three disease groups alone account for three quarters of all deaths and about a quarter of all medical costs. In addition, there are chronic diseases of the musculature, bones, and joints as well as of the psyche, impaired vision, or hearing problems. And one in ten Germans is now diabetic!

Now you might say to yourself that your blood pressure medication lowers your blood pressure after all if you take it regularly—in which, by the way, only one-fifth of all blood pressure patients do. But what exactly happens when you take it? Your blood pressure medication can work in two main ways. It can cause your blood vessels to dilate, in which—surprise, surprise!— your blood pressure drops, much like how in a garden hose the pressure drops as the diameter of the hose gets larger. Another type of blood pressure medication causes your heart to beat more slowly. So, less blood is pumped into the blood vessels, and that's another way your blood pressure drops—kind of like turning off the faucet your garden hose is barely connected to.

But why is this not enough? Let's stay with the example of the garden hose outside the house. The garden hose itself will not be the problem. But maybe, for example, the water pump in your house is defective, and thus the pressure in the whole house is much too high. But you don't know this possible cause, and so the symptom is treated at the garden hose until, yes, at some point, a water pipe bursts in the house, the house is flooded, and huge, perhaps irreparable water damage has occurred.

The same applies to your blood pressure. Why your blood pressure has risen and whether your blood pressure rise has the same cause as that of other patients remains unclear in most cases; in the case of high blood pressure, this applies to 95% of all patients. As a high blood pressure patient, you come to the doctor's office regularly from now on, you get your prescription, at some point you don't even see the doctor anymore, but only call the receptionist that you need another prescription, and so on. Still all good? No. Whether there were alternatives to drugs and whether you will really benefit from these blood pressure drugs will remain unanswered for you until the same thing happens as with the house water pipe. Serious damage occurs. In the case of high blood pressure, this could be sudden cardiac death or cerebral haemorrhage, for example. Only a few of these complications are prevented by anti-hypertensives. But we will come to that later.

It is the same with cholesterol. Your corresponding value in the blood drops because you take one of the so-called cholesterol-lowering drugs. They work mainly in the liver and cause cholesterol to be transported out of the blood. The cholesterol level in your blood drops. Everything okay? No. Why cholesterol levels had risen, whether there were alternatives to drug treatment, and whether you will really benefit from these cholesterol-lowering drugs will remain unanswered for you throughout your life until, as with the blood pressure-lowering drugs in the above example, you do have a heart attack or stroke at some point—because only very few of the heart attacks and strokes are prevented by cholesterol-lowering drugs.

And the same can be said for heart failure and asthma. In the case of heart failure or cardiac insufficiency, about half of all forms are not even symptomatically treatable, and one in ten patients die within 2 years. This is a worse prognosis than for many cancers.

As an asthmatic, they take either medications that dilate the airways (again, like the garden hose example and high blood pressure) or those that have anti-inflammatory effects. But why your airways narrowed or why they were inflamed remains unanswered in most cases. The symptoms are eliminated; nothing more is possible. In the case of asthmatics, it can at least be said that their life expectancy is the same as that of a healthy person if they are treated appropriately and their quality of life need by no means be restricted either. Nevertheless, the cause remains undetected and untreated.

Medicine and our healthcare system are therefore essentially geared towards illness, do not know the causes of the illnesses, and treat patients symptomatically to try to prevent more serious consequences—and chronically, since a cure cannot be achieved in this way. For example, 10% of all 18- to 29-year-olds are already classified as chronically ill; from 30 onwards, one in five; from

60 onwards, over a third; and from 70 onwards, one in two. That diseases increase with age may still be expected—but why are so many diseases chronic?

All Are Satisfied

There are many reasons for this, and although all those involved in the system, such as doctors, health insurers, patients, drug manufacturers, and so on, have somehow come to terms with this situation, including financially, I would not accuse anyone of doing so out of commercial interest. We simply cannot do any better in medicine at present.

The cause is unclear not only in my favourite example hypertension (because it is so common and grotesque) but also in almost all diseases, especially chronic ones. By cause, we mean the exact molecular mechanism that causes the symptoms. By molecular mechanism, we mean the exact knowledge of which molecules, messengers, hormones, or signalling pathways in our body are altered so that the symptoms arise but also the long-term serious consequences, such as a heart attack or stroke. It makes a huge difference whether I look at symptoms or causes. If I only treat symptoms and not the causes, the symptoms will keep coming back and must be treated again and again. Only when I have found the cause is there any hope of a cure in principle. But since this is not the case with most illnesses, the patient is defined as chronically ill, and the symptoms recur again and again and must be constantly suppressed.

Mostly the symptom treatment is done with drugs. Approximately 70% of all medical measures involve the prescription of a drug. What is the state of the art or what is considered to be the state of the art within a country or healthcare system is laid down in so-called treatment guidelines. Ideally, these are based on solid scientific findings, but often they are based on expert opinions. We have seen how these can diverge fundamentally in the Corona pandemic.

It is important for the system that guideline-based treatment is reimbursed by the health insurance companies. This way, everyone is satisfied: You as a patient think—at least until you have finished reading the first part of my book—that you have been treated well. You are a chronic patient. The doctor has a regular patient with you, who has his insurance card scanned every quarter, because you need a new prescription—officially, of course, only after a personal discussion with the attending physician, which can be billed to the health insurance company, and not just with the receptionist at the front desk. Also, the pharmacy is content, a prescription and perhaps still another auxiliary sale each quarter (an incentive to advise critically does not exist, since pharmacists do not get their medicament consultation but exclude their costs after delivered medicaments refunded). The pharmaceutical industry is also satisfied and so is the hospital, since the symptoms occasionally become more serious and hospitalization is necessary (Fig. 1.2).

Everything goes hand in hand. Not perfect, but everyone involved has somehow settled in. But what is the catch in this disease system? It lies in the fact that the outcome, in terms of consequences relevant to the patient, is completely uncertain. Because treating the symptoms is often not what the patient really cares about, it's the long-term consequences: Blood pressure doesn't hurt but the sudden cardiac death or cerebral haemorrhage associated with it; even the elevated blood cholesterol doesn't hurt but the heart attack or stroke associated with it; the occasional shortness of breath doesn't hurt but the fatal heart failure associated with it; even the elevated sugar levels don't bother the diabetic for a long time, but the more important question is whether he is protected from kidney failure, nerve damage, and blindness. No doctor can promise all these to the patient. The outcome is and remains uncertain. But please come back next quarter for the prescription. Can you at least assume that you are getting at least some small benefit from the drug you are taking? No, on the contrary, you can assume that you won't get any benefit.

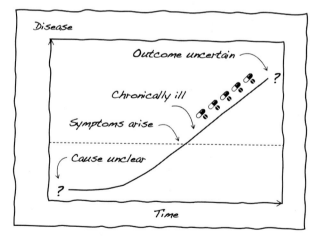

Fig. 1.2 The development of a chronic disease. Below the timeline, on the left the worsening of the symptoms or disease. For a long time, nothing happens; you don't even know that a disease is bubbling up inside you. Its causes are also unclear. Then suddenly symptoms appear that need treatment. But the cause is still unclear. So, only your symptoms can be cured again and again by taking pills regularly. The actual cause of the disease, however, continues to bubble up inside you, and whether you will suffer a serious complication at some point as a result or die earlier remains uncertain throughout your life

2

Don't Rely on Your Prescription

Most likely it's not working for you. When you are prescribed a medicine and take it, you do so in the hope that you will have a benefit from it. Why else would you take it? But, unfortunately, in far too many cases, that hope is deceptive. Because every day, millions of people take medications that won't benefit them.

How do I come up with this? Well, for example, all clinical studies on the ten best-selling drugs in the USA in 2015 showed that they help only every fifth or even only 1 in 25 patients. This means that 4 out of 5 or 24 out of 25 patients get no benefit from their prescription drug at all!

These are not selected examples but rather the rule and can in principle be applied to almost all drugs. For some drugs, such as the cholesterol-lowering drugs routinely used to lower cholesterol levels, known as statins, only 1 in 50 patients benefits.[1] Moreover, there are drugs that are harmful to certain ethnic groups because most trials are tested on white Western patients. One example is long-acting drugs that dilate the airways, which can[2] cause life-threatening side effects and deaths in African Americans.

One reason for this lack of precision in drug therapy is again the difference between symptom and cause. In most drug approval studies, only a handful of measurements are made and only on a few hundred to thousand patients. What is currently important in these studies to companies and regulators is not whether each patient had a benefit but just whether on average, i.e. when

---

[1] Mukherjee D & Topol EJ (2002) Pharmacogenomics in cardiovascular diseases. Prog Cardiovasc Dis 44:479–498, https://doi.org/10.1053/pcad.2002.123467

[2] Currie GP et al. (2006) Long-acting beta2-agonists in asthma: not so SMART? Drug Saf 29:647–656, https://doi.org/10.2165/00002018-200629080-00002

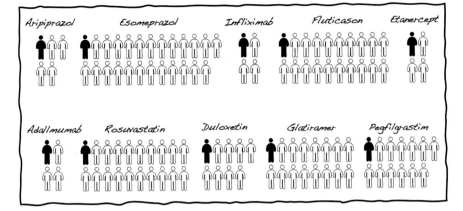

Fig. 2.1 Only the patients shown in black have a benefit from their drug; patients in white have none or, in the worst case, may suffer from side effects. There are hardly any possibilities to differentiate between the two patient groups before starting a therapy. (Adapted from: Schork NJ (2015) Personalized medicine: time for one-person trials. Nature 520:609–611, https://doi.org/10.1038/520609a)

comparing the combined values of all patients in the treated versus those in the untreated groups, a statistically significant benefit could be measured. As you can derive from the above examples in Fig. 2.1, a positive effect in 1 in 50 or more patients may be sufficient to reach this significance (and registration of the drug).

However, to reach this one patient, we unnecessarily expose the other much larger fraction of patients to the risk of side effects with no associated benefit. Table 2.1 shows, by way of example, six clinical drug trials that are considered landmark successes in cardiovascular medicine and based on which new drugs were included in important therapeutic guidelines that affect millions of patients, e.g. cholesterol-lowering drug simvastatin, the blood pressure-lowering drug ramipril, and blood thinners such as aspirin, clopidogrel, abciximab, and other thrombolytics.

You may be surprised to learn that even though only 1.9–9% of patients benefited from their medication and 91–98.1% had no benefit or only a risk of adverse side effects, these drugs were registered and included in all major guidelines for the treatment of cardiovascular disease. You might say to yourself: These are disappointing results, and therefore these imprecise drugs should not have been approved or marketed in the first place. Unfortunately, compared to many other drugs and their precision, these are quite good data! This is the best we can do now, and we cannot leave these patients untreated; otherwise, we would not even be protecting the 1.9–9% of patients for whom the drugs were of help, often saving their lives. This is the disadvantage of pursuing patient-relevant goals (i.e. preventing heart attacks, strokes, or

Table 2.1 Six clinical trials the led to the registration of new drugs and the percentage of patients that had a benefit or no benefit from them[a]

Drugs	Symptom (indication)	Therapeutic goal relevant for patients	Patients having		Study name
			A benefit (in %)	No benefit (in %)	
Simvastatin	Elevated cholesterol	Coronary heart disease	9	91	4S
Ramipril	Increased blood pressure	Heart attack or stroke	3.8	96.2	HOPE
Aspirin		Heart attack or stroke	4	96	APTC
Clopidogrel		Angina pectoris	2.2	97.8	CURE
Abciximab		Acute myocardial infarction	4.5	95.5	EPIC
Various thrombolytics		Acute myocardial infarction	1.9	98.1	FTT

[a] Abbreviations: 4S: J Kjekshus, TR Pedersen Reducing the risk of coronary events: Evidence from the Scandinavian Simvastatin Survival Study (4S) Am J Cardiol, 76 (1995), pp. 64C–68C; HOPE: S Yusuf, P Sleight, J Pogue, et al. Effects of an angiotensin-converting-enzyme inhibitor, ramipril, on cardiovascular events in high-risk patients. The Heart Outcomes Prevention Evaluation Study Investigators N Engl J Med, 342 (2000), pp. 145–153; APTC: Antiplatelet Trialists' Collaboration. Collaborative overview of randomised trials of antiplatelet therapy-I: Prevention of death, myocardial infarction, and stroke by prolonged antiplatelet therapy in various categories of patients. Br Med J, 308 (1994), pp. 81–106; FTT: Fibrinolytic Therapy Trialists' FTT Collaborative Group Indications for fibrinolytic therapy in suspected acute myocardial infarction: Collaborative overview of early mortality and major morbidity results from all randomised trials of more than 1000 patients. Fibrinolytic Therapy Trialists' (FTT) Collaborative Group Lancet, 343 (1994), pp. 311–322; EPIC: The EPIC Investigation. Use of a monoclonal antibody directed against the platelet glycoprotein IIb/IIIa receptor in high-risk coronary angioplasty. N Engl J Med, 330 (1994), pp. 956–961; CURE: S Yusuf, F Zhao, SR Mehta, et al. Effects of clopidogrel in addition to aspirin in patients with acute coronary syndromes without ST-segment elevation N Engl J Med, 345 (2001), pp. 494–502

death) but only being able to treat symptoms or risk factors (cholesterol, blood pressure).

However, there is another downer, because these success rates are probably not transferable to you as a patient. In such studies, the participating patients are rather hand-picked to ensure that the study will be positive; these patients may have little to do with you. For example, they may be middle-aged, have no other disease (comorbidity), and so on. In addition, patients participating in clinical studies are monitored very closely to ensure that they take their medicines regularly and in the correct amounts. In the real world, unfortunately, things are quite different. Even I find it difficult when I must take an antibiotic for a few days and remember taking it every morning and evening. However, older patients are often prescribed four or more medicines, and it is obviously easy to forget one of them by which the so-called compliance decreases and the medication may on one day be forgotten and, on another day, taken twice.

A typical example of poor patient compliance is beta-blockers and their use to lower blood pressure. One of their side effects is that they paradoxically constrict the blood vessels in the hands and feet but also in the penis. One possible consequence is therefore erectile dysfunction. Because of this, patients like to skip the beta-blocker occasionally or even for a longer period. Shortly before the next visit to the doctor, of course, they take them again, the blood pressure is then normal, and everyone (the patient and the doctor) is happy. Now you might think: Never mind, the chance that the beta-blocker will help the patient is small anyway, according to what I wrote above. It is small, that is true, but this patient could be just the "lucky" one for whom the beta-blocker would have saved his life, and during all the days when he did not take it, this—albeit small—protection was not there (see also further down in Sect. 2.1).

On the other hand, in large studies, which, after many millions of euros have been invested in development, are ultimately about approval, the patient groups are put together in such a way that the probability of a positive effect is as high as possible. This can mean selecting patients with high-risk or severe symptoms, those who are not too old but also not too young, and those with as few additional diseases as possible. After approval in everyday medical practice, patients with milder symptoms or lower risk, also older patients than in the study, and also those with additional diseases are then treated, of course. The consequence of this in such so-called "real-world" patients is that the effect is even less or the side effects are more severe than in the original approval study. In the case of some drugs such as statins, which are routinely used to lower cholesterol levels, it is possible that only 1 in 50 normal patients will benefit, and in the case of antihypertensives, only 1 in 100. As a reminder, this means that for 49 or 99 patients, it will make no difference to them in the example whether they take their drugs or not; they will have no advantage but rather disadvantages.

Since we currently have for most drugs no way to distinguish between those patients who will have a benefit and the many others who will not, we must treat all of them. Please do not (!) take all these examples as a reason to now discontinue any of your medications. You don't know to which group you belong, perhaps exactly to the one for whom the drug would have been a lifesaver, e.g. prevented a serious heart attack or a stroke. We simply don't know and neither does your doctor. So, it is not a mistake on your doctor's part to prescribe you this drug. There is currently no better alternative. It is probably not even a mistake on your doctor's part not to tell you about the lack of precision of your drug and the low probability that you will benefit from it. If he did that with all patients, it is quite likely that soon none of his patients would be taking his medication, not even those whose lives he could have saved. So, if the potential side effects are not too serious, you just accept that risk. You must accept it.

You might be thinking to yourself that this almost sounds like a scandal. Or you may question me. Have I possibly picked out a few extreme examples of drugs to dramatize and make my point? You may think, "After all, don't many of the other drugs work for most patients?" No, let's dive even deeper into numbers (not too much, don't worry; I'm not a fan of math, but it's important and enlightening), namely, the key term in all of this, the "number needed to treat".

The Number Needed to Treat

There is a way to understand or calculate how much a medicine has to offer to an individual patient. It is a simple statistical concept called the "number needed to treat" or "NNT" for short, i.e. the number of patients that must be treated so that one patient has a benefit. The NNT measures the effect of a drug or other therapy, such as a surgery, by estimating the number of patients who need to be treated to achieve a positive, desired effect for one person, such as preventing a disease risk like heart attack or a stroke. The concept is somewhat dry statistics, but still plausible, since we now know that not all people benefit from a drug or intervention—some benefit, some are harmed, and some remain unaffected.

The NNT can be calculated from any clinical trial of a drug or other intervention such as surgery, etc. Since most drugs and interventions have been studied in a clinical trial at some point, we can estimate an NNT for many (if not most) of the medical treatments. This means that physicians and their patients can easily determine the likelihood that a patient will be helped or harmed by a particular drug or procedure. You can research the NNT for any drug and its use on the NNT Team website.[3] This group of physicians, established in 2010 and led by the emergency medicine physician Shahriar

---

[3] The NNT. Therapy (NNT) Reviews https://www.thennt.com/home-nnt/

Zehtabchi, has developed a unique system to evaluate either therapies (based on their patient-relevant benefits or harms, respectively) or diagnostics (based on symptoms, lab tests, or clinical trials) in a way that is very easy for anyone to understand.

In addition to the NNT, another not unimportant figure can be calculated, namely, the "number needed to harm" (NNH), i.e. the number of patients that must be treated until one patient will experience a relevant, severe side effect due to drug. One can then compare both numbers in order to establish a so-called benefit-risk ratio.

The NNT team uses only the highest quality evidence-based studies[4] and does not accept third-party funding or advertising. For example, you can search there for the cholesterol-lowering drugs called statins, and you will find different options (Table 2.2): for cardiovascular prevention in a patient with or without pre-existing risk, for a patient with a known heart disease, or for a patient with acute angina or myocardial infarction. Let us consider the most common case: a patient without any previous heart disease, who is prescribed a statin on the basis of his personal risk profile and elevated blood cholesterol levels, to prevent serious cardiovascular diseases, e.g. a heart attack or a stroke or even death.

It is surprising that not a single life is saved and only two serious events such as a heart attack or stroke are prevented, for which, however, a total of 258 patients (104 + 154) had to be treated. A caveat to these figures is that it is controversial whether statins reduce mortality in this group of patients. The NNT team does not believe that this is the case but is aware that others interpret the available data differently.

The most common side effect of statin treatment is severe muscle pain or muscle damage, a side effect that is still relatively easy to notice and attribute to statins. The frequency of 1 in 10 listed here, i.e. 10%, is intensely discussed

Table 2.2 Benefit (number needed to treat, NNT) and risk (number needed to harm, NNH) of cholesterol-lowering statins in patients at risk but without prior heart disease[a]

Advantage	NNT	Disadvantage	NNH
Lives saved	0	Diabetes developed	1 in 30
Heart attack prevented	1 in 104	Muscle damage	1 in 10
Stroke prevented	1 in 154		

[a] The NNT. Statin Drugs Given for 5 Years for Heart Disease Prevention (Without Known Heart Disease) https://www.thennt.com/nnt/statins-for-heart-disease-prevention-without-prior-heart-disease-2

---

[4] Cochrane Germany. Cochrane systematic reviews https://www.cochrane.de/de/systematische-uebersichtsarbeiten

and may be a relatively conservative estimate for this side effect.[5] However, this side effect may be one of the main reasons why patients so often discontinue statins on their own or at least take them irregularly.[6]

Another worrying side effect is new diabetes mellitus induced by statins.[7] The risk of 1:50 is estimated again rather conservatively. Since up to 10% of all Western industrialized societies are already diabetic, these patients are at risk of worsening their existing (pre)diabetes, making them incapable of ever controlling or curing their diabetes with lifestyle changes. Because such patients are usually excluded from statin trials, this risk can only be estimated. Also, the sources of most of these data are industry-funded studies, suggesting that the above figures (1:50 risk) represent more of a best-case scenario.

So, are statins an appropriate choice for the prevention of a heart attack or stroke? At the very least, this example illustrates that the symptom of "elevated cholesterol" does not necessarily mean that one should immediately take a statin. This should be carefully considered together with one or more physicians—of course also with a view to the individual preferences of the patient and their ability and willingness to first try lifestyle changes. In the best case, there is a benefit to statins, but the potential harm is easily underestimated. The alternative of lifestyle changes such as a more or purely plant-based diet may be more effective than statin drugs in achieving cardiovascular benefits and without causing potential harm.

To hide these unattractive NNT figures, industry plays a trick to make the risk reduction by a drug look much better than it is and use it for marketing purposes. And I think that many a doctor have already fallen for this and still do. Unfortunately, we must dive into mathematics a little bit further. Please follow me; it's worth it.

Absolute and Relative Risk

With a drug therapy, I want to reduce or ideally eliminate a serious disease risk. There are two ways of presenting this risk reduction: in absolute or relative values. In controlled clinical trials of a medical intervention (drugs, surgery, etc.), there is typically an endpoint that is as patient relevant as possible

---

[5] Fernandez G et al. (2011) Statin myopathy: a common dilemma not reflected in clinical trials. Cleve Clin J Med. 78:393–403.

[6] Jackevicius CA et al. (2002) Adherence with statin therapy in elderly patients with and without acute coronary syndromes. JAMA. 2002; 288:462–467.

[7] Culver AL et al. (2012) Statin use and risk of diabetes mellitus in postmenopausal women in the Women's Health Initiative. Arch Intern Med 172:144–52.

and allows to measure whether the intervention was superior to standard therapy or not. In the most extreme case, this can be fewer deaths or not experiencing a heart attack or a stroke. In Fig. 2.2, I have simplified the numbers a bit to make them easier to calculate, but in principle they match real clinical trial examples as in Tables 2.1 and 2.2. Let's assume for a drug an NNT of 50 to avoiding one death. This means in percent that 2% of all treated patients have a major benefit because they will not die for the duration of the trial, e.g. 5 years. Now, fortunately, very few patients die at all during such trial. Let's assume that, without treatment, out of 100 patients there are 10 patients who will die, and now, with treatment, there are 2 less, i.e. only 8, but5 these 8 still die despite of the therapy. The absolute risk reduction (ARR), i.e. taking all patients into account that have been treated, is then 2%. Marketing-wise this doesn't sound particularly impressive, but it is honest and includes all patients who took the drug. Accordingly, 98% of the patients have no advantage: 90% would not have died anyways—with or without the drug—and 8% died despite taking the drug. What pharma marketing, however, does is to calculate another value, which is not fundamentally wrong but can be used to mislead doctors and patients if the ARR is no longer mentioned. Here, the relative risk reduction (RRR) is calculated by looking solely at the deaths and

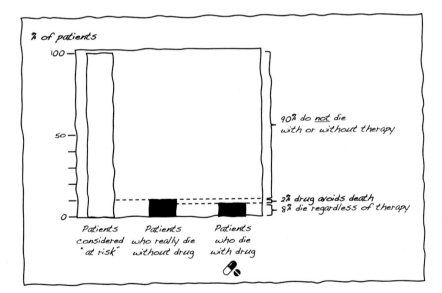

Fig. 2.2 How to present risk honestly and for marketing. One hundred patients are treated. Ten would die if untreated (white bars) and only eight if treated (black bars), equal to a benefit for two patients. The ARR is 2%, and the RRR 20%. Twenty percent sounds better

ignoring all other patients, who still took the medicine. Accordingly, ten die without therapy and only eight with therapy, which can be expressed as a 20% reduction in relative risk (RRR). Twenty percent sounds of course much more impressive than 2%. It is not incorrect but hides the many patients that were never at risk and still took the medication according to in inclusion criteria or—later in real life—according to therapeutic guidelines.

The problem with this kind of data presentation is that, while mathematically and semantically correct, it is deeply misleading. This is because, after all, both patient and doctor have no way of knowing before treatment begins whether a patient will be helped, harmed, or not affected at all by the treatment. If, in a conversation with a patient, the RRR is used to describe how likely it is that the therapy will succeed (i.e. it reduces the chance of dying by 20% in the above example), then we have ignored the much greater probability of 98% that a patient will have no benefit of the drug.

Individuals or groups with a commercial profit motive may thus attempt to influence a patient in a particular direction. This is where the NNT would be most valuable, as a tool to standardize communication. The NNT uses only the ARR. When patients and physicians use the NNT, there is no deception or exaggeration as to the expected effect. Once the calculation and concept of the NNT is understood, it is easy to use. But as obviously useful as the NNT is, it is unfortunately not used in everyday medical practice. Many physicians are even surprised at how high the NNT is for the drugs they routinely prescribe—even though every physician should be able to read clinical studies correctly and interpret them critically.

Now there is one more complication missing for all these considerations, the change from relatively artificial study conditions to the real world, i.e. data with relevance for the average patient, not only those hand-picked for the industry's pivotal registration study. By their very nature, these real-world data can only be collected after approval in so-called follow-up studies, when the new drug is used in everyday life, i.e. in "normal" patients and not those who have been selected for an industry approval study and optimally adjusted in terms of drug dosage. Under these so-called "real-world" conditions, the ARR and the NNT can then deteriorate significantly, often even to such an extent that a new drug is reassessed as without any benefit compared to the previously existing standard therapy and sometimes even withdrawn from the market if, for example, previously unobserved side effects are added. New drugs are always riskier. Old drugs have been prescribed millions of times and we know their risks. A major risk that occurs in every 1000 patients will most likely be missed in a trial that enrolled only 500 patients.

This scenario gets even harder if there is already an effective therapy on the market. In that case, any new drug must not be tested against no drug but against the existing one and show an additional benefit, either a higher benefit or less side effects. This is, of course, even more difficult to achieve, in particular because of our current imprecise disease definitions, i.e. mainly symptoms. Then, even several thousands of patients are included in a study to distil out minute added benefits. If one follows up after the approval of a drug whether this trial benefit is maintained in the real world, nothing of the benefit sustains. Does this rarely happen? Surprisingly, no. In fact, it is rather the rule: Sometimes the harm may even begin to outweigh the benefit, and the drug must be taken off the market.

New Drugs Mostly Without Any Benefit

Standard of care is an approved and reimbursed measure for which a benefit has been demonstrated according to the standards of evidence-based medicine, i.e. based on studies with patient-relevant outcomes such as mortality, disease incidence, or health-related quality of life. The added benefit of a new drug is primarily determined by a direct or appropriate indirect comparison with this standard of care using the same endpoints. Evidence requires a statistically significant benefit for the patient-relevant outcomes in a clinical trial. To enter the market, the responsible drug company must submit a standardized dossier containing all available evidence of the additional benefit of the drug compared to standard of care. After market entry, independent authorities conduct a benefit assessment. The results of this serve as the basis for the final decision on whether there is an added benefit.

The conclusions on an added benefit have two important functions. First, they serve as a basis for price negotiations between health insurers and the drug manufacturer. Even if it is concluded that a new drug has no added benefit, the drug may remain on the market but may then not cost more than standard of care. Second, the conclusions can be subsequently used for medical treatment guidelines by medical societies facilitating then individual treatment decisions by your doctor.

In 2019, an overview was published of drugs assessed between 2011 and 2017 that entered the market after approval: a total of 152 new active substances and 64 already approved drugs but in a new indication.[8] Only 54 of the 216 drugs (only 25%) were classified as having considerable or major added

---

[8] Wieseler et al. (2019) New drugs: where did we go wrong and what can we do better? BMJ 366:l4340.

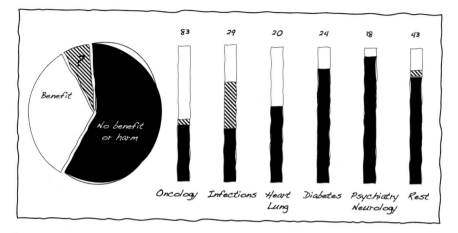

Fig. 2.3 Added benefit of new drugs. White, drugs with additional benefit compared to standard of care; black, without. Bars show the same data differentiated by indication

benefit. For 35 (16%), the added benefit was either minor or could not be quantified. For 125 drugs (58%), i.e. well over half, no additional benefit over standard of care could be demonstrated in terms of mortality, disease frequency, or health-related quality of life in the approved patient population (Fig. 2.3).

If these data are broken down even further between different medical specialties, the situation is in some areas downright alarming. For example, in psychiatry/neurology and diabetes, an additional benefit was proven in only 6% (1/18) and 17% (1/6) of the assessments, respectively (right part of Fig. 2.3). The numbers above the bars in Fig. 2.3 also show that the development and approval of drugs is not evenly distributed across different indications. There is a strong tendency of the pharmaceutical industry to develop more cancer drugs and fewer psychiatric or neurological drugs. Many companies have almost withdrawn from the last two indications.

Currently, all drug regulators worldwide pursue a strategy of speeding up drug approval[9] based on the assumption that faster access to new medicines will benefit patients. The rhetoric of novelty and innovation creates a belief that new medicines are always better than existing ones. While there have been undoubtedly dramatic gaps in the drug arsenal (see the previous chapter) since the 1970s, only a limited number, under 15%, of new drugs offer real advances over existing drugs and without a trend toward improvement. Drug regulators wanted—or were pushed—to provide early access to new drugs.

---

[9] Makady A et al. (2018) Using real-world data in health technology assessment (HTA) practice: a comparative study of five HTA agencies. Pharmacoeconomics. 36:359–368, https://doi.org/10.1007/s40273-017-0596-z

The hope was to compensate for the lack of limited information at the time of accelerated regulatory approval by ensuring that subsequent widespread patient use and research would eventually prove the benefit to patients.[10] However, the reality is quite different. For example, a systematic review of cancer drugs approved between 2009 and 2013 showed that most of them had been approved without evidence of clinically meaningful benefit for patient-relevant outcomes (survival and quality of life), and a few years later this situation had hardly changed.[11] Perhaps even more worryingly, a large systematic review of new drugs for over 100 indications found that superior efficacy was confirmed in less than 10% and 20% of[12] cases,[13] respectively. In addition, such post-marketing studies, in which the drug companies are obliged to conduct after registration, are often not carried out, and only half of them are completed on time or within 5–6 years.[14] Regulators worldwide do little to sanction noncompliant companies.

Pseudo-Innovative "Me Too" Drugs

Even among drugs with an additional benefit, there are many pseudo-innovations, so-called "me too" drugs. Once a company has discovered a new effective drug principle, other companies follow suit and want to market similar drugs based on the same principle. It's like the car industry: If one company starts selling SUVs successfully, everyone wants to do it. If another company starts selling mini-SUVs, everyone follows suit. That's not what innovation is about; at least no carmaker would dare to claim that.

As a result, 12 out of 48 (25%) recent successful drug evaluations in oncology all had the same mechanism of action. Similarly, all recent drugs that showed an added benefit in hepatitis C use one of the same three mechanisms or combined them. When a drug is similar, this does not automatically mean

---

[10] Eichler HG et al. (2015) From adaptive licensing to adaptive pathways: delivering a flexible life-span approach to bring new drugs to patients. Clin Pharmacol Ther 97:234–46, https://doi.org/10.1002/cpt.59 pmid:25669457.

[11] Davis C et al. (2017) Availability of evidence of benefits on overall survival and quality of life of cancer drugs approved by European Medicines Agency: retrospective cohort study of drug approvals 2009–13. BMJ 359:j4530, https://doi.org/10.1136/bmj.j4530 pmid:28978555.

[12] Gyawali B et al. (2019) Assessment of the clinical benefit of cancer drugs receiving accelerated approval. JAMA Intern Med, https://doi.org/10.1001/jamainternmed.2019.0462 pmid:31135808.

[13] Pease AM et al. (2017) Postapproval studies of drugs initially approved by the FDA on the basis of limited evidence: systematic review. BMJ 357:j1680, https://doi.org/10.1136/bmj.j1680 pmid:28468750.

[14] Woloshin S et al. (2017) The fate of FDA postapproval studies. N Engl J Med 377:1114–7, https://doi.org/10.1056/NEJMp1705800 pmid:28930510.

it is the same. And the future does not bode well either. Analyses of drug development pipelines show a similar pattern. Many ongoing and planned trials in oncology are investigating drugs with the same mechanism.[15] From a patient perspective, this is concerning on two fronts. On the one hand, patients participate in industry-sponsored studies (financially attractive to conduct for hospitals) but are not expected to experience any real improvement over standard therapy, and, on the other hand, these same patients cannot be recruited into other possibly more innovative investigator-initiated studies (which cost money to hospitals or require the extra effort of attracting research grants). Thus, money is wasted on superfluous developments, and new approaches with innovative mechanisms of action are not developed and tested. The me-too trend is one of the biggest obstacles to medical progress with respect to drug therapy.[16]

Given the current information gaps, it is not possible to provide doctors, and especially patients, with impartial and complete information about what to expect from a particular treatment, including information about the benefits of alternative treatments or no treatment. This impairs the ability of patients to make informed treatment decisions consistent with their preferences. Ultimately, this leads to an unethical situation for any healthcare system that claims to be patient centred.[17] Since drug development, approval, reimbursement, and pricing are highly regulated, the current situation ultimately points to a profound failure of health policymakers and regulators. Often, the final counterargument is that several "me too" drugs on the market would drive down costs, as the healthcare system would then not be confronted with a monopoly and possibly persistently high prices. Unfortunately, in most cases, this hope for competitive price reductions does not materialize.[18] And even if there were a significant impact on pricing, it still would not require the immense "me too" development that is currently the case.[19]

---

[15] Tang J et al. (2018) Comprehensive analysis of the clinical immuno-oncology landscape. Ann Oncol 29:84–91, https://doi.org/10.1093/annonc/mdx755 pmid:29228097.

[16] Fojo T (2017) Cancer therapies and the problem of me too many. Semin Oncol 44:113, https://doi.org/10.1053/j.seminoncol.2017.06.004 pmid:28923208.

[17] Weeks JC et al. (2012) Patients' expectations about effects of chemotherapy for advanced cancer. N Engl J Med 367:1616–25, https://doi.org/10.1056/NEJMoa1204410 pmid:23094723; London AJ & Kimmelman J (2016) Accelerated drug approval and health inequality. JAMA Intern Med 176:883–4, https://doi.org/10.1001/jamainternmed.2016.2534 pmid:27295005.

Wise PH (2016) Cancer drugs, survival, and ethics. BMJ 355:i5792, https://doi.org/10.1136/bmj.i5792 pmid:27920029.

[18] Gordon N et al. (2018) Trajectories of Injectable Cancer Drug Costs After Launch in the United States. JCO 36:319–325.

[19] Tang J et al. (2018) Comprehensive analysis of the clinical immuno-oncology landscape. Ann Oncol 29:84–91.

The issues with the current drugs do unfortunately not stop here. Even the most effective and safe drug, when given alone, can still create problems, when combined with others. Who takes most of the drugs? Older people. And they usually have more than one condition, and so, over time, many take a difficult-to-manage number of drugs prescribed by different doctors plus over-the-counter drugs purchased by themselves. This day-to-day therapeutic reality is called polypharmacy, and it can create problems that patients would never have had without their drugs.

Polypharmacy or Polymedication

Through our aging societies and the chronification of disease because we can't cure them, we are entering an era of polypharmacy, using more and more drugs simultaneously to treat, for example, just cardiovascular diseases. A typical guideline-appropriate drug regimen for heart failure includes four or more drugs for the same patient. Most patients with coronary artery disease receive aspirin, β-blockers, nitrates, ACE inhibitors, statins, and clopidogrel. Thus, 80-year-old patients can easily receive an average of eight drugs. This is hardly surprising when one realizes that every therapeutic guideline recommends an average of three drugs per diagnosis. However, the term polypharmacy is unfair. It suggests that many medicines are dispensed uncontrolled by pharmacies. This is not the case; most problems result from different doctors prescribing several drugs for the same patient without cross-checking the prescriptions of the other doctors plus any self-medication by the patient. So, to be fair, it is rather a physician and data integration problem. Let's call it a polymedication problem.

From a medical and drug therapy point of view, elderly people, children, and pregnant women are considered a special patient group. Elderly people differ greatly from the rest of the population in the way their bodies interact with medicines. This concerns absorption into the body, for example, from a tablet, how the drug is distributed in the body, how it is metabolized, and how it is excreted. For example, if liver function is impaired, many drugs are metabolized more slowly, which can lead to higher blood levels and a much too strong effect. Similarly, kidney function may be impaired, which also leads to a drug being excreted more slowly through the urine, again increasing blood levels and therefore potency over a longer period. For a single drug, this could still be adjusted via a change in dosage by a careful prescribing physician who considers, for example, a patient's liver and kidney function. The problem, however, is that older people often take multiple medications as more and more disease diagnoses are added with age. One third of all men and women over the age of 65 take five or more medications.[20] People over the age of 80 have an average of three diagnoses,[21] which further aggravates polymedication.

This means that older people are almost seven times as likely as younger people to suffer adverse drug reactions requiring hospitalization.[22] Adverse drug reactions are a relevant reason for emergency room visits, accounting for an average of 6.5%, frequently lead to hospital admissions,[23] and are the fourth leading cause of death.[24] Since elderly people are often excluded from drug studies (companies want to demonstrate a safety profile as good as possible), there are usually hardly any data regarding safety, efficacy, risks, and benefits of drug therapy for the elderly and consequently very few clear therapeutic guidelines for this age group. This is often presented as a special case of "gerontomedicine" or "gerontotherapy"; however, quantitatively it represents rather the rule in everyday medicine, not a special case. There is therefore a great need to improve the quality of the individualization of pharmaceutical care and thus ultimately the quality of life of older people.

A similar risk holds true for drug therapy in children. There are almost no clinical studies, and all dosages in children are estimates. Many drugs used in children have not been sufficiently tested in children (most parents will not make their child available for a drug study unless it is a life-threatening situation and last resort) and are therefore not approved for children. Therefore, the appropriate dosage—that is, the dosage that is both effective and safe—is usually not known at all. In addition, there is often a lack of dosage forms suitable for children. Thus, paediatricians are often dependent on using drugs that have only been adequately tested on adults. At least children do typically not have a polymedication problem as they usually take only a few drugs or only occasionally.

Another issue in elderly patients goes beyond drug-drug interactions but pertains to the drug effects themselves. Many drugs lower muscular tone, walking speed (or gait), and safety and thus increase the risk of falls; they may

[20] Barmer GEK Drug Prescription Report 2013, www.khbrisch.de/files/barmer_gek_arzneimittelreport_2013.pdf

[21] Van den Akker M et al. (1998) Multimorbidity in general practice: prevalence, incidence, and determinants of co-occurring chronic and recurrent diseases. J Clin Epidemiol 51:367–75.

[22] Budnitz DS et al. (2006) National surveillance of emergency department visits for outpatient adverse drug events. JAMA 296:1858–66.

[23] Schurig A et al. (2018) Adverse drug reactions (ADRs) in hospital emergency departments. Dtsch Arztebl Int 115:251–8, https://doi.org/10.3238/arztebl.2018.0251

[24] Light D (2010) Bearing the risks of prescription drugs. In: Light DW, ed. The Risks of Prescription Drugs. New York, NY: Columbia University Press, pp. 1–39.

promote cognitive impairment and even drug-induced dementia and prolong hospital treatment times. To make drug therapy safer for elderly patients and to avoid polymedication-related hospital admissions and deaths, so-called negative lists have been developed, for example, the Beers Criteria list, the STOPP criteria (Screening Tool of Older Persons' Prescription), or the PRISCUS list.[25] They have been developed to support the optimization of medication regimens by deleting drugs. Such "negative lists" are easy to apply because they are clear recommendations that do not require in-depth knowledge about the patient.

One core document for polymedication to prevent or reduce risks would be a thorough medication plan, at least for special patient groups, in particular elderly patients, but this is rarely in use or if it exists has many gaps not patient-friendly designed. In that respect, pharmaceutical competence is clearly underused in many countries. Whereas in some countries it is common practice that the diagnosis is the responsibility of the physician, but the medication is at least in part the responsibility of the pharmacist, in others physicians are still completely in charge of both. For example, the USA has up to 17.5, and the UK has an average of 4.4 pharmacists per 100 hospital beds, but others such as Germany have less than 0.4. In the USA, pharmacists calculate each dosage and compile the drugs on the basis of lists of interactions and the doctors' instructions; in most German hospitals, the pharmacist only visits the ward twice a year as part of the legally required inspections.[26] This also coincides with highly diverse curricula for pharmacy students. In the Netherlands, the curriculum is highly modern and therapeutically orientated; in Germany, students spend a large part of their time dealing with last century chemical analysis and synthesis methods as well as herbal biology, which they will hardly ever need in their later professional life.

Well-trained clinical pharmacists can distinguish the symptoms of a polypharmaceutical prescription cascade from those of a disease. However, this could deprive hospitals in some healthcare systems of income, where every new diagnosis can be labelled and charged to health insurance funds. In the case of simple drug side effects or interactions, the causative drug would simply be discontinued or exchanged, whereupon the symptoms of the side effect or interaction (and thus the revenue-generating diagnosis) would disappear. In this way, hospital pharmacists would put the brakes on the diagnosis and

---

[25] Wehling M (2011) Guideline-driven polypharmacy in elderly, multimorbid patients is basically flawed: there are almost no guidelines for these patients. J Am Geriatr Soc 59:376–77.

[26] Chamber of Pharmacists of Lower Saxony. 2017. For more patient safety: Why do we need ward pharmacists? https://www.apothekerkammer-niedersachsen.de/index.php?did=26&view=3319,4&print=1

remuneration turbo triggered by some healthcare systems. However, the patient would benefit, and this is what should count.

Official medication plans should remedy the risk of polymedication, i.e. from three or more medicines upwards. However, patient surveys have shown that many patients misunderstand these plans and abbreviations. Of the patients, 50% had difficulties in understanding and 18% did not understand the plan even after explanation by the doctor. In addition, the medication plan provides very little space for patient-relevant information on medication use and precautions. The family pharmacy would be the ideal point of contact for such a medication plan, since this is also where the information on the medicines purchased over the counter by the patient is on file and can be integrated. If a patient has one general practitioner and several specialists, confusion sets in and information on self-medication depends solely on the patient's memory. So far, however, medication plans have been anything but common. Only 23% of patients have a medication plan at all, and, of these, only 60% are issued by physicians. The rest are made up by patients themselves and relatives. The plans look correspondingly different. Sometimes medications are noted twice—and are obviously taken twice. Other medications that should not be taken together are listed to be taken at the same time. Often the times of taking the medication and the mode of taking the medication (before the meal/after the meal) are not considered. Electronic prescriptions could be a solution as these will be in the cloud or electronic patient record and thus equally visible to all parties involved—doctor, pharmacist, and patient.

But polymedication, more side effects, and the resulting occasional hospital admissions are ultimately the least of the problems associated with being "chronically ill." Being chronically ill is lonely and costs quality of life and years of life, so that in some countries life expectancy is beginning to decline—not exactly what we hope for from progress in medicine.

3

Chronic Disease?

There is no uniform definition for being "chronically ill" or even "chronic"; not even the duration is defined.[1] Is one chronically ill from 1 year of suffering? Or already from 6 months or only from 2 years? For sure, chronically ill patients are under lifelong medical control and treatment.

Most chronic diseases—with only a few exceptions—are not transmissible, i.e. not contagious; they are therefore not infectious diseases. Apart from that, in chronic diseases, very different organs and bodily functions can be affected, sometimes at the same time: joints (e.g. osteoarthritis, arthritis), heart (e.g. coronary heart disease, heart failure), lungs (e.g. asthma, chronic obstructive pulmonary disease), brain (mental disorders and dementia), kidney (diabetes), and, in cancer, in principle all organs.

Not understanding the causes of diseases and thus making them chronic has implications far beyond having to take medicines permanently or polymedication. The number of chronically ill patients and the extent of multimorbidity—i.e. the permanent suffering from several diseases at the same time—cost quality of life and shorten life. Moreover, our entire healthcare system is mainly aligned to focus on treating or managing chronic diseases, alas, with little success. The supposed progress in healthy life expectancy is stagnating; indeed, in some industrialized countries such as the USA and UK, total life expectancy is already falling. "Pumping" more money into such systems is obviously not the answer. The problems and causes are conceptual.

---

[1] Compendium "Chronisch Kranksein in Deutschland Zahlen, Fakten, Versorgungserfahrungen", Institute of General Medicine, Goethe University Frankfurt http://publikationen.ub.uni-frankfurt.de/frontdoor/index/index/docId/55045

Chronic Sickness Costs Quality of Life

The social and family consequences for the chronically ill patients and their relatives are often dramatic. This is because, in addition to a doctor, they have many different points of contact with the health and care system, from nursing to the social court. These are usually much more frequent and more unpleasant and stressful than those of a "normal" sick person. Both too many contacts and interventions and constantly changing contact persons in the care system can become a considerable burden. Great deficits exist as well, for example, in the support of mentally ill people with dramatic consequences.

The trend to deinstitutionalize (i.e. remove disabled people from custody and segregation in homes and institutions to a supervised everyday life) mentally ill people, but at the same time have a lack of parallel, supportive measures, leads among other things to high unemployment rates and—in extreme cases—to homelessness due to the shortage of cheap housing. Thus, mental illness is much more prevalent among homeless people compared to the general population. Ninety-three percent have met the criteria for at least one psychiatric diagnosis (excluding personality disorders) during their lifetime.[2] When examining whether homelessness causes the mental illness, or mental illness causes the homelessness, for two-thirds of respondents, the mental health condition existed 6.5 years before they lost the roof over their heads. This suggests that poorly served mentally ill people slide disproportionately into homelessness. Although this is an extreme example, it shows that the problems of the chronically ill go far beyond symptoms, medication, and other therapy.

The rest of the population, however, notices little of this, because being chronically ill makes people lonely and invisible. Moreover, loneliness perpetuates or intensifies an illness.[3] Loneliness is becoming the defining condition of the twenty-first century.[4] The risk of loneliness and social isolation, for example, due to illness, also has economic causes in many cases, or these social conditions increase the risk for loneliness. The proportion of people with few or no social relationships increases as income falls. People in the lower income bracket are much less involved in social relationship networks than the average

---

[2] Fichter et al. (2000) Dt Ärztebl 97:A-1148–1154, https://www.aerzteblatt.de/archiv/22758/Praevalenz-koerperlicher-und-seelischer-Erkrankungen-Daten-einer-repraesentativen-Stichprobe-obdachloser-Maenner; Bäuml J et al. (2016) Homelessness or mental illness - which came first? Results of the Munich SEEWOLF study (Mental illness rates in homelessness facilities in the greater Munich area), Gesundheitswesen 78:V83, https://doi.org/10.1055/s-0036-1578898

[3] Loneliness and health. In: The loneliness book. How health professionals can understand, accompany and integratelonely people, 2018, ed. Hax-Schoppenhorst, T., hogrefe AG, Bern, Switzerland.

[4] Hertz N, The Lonely Century, Sceptre, 394 p., 2020.

Fig. 3.1 Mortality rates for all causes (dashed line), noninfectious causes (solid line), and infectious diseases (dotted line) in the USA from 1900 to 1996

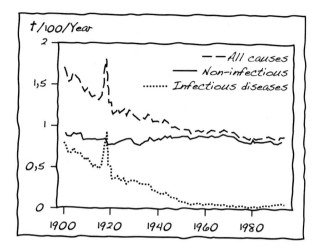

population.[5] Chronic illnesses therefore have a dramatic to existential impact on quality and enjoyment of life, which should be unacceptable enough for our solidarity society. Unfortunately, the effects of chronic illness go even further.

Chronic Illness Shortens Life

You might ask yourself: Why does being chronically ill shorten one's life when our high-tech medicine has achieved so much, especially an ever-increasing life expectancy and decreasing mortality? You read about this everywhere. In fact, at least in relatively highly developed countries, mortality has fallen significantly since 1900, and life expectancy has increased (Fig. 3.1). So, we are healthier and living longer. But to what is this due? In the very largest part, this is a result of our ability to prevent infections or, if an infection has occurred, to treat it effectively. Three components have contributed to this:

1. Better hygiene
2. The possibility to be vaccinated
3. Effective antibiotics in cases of infection

If you take out the share of these three measures and therapies, there is not much left for medical innovation. Some causes of death have decreased;

[5] European Foundation for the Improvement of Living and Working Conditions, European Quality of Life Survey, 2003, https://www.eurofound.europa.eu/de/surveys/european-quality-of-life-surveys/european-quality-of-life-survey-2003/eqls-2003-main-findings; Eurostat, "European Union Survey of Income and Living Conditions" (EU-SILC), 2006, https://ec.europa.eu/eurostat/de/web/microdata/european-union-statistics-on-income-and-living-conditions; European Social Survey (ESS), 2008, https://www.europeansocialsurvey.org

others—especially those caused by chronic diseases—have increased. Surprisingly, if one excludes the effect of being able to prevent or treat infections more effectively, not much improvement in mortality or life expectancy since 1900 remains.[6] The decline in mortality from infectious diseases paralleled the decline in overall mortality in the first half of the twentieth century. The mortality rate from all other noninfectious causes has been surprisingly constant since 1900, with only some small fluctuations from year to year. Whenever there has been an increase in overall mortality, it has generally occurred in the same years that the mortality rate from infectious diseases increased. Now you might think, "As people get older, new diseases come along, such as cancer or Alzheimer's, which then contribute to mortality again". Or: "In the past, people didn't have cancer because they didn't get old enough to experience their cancer in the first place". But this is not true; the shape of these curves changes little when the data are age-adjusted to the 2000 population. Similarly, adjusting the data to account for changes in disease classification (i.e. less cardiovascular disease and more lung disease and cancers) results in little change in the overall shape of the curve.

Mortality from infectious diseases declined markedly during the first eight decades of the twentieth century, from 1900 to 1980. However, the decline was abruptly interrupted by a catastrophically large increase in mortality caused by the so-called Spanish flu of 1918. From 1938 to 1952, the decline in mortality per year was particularly rapid. Throughout the twentieth century, pneumonia and influenza (flu) accounted for most of all deaths from infectious diseases, but, after 1945, tuberculosis accounted for hardly any, and pneumonia and flu accounted for significantly fewer. In the 1980s and early 1990s, the emergence of AIDS was added; in late 1997, an outbreak of avian influenza in Hong Kong from the H5N1 viral strain, previously unknown to infect humans, served as a reminder that pandemic viral influenza remained a threat.[7] While many Asian countries then prepared for[8] a similar outbreak with prevention and pandemic control scenarios, almost all other countries failed to do so, which would be avenged in the COVID-19 pandemic caused by SARS-CoV-2 starting in 2019. The COVID-19 pandemic triggered significant mortality increases of a magnitude not witnessed since World War II in Western Europe or the breakup of the Soviet Union in Eastern Europe. Females from 15 countries and males from 10 countries ended up with a

---

[6] Armstrong, G. L. (1999). Trends in Infectious Disease Mortality in the United States During the 20th Century. JAMA, 281(1), 61. https://doi.org/10.1001/jama.281.1.61

[7] Centers for Disease Control and Prevention (1998) Update: isolation of avian influenza A(H5N1) viruses from humans-HongKong, 1997–1998. MMWR Morb Mortal Wkly Rep. 46:1245–1247.

[8] Caballero-Anthony M (2009) Pandemic Preparedness in Asia, RSIS, NTU, Singapore.

lower life expectancy at birth in 2020 than in 2015.[9] But, unfortunately, it gets worse, beyond COVID-19.

Mortality Is on the Rise

Not only has life expectancy stagnated since 2000, but it is also actually starting to fall in some industrialized countries. The USA and the UK are the inglorious "pioneers" in this respect, but it will not be long before this development also affects other countries. In the USA, life expectancy declined in 2019 for the third year in a row.[10] This change reversed decades of medical progress in reducing mortality—even if this was largely due to the narrow field of hygiene in infectious diseases, vaccinations, and antibiotics.

The causes of this are to some extent USA-specific as one major reason for early deaths there was the relatively unique crisis caused by the irresponsible prescription of powerful painkillers (which in most other countries are covered by Narcotics Acts and thus much better regulated) but also by chronic alcohol abuse, suicides, obesity, hypertension, diabetes, and other chronic diseases. For 30–34-year-olds with diabetes, the expected healthy lifespan for women is 11 years and for men 12 years less than for age-matched people without diabetes. The USA affords the most expensive healthcare system in the world, at least per capita; however, its population is no healthier than anywhere else. On the contrary, in terms of life expectancy, the USA is below average compared to other industrialized countries. There has been a shocking increase in mortality among rural white male Americans of working age.[11] The gap with urban areas has almost tripled in the last two decades where mortality rates had fallen. Reasons include the so-called "diseases of despair", a combination of alcohol excesses, suicides, and an unhealthy lifestyle with smoking, dietary deficiencies, lack of exercise, and obesity, which all add up to shorten life. There has even been an increase in mortality of the younger white rural population exacerbated by the fact that numerous rural clinics have been closed for economic reasons.

---

[9] José Manuel Aburto, Jonas Schöley, Ilya Kashnitsky, Luyin Zhang, Charles Rahal, Trifon I Missov, Melinda C Mills, Jennifer B Dowd, Ridhi Kashyap, Quantifying impacts of the COVID-19 pandemic through life-expectancy losses: a population-level study of 29 countries, International Journal of Epidemiology, 2021; dyab207, https://doi.org/10.1093/ije/dyab207

[10] Bokhari A & Sharfstein JM (2019) Declining US Life Expectancy and the 2020 Presidential Election. JAMA Health Forum, https://jamanetwork.com/channels/health-forum/fullarticle/2759637

[11] Cross SH, Califf RM, Warraich HJ. Rural-Urban Disparity in Mortality in the US From 1999 to 2019. JAMA. 2021;325(22):2312–2314. https://doi.org/10.1001/jama.2021.5334

In the UK, it was noticed for the first time in 2013 that the rise in life expectancy started to slow down. In 2019, for the first time in 100 years, Britain's residents began to die earlier. Britain currently has the worst health trends in all Western Europe. Elderly people, the poor, and newborns are the most affected. Men aged 65 will die at 86.9, earlier than the previous 87.4; women now aged 65 are likely to die at 89.2, a drop from the previous 89.7. In other words, the life expectancy of people entering retirement age has dropped by about 6 months of life. Now you might think, "Haven't people simply reached the peak of their possible longevity. After all, you can't expect life expectancy to increase forever". However, the latest figures from the USA and the UK contrast with the fact that life expectancy in many other places in the world, including Hong Kong, mainland China, Japan, and Scandinavia, for example, is not falling and is well above the UK levels.

Similarly, within Europe, Germany has the most expensive healthcare system, next to Switzerland. Nevertheless, it ranks in the bottom third in terms of life expectancy in a Europe-wide comparison, and the same applies to the health of the population. Thus, in industrialized countries, population health is not a matter of money. Of course, the conditions in Europe are not yet like in the USA and unlikely to reach this catastrophic level where millions live without health insurance. However, even industrialized societies have profound social inequalities, and too little attention is paid to the links between social status and health. After all, the greatest threat to health comes from poverty, lack of education, loneliness, and insecure financial circumstances. Health policy is virtually unconcerned with these important aspects of well-being, and doctors and clinics are neither trained nor equipped for this and must leave people alone to deal with this. Completely different disciplines would be required for a more holistic healthcare: social workers, psychologists, coaches, and nutritionists. But the money pot for health seems to be exhausted. But is it money alone that makes the difference?

More Money? No

As we noted, more money alone does not automatically mean better health. The graph compiled for the World Economic Forum by researchers at the Boston Consulting Group using data from the World Health Organization and World Bank (see Fig. 3.2) shows health-adjusted life expectancy, i.e., the expected number of years a person will live disease-free, worldwide for various countries on the left axis and annual per capita health spending on the bottom axis.

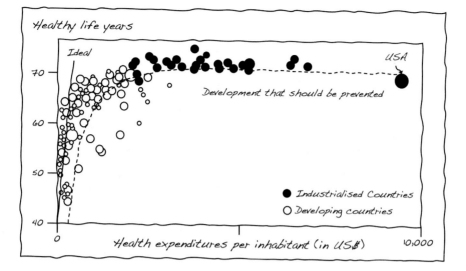

Fig. 3.2 More inputs do not produce more outputs (World Economic Forum (2016) Health Systems Leapfrogging in Emerging Economies: Ecosystem of Partnerships for Leapfrogging. https://image-src.bcg.com/Images/WEF_Health_Systems_Leapfrogging_Emerging_Economies_report_tcm55-85769.pdf). Distribution of health expenditure (in US dollars) per inhabitant and the effect on healthy life years (as of 2015) in various countries. Circles symbolize developed and developing countries. The size of the circles shows health expenditure as a percentage of gross national product (as of 2014)

Ideally, the countries' points would all be in the upper left-hand area of the graph, as this is where healthy life expectancy increases without a significant increase in expenditure (indicated as the "ideal" line). Many on this line, especially developing countries (the open circles), are obviously achieving a high standard of health for their populations with relatively little expenditure. But this graph also shows that in large parts of the world, almost the opposite has occurred for developed countries (the black circles on the right half of the graph): healthy lifespans are not increasing any further in these countries, even though up to ten times more money per inhabitant is spent on healthcare, around eight trillion dollars annually worldwide for the supposedly developed nations.

It is striking that the USA has the highest costs per capita and per gross national product and yet achieves among the lowest health-adjusted life expectancy for its citizens of any industrialized nation. Americans spend more than five times what Chileans spend, for example, even though the Chilean population lives longer than the US population.

There are several aspects that contribute to the fact that the USA and the UK are (still) outliers in international comparisons, even when compared to other rich countries. Administrative costs in the health sector in the USA are high. Large social inequalities in health spending also appear to be a driver. A growing number of expenditures are not covered by health insurance, resulting in healthcare services being heavily concentrated among the top 5% of patients in terms of income; these account for nearly half of expenditures. Those of the top 1% of patients account for nearly 20% of expenditures. Moreover, a plethora of different health insurance companies lead to a fragmented and complex healthcare system with an administrative cost component of 30% (as compared to 8% in most other countries), and prices, e.g. for drugs and procedures, are high and lack transparency.[12]

In Europe, too, the healthcare system is increasingly driven by commercial interests and optimization. However, nearly everyone has health insurance, and, whether private or statutory, treatment will in principle be equally good. Nevertheless, there are false incentives (see Chap. 6), and, contrary to all assurances by politicians that this is not the case, the importance of privately insured persons for the financing of healthcare systems continues to grow. However, since privately insured persons are reimbursed for treatment costs without budget limits, they pay higher fees for many medical services. If they had statutory insurance, the system of healthcare providers would lose over a third of their income. In the outpatient sector, the revenue loss would be particularly high, and many physicians claim that without private patients, they would not be able to keep their practice alive. No wonder that private patients are preferred, whether this is said publicly or concealed as politically incorrect; it is a fact. And who wouldn't give preference to the best clientele, essential to the survival of the practice? In the hospital sector, by the way, the share of additional turnover is much lower, which is because here privately and statutorily insured patients are billed according to the same remuneration system, except possibly for accommodation in a single or double room or treatment by the head physician—a dubious advantage, by the way.

So, money alone does not make you healthy, or too little money does not explain the high proportion of chronically ill people and the impending loss of healthy years of life in our country too. It should be noted that life expectancy has increased in many parts of the world over the last 100 years, but this increase is now stagnating and is beginning to decline in some industrialized countries. All the while, the proportion of a person's lifetime spent living with disability and illness at the end of their life is growing, especially for women. Let's dig deeper into the causes of all this.

---

[12] Papanicolas, I. TEDMED, https://youtu.be/ZXCqHOFFMOc

4

No Prevention

Let's do a little research into the causes of the many chronic diseases and why they threaten to shorten our life expectancy, as they are already doing in the USA and Great Britain. Of all chronic diseases, 80% are caused by 15 symptoms and complaints:[1]

1. Depression
2. Back pain
3. Arthritis
4. Overweight to obesity
5. Diabetes
6. Elevated cholesterol
7. Hypertension
8. Coronary artery disease or disease of the coronary arteries, angina pectoris
9. Heart failure, cardiac insufficiency
10. Allergies
11. Asthma
12. Sinusitis
13. Chronic obstructive pulmonary disease (COPD)
14. Kidney disease
15. Cancer

---

[1] Kompendium Chronisch Kranksein in Deutschland Zahlen, Fakten, Versorgungserfahrungen, Institute of General Medicine, Goethe University Frankfurt http://publikationen.ub.uni-frankfurt.de/frontdoor/index/index/docId/55045

They represent the "daily bread" of every family doctor. As already mentioned, since we do not know the exact molecular causes, i.e. because we do not know which molecules, hormones, and signalling pathways are dysregulated, we cannot cure the cause but only treat the symptoms. In treating the symptoms diabetes, high cholesterol, high blood pressure, coronary heart disease, and cardiac insufficiency, we hope to prevent their long-term and life-threatening consequences, i.e. heart attack or stroke.

However, we also know that these diseases are not exclusively genetically determined, i.e. they are not fated. All of them are influenced or possibly triggered by other modifiable lifestyle factors. Different people therefore carry different, probably genetically or epigenetically (more on this later) defined risks, the onset of which, however, they have the power to influence.

Of course, it may be that you have such favourable genes that even with the worst lifestyle you will live to be 100 years old. And we all know such examples as Helmut Schmidt, Germany's chancellor from 1974 to 1982, who smoked not only cigarettes but even menthol-containing ones and lived to be almost 100 years old, or Winston Churchill, who became 90 despite smoking cigars and indulging in whiskey and champagne (however, the quote "No Sports" is wrong; Churchill never said this). Getting very old is therefore not necessarily the result of a healthy lifestyle. Neither do very old people eat healthier, nor do they exercise more. They are also just as likely to smoke or drink. Nevertheless, for most of us, such lifestyle habits are, unfortunately, not a good choice.

The problem is that we don't know the "longevity-despite-an-unhealthy-lifestyle" genes yet. It's like drug efficacy, where we can't pick out the one patient who will benefit from a drug; similarly, we can't filter out the person to whom we can say, "You have such longevity genes; you can do (almost) whatever you want, you'll live to be 100". Conversely, the same is true the other way around. There are also high-risk people who should be monitored and coached from a young age on, and certain lifestyle aspects should be strictly modified so that they can enjoy a normal life expectancy. These we can't pick out either with high precision. The only clue we may have is a serious illness from the above group of 15 in either a parent or siblings, but such risk predictors are very vague and imprecise. Far away from precision prevention.

What we know, however, is that there are at least eight risks or lifestyles that can trigger a chronic disease, possibly based on a genetic profile.[2] Of these eight, seven are self-influencing misconduct (Fig. 4.1):

---

[2] Centers for Disease Control and Prevention (2009) The Power of Prevention: Chronic disease … the public health Challenge of the 21st Century, https://www.cdc.gov/chronicdisease/pdf/2009-power-of-prevention.pdf

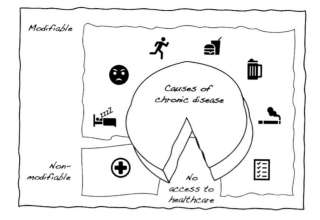

Fig. 4.1 Eighty percent of the costs of the most frequent chronic diseases are preventable by omitting seven modifiable causes or lifestyle errors (sleep, stress, physical fitness, nutrition, alcohol, smoking, check-ups) plus one for an individual non-modifiable factor (presence of a high standard medical care; lower left)

1. Insufficient sleep
2. Too much stress or lack of ability to avoid or cope with stress
3. Too little physical fitness (endurance, musculature, and mobility)
4. Unhealthy diet (too many calories, too few vegetables, too much red meat and sugar)
5. Excessive drinking
6. Smoking
7. Not taking advantage of medical services and preventive care facilities

If all these modifiable risks were avoided, 80% of the costs in the healthcare system for chronic diseases could be saved. Thus, all of these are typically suggested to every patient, which is quite overwhelming and demotivating. Perhaps only one of these would be sufficient, e.g. not to smoke, because a patient has a very high lung cancer risk, but on all the others he could take it easy. This would be truly precision prevention, not possible at the moment. Only the presence or absence of environmental factors and medical and preventive services are beyond your personal control. What is, however, common is the underuse of preventive services, particularly by men (see Chap. 5). In industrialized countries, men are screening muffle heads and make disproportionately low use of such offerings.[3]

Preventive lifestyle changes, i.e. the avoidance of the six modifiable misbehaviours plus the use of preventive services, can prevent the onset of 15

---

[3] Pies C (2019) Männer-TÜV: Das Praxishandbuch zur Männergesundheit, Herbig-Verlag, Stuttgart.

chronic diseases or at least reduce the severity of symptoms or the overall course.[4]

The incidence of the above chronic diseases that can be influenced by lifestyle is thus an important measure of the health status of a population and reflects the existence and effectiveness of health education and prevention programmes. Consistently implemented, a large gain in life expectancy and quality of life can be achieved with relatively little financial expenditure. Conversely, being late with lifestyle changes, namely, only when a disease is diagnosed or when symptoms have appeared ("My blood pressure is high", "I should…", "I urgently need to lose weight…", "My bronchitis is slowly becoming chronic", "I need to stop smoking…"), also means that at this point real prevention is no longer possible. However, even at that stage a lifestyle change may still be sensible, i.e. secondary prevention. Better late than never.

Hardly Real Prevention

So, what about the access, financing, and use of prevention? At present, most prevention programmes refer almost not at all to lifestyle but essentially to vaccinations against various bacterial and viral pathogens. You will remember that the control of infectious diseases remains the major factor in our gain in life expectancy. Added to this, as we age, is only a small set of cancer screening examinations, which cannot be called preventive care, since they are usually aimed at detecting an early stage of a pre-existing tumour. In the important age of 18–35 years, when prevention would really make sense, there is a big gap. It is only from the age of 35 that a general check-up (heart, circulation, diabetes, kidney, blood count) is recommended in regular intervals, e.g. an ultrasound examination to detect a dangerous enlargement (aneurysm) of the abdominal aorta.

So essentially, it's mainly vaccinations and early detection of cancer, with men being a little lazier about preventative care than women, as already mentioned, who are better monitored health-wise already because of the obligation to have a physical examination as part of the prescription for the anti-baby pill. That leaves only the regular check-ups at the GP and the occasional visit to the dentist. And what do they achieve?

---

[4] WHO (2005) Preventing chronic diseases: a vital investment, WHO global report, https://www.who.int/chp/chronic_disease_report/contents/en/

Check-Ups with the Family Doctor Useless

To be useful, health checks must reduce disease rates and prolong life. One would assume that this is self-evident. For example, the detection of elevated risk factors such as high blood pressure or cholesterol and subsequent treatment should lead to a reduction in heart disease and death (well, we've already discussed how "effective" treatments in heart disease are). Other tests can detect precursors to disease, such as precancerous lesions, the treatment of which can prevent cancer from developing. In general, it would have to be beneficial to detect signs or symptoms of a manifest disease that the person had not noticed or considered important. Some people may improve their lifestyle because of test results and advice, and healthy people may feel reassured.

But, as always, it's better to double-check. And so the Nordic Cochrane Collaboration conducted a meta-analysis on this.[5] It included 17 different studies with a total of 251,891 randomly selected or assigned participants, in which adults with and without check-ups were compared. Studies on very old patients were not included, as the aim was to investigate preventive rather than follow-up care. A health check was defined as screening for more than one disease or risk factor in more than one organ system, i.e. the way this is usually done at the family doctor's office. The surprising but little communicated result was that health checks have little or no effect on all-cause mortality or cancer mortality, probably little or no effect on cardiovascular mortality (i.e. fatal heart attack or stroke). So general check-ups, at least as they are done today with the resources available, are probably not beneficial. So they are more of a ritual for conscience relief.

One criticism of this very large analysis was that it covered a large period of time and therefore old data from times when, following the check-ups, possibly now outdated and less effective drugs were prescribed distorted the statements. For this reason, the "Inter99" study on the effect of health checks in a modern setting was subsequently carried out. Here, check-ups were additionally combined with an individually tailored intervention programme, screening for the risk of heart disease, and lifestyle intervention over 5 years. Result after 10 years is as follows: no effect on heart disease, stroke, or mortality.[6]

---

[5] Krogsbøll LT et al. (2019) General health checks in adults for reducing morbidity and mortality from disease. The Cochrane database of systematic reviews, https://doi.org/10.1002/14651858. CD009009.pub3

[6] Jørgensen T et al. (2014) Effect of screening and lifestyle counselling on incidence of ischaemic heart disease in general population: Inter99 randomised trial. BMJ 348:g3617, https://doi.org/10.1136/bmj.g3617

And in 2021 another major study investigated the benefit of check-up with the same result, no health benefit. The editor concluded that this is it; no further studies on this are needed. This case is closed until something fundamentally would change in the healthcare system, e.g. putting instead emphasis on providing equitable universal access, eliminating financial incentives to provide unnecessary tests and treatments, reducing medical error, improving patient safety, and building in adequate time for doctors to spend with their patients.[7] We will come to all these points in more detail.

What could be the reasons that the present form of check-up doesn't work? People who accept an invitation to a health check in the first place are possibly more health conscious to begin with and tend to have a higher socio-economic status, a lower risk of cardiovascular disease, and lower mortality. Systematic health checks may therefore not reach those most in need of prevention at all, a phenomenon known as "inverse care", that is, those who need the care do not use it, and those who hardly need it do.[8]

In summary, great scepticism about the current check-up practice is called for. In addition, the possibilities to generate measured values are almost unlimited: Metabolic, hormonal, whole-body scans, and much more are technically available, advertised, and carried out as quite lucrative "individual health services". These are services for which the health insurance companies are not obliged to pay, i.e. which are paid for privately. If they were evidence-based and had a clear benefit, they would have to be covered by the health insurance companies. Very few of these measures are scientifically monitored, and the benefit for the participants is often—to put it mildly—unclear.

The fact that routine check-ups by general practitioners have no clear benefit, at least for the already health-conscious patient group that currently makes use of them, does not mean, of course, that doctors should generally discontinue tests and preventive measures when a disease is suspected. One reason for the lack of benefit from regular check-ups could be that health-conscious patients visit the doctor at the first sign of a disease and therefore nothing new is found in a later check-up.

However, there is another group of doctors who offer their own check-ups: dentists. You and I would have expected here that this form of check-up at the dentist is beyond any doubt. But you will be as surprised as I was when I first

---

[7] Liss DT et al. (2021) General Health Checks in Adult Primary Care: A Review. JAMA 325:2294–2306, https://doi.org/10.1001/jama.2021.6524; Brett AB (2021) The Routine General Medical Checkup: Valuable Practice or Unnecessary Ritual? JAMA 325:2259.

[8] Waller D et al. (1990) Health checks in general practice: another example of inverse care? BMJ 300:1115–8.

read the studies on this, which wanted to check the seemingly self-evident to be on the safe side.

Check-Ups at the Dentist Useless

Although diseases of the teeth would be largely preventable, they persist unabated. Worldwide, the most frequent and most consequential are caries, periodontitis, and tooth loss. How can it be that these do not decrease significantly despite all early detection and treatment measures? As in the case of chronic diseases in general practice (see Fig. 4.1), the main risk factors are again diet (especially sugar consumption), alcohol, and tobacco consumption. Dentists have a hard time with real prevention and focus too much on therapy.[9] It is unclear what the reason for this is:

- The dentists themselves and the need for prevention to be more firmly anchored in the training of dentists or dental assistants.
- The differences in remuneration between prevention and therapy.
- The patients who are resistant to advice.

Ever since Pierre Fauchard stated in 1746 that one should visit the dentist every 6 months, this has been set in stone and is a cornerstone of dental practice.[10] Although recommendations on the optimal interval vary slightly from country to country, the majority of dentists therefore recommend 6-monthly visits for a visual examination and probing, which is covered by most health insurances, to detect and treat caries, as well as tartar removal and tooth polishing to prevent periodontal disease, for which typically a fee is charged. Surprisingly, however, there is no scientific evidence as to whether this routine brings any patient benefit and whether longer intervals, for example, annually or biennially, would not suffice.[11] There are essentially correlations, for example, that children who only go to the dentist when they have problems have

---

[9] Peres M et al. (2019) Oral diseases: a global public health challenge. The Lancet 394:249–260, https://www.thelancet.com/journals/lancet/article/PIIS0140-6736(19)31146-8/fulltext; Watt RG et al.: The Lancet, 20 July 2019 https://www.thelancet.com/journals/lancet/article/PIIS0140-6736(19)31133-X/fulltext

[10] Adolfo Patiño G (1985) The surgeon-dentist Pierre Fauchard. Revista de la Federacion Odontologica Colombiana 34:117–23; Kay EJ (1999) How often should we go to the dentist? About once a year-but rates of disease progression vary greatly. BMJ 319:204–205, https://doi.org/10.1136/bmj.319.7204.204

[11] Riley P et al. (2013) Recall Intervals for Oral Health in Primary Care Patients. Cochrane Database of Systematic Reviews 12:CD004346; Lamont T et al. (2018) Routine Scale and Polish for Periodontal Health in Adults. Cochrane Database of Systematic Reviews 12:CD004625.

more decayed and filled teeth than children who also go to the dentist regularly without having symptoms. Also, regular dentist-goers have fewer teeth pulled than those who only go to the dentist when they have problems. At first glance, yes, it sounds plausible that those who go to the dentist for routine check-ups before symptoms appear have less dental disease. But beware! This is only apparently the case.[12]

One of the biggest mistakes made time and again in medicine is to draw forward-looking conclusions about cause and effect from backward-looking correlations. Just like any other chronic disease negatively influenced or exacerbated by unhealthy lifestyle, oral health exhibits the same social gradient.[13] The affluent and better off suffer less from dental disease than the poorer and most disadvantaged groups. People in higher socio-economic classes are also more likely to register with a dentist and to go for dental check-ups even when they have no symptoms. Thus, the correlation between going to the dentist and lower risk of disease may simply be a social or educational phenomenon and may be due to general differences in lifestyle and healthier diets, for example, lower in sugar, rather than the effectiveness of dental check-ups.[14]

Even if the preventive dental visits were reasonable, there is still the question of whether it must be the usual 6-month interval or whether longer intervals would suffice. The debate about the appropriate interval duration between dental check-ups for patients in primary care was first initiated in 1977. After all, it is crucial for the dentist to detect and intervene before caries progresses irreversibly into the dentin (tooth bone). Depending on how deeply caries sits in the enamel, this can take up to 3 years.[15] In addition, there are variations between different patients, and all dentists are not equally diligent about this either. All this resulted in optima for the dental check-up that ranged from 13 months to 10 years (!). However, every 6 months was far too frequent and unnecessary in every case. For both children with primary teeth and adolescents with permanent teeth, a dental check-up every 2 years seems optimal on average. Given the duration of this debate and the potential impact of changing check-up intervals on dental healthcare costs and outcomes, it is difficult to understand why there are few high-quality, reliable

---

[12] O'Brien M (1994) Children's dental health in the United Kingdom 1993. London: HMSO; Todd JE & Lader D (1989) Adult dental health 1988 United Kingdom. London: HMSO.

[13] Tickle M et al. (1999) The effects of socio-economic status and dental attendance on dental caries experience, and treatment patterns in 5 year old children. Br Dent J 186:135–137.

[14] Eddie S & Davies JA (1985) The effect of social class on attendance frequency and dental treatment received in the General Dental Service in Scotland. Br Dent J 159:370–372.

[15] Sheiham A (1977) Is there a scientific basis for six-monthly dental examinations? Lancet 2:442–444, https://doi.org/10.1016/s0140-6736(77)90620-1; Kay EJ et al. (1995) Restoration of approximal carious lesions-application of decision analysis. Comm Dent Oral Epidemiol 23:271–275.

studies on this issue. The largest multicentre randomized controlled trial to date, INTERVAL, is expected to provide some clarity[16] but has not yet been published.

The situation is different for the second routine dental measure, which, unlike the check-up, is usually paid for privately: professional tooth cleaning with subsequent polishing. Almost half of all adults show signs of gum disease (periodontitis), making it the most common chronic disease worldwide with significant health and economic implications. You most likely are convinced that professional teeth cleaning can only be a good idea and that there will be plenty of studies proving its benefits. After all, you pay for it. "Do we even need to examine something like that?", you might think, "Isn't it obviously sensible?" It is recommended everywhere, and everyone you know probably has it done. As so often in medicine, it is always worthwhile to question or at least test dogmas[17] and not to let go until evidence is presented, or not.

In fact, there is a lack of reliable evidence which of the different dental procedures—oral hygiene advice on self-care up to professional tooth cleaning and polishing—are effective and cost-effective.[18] This is what the Improving the Quality of Dentistry (IQuaD) study set out to do.[19] It was, indeed, a ground-breaking study and the largest ever conducted in dentistry. It was not retrospective and reliant on weak correlations (see above), but prospective, and aimed to find out whether dental oral hygiene advice on self-care, or professional teeth cleaning and polishing, worked and provided value for money. Surprisingly, however, after 3 years it made no difference whatsoever to gum health whether professional dental cleanings had previously been performed every 6 or 12 months or not at all. There was even no benefit from oral hygiene advice on self-care. These results were later confirmed again[20] but have not found expression in treatment guidelines. Because these data

---

[16] Clarkson JE et al. (2018) INTERVAL (investigation of NICE technologies for enabling risk-variable-adjusted-length) dental recalls trial: a multicentre randomised controlled trial investigating the best dental recall interval for optimum, cost-effective maintenance of oral health in dentate adults attending dental primary care. BMC Oral Health 18:135.

[17] Frame PS et al. (2000) Preventive Dentistry: Practitioners' Recommendations for Low-Risk Patients Compared with Scientific Evidence and Practice Guidelines. American Journal of Preventive Medicine, https://doi.org/10.1016/s0749-3797(99)00138-5

[18] Worthington HV et al. (2013) Routine periodontal health scale and polish in adults. Cochrane Database Syst Rev 11:CD004625.

[19] Ramsay CR et al. (2018) Improving the Quality of Dentistry (IQuaD): A Cluster Factorial Randomised Controlled Trial Comparing the Effectiveness and Cost-Benefit of Oral Hygiene Advice And/or Periodontal Instrumentation with Routine Care for the Prevention and Management of Periodontal Disease in Dentate Adults Attending Dental Primary Care. Health Technology Assessment 22:1–144.

[20] Lamont T et al. (2018) Routine Scale and Polish for Periodontal Health in Adults. Cochrane Database of Systematic Reviews 12:CD004625.

fundamentally called into question the entire routine dental practice to date, the even larger INTERVAL study was initiated, which is now being conducted over 4 years instead of 3.[21] Let's wait and see. Until then, I personally still go for a dental check-up every 12 months. However, I will hold back on professional dental cleanings and polishing for the time being.

But what could now represent real dental prevention, if the regular visit makes only limited sense and scaling and polishing, at least over 3 years, no sense? In addition, all these measures are not real prevention but—as in the general medical routine—only early detection and treatment of one of the chronic diseases, caries, and periodontitis. If we wanted real prevention, we would have to start somewhere entirely else, namely, by tackling the main cause of sugar, the global sugar industry, and its sophisticated corporate strategies to promote sugar consumption.[22] When the sugar industry could no longer deny the role of sugar in dental caries in the face of scientific evidence (we are reminded of the tobacco industry), it developed an almost global strategy. To avoid restricting sugar consumption, attention was to be directed to public health interventions. Tactics included working with allied food industries to fund research with questionable potential, for example, on enzymes to break down plaque and a rather grotesque project to develop a vaccine against tooth decay. In addition, the sugar industry established close relationships with professional dental associations and members of dental expert panels in many countries.

The sugar industry influences dental research and oral health policy through lobby organizations.[23] Under the guise of an independent scientific educational campaign according to the motto that sugar is by no means the main cause of caries, and one only has to brush one's teeth well, action games were offered for kindergartens, and it is claimed that one can eat sugar safely; the only decisive factor is the energy balance.

So if we want real, dental-health prevention, there is an urgent need to curb the influence of the sugar industry on research, policy, and practice, for example, through clear and transparent guidelines. Advising or receiving money from the sugar industry must strictly preclude membership of dental

---

[21] Clarkson JE et al. (2018) INTERVAL (investigation of NICE technologies for enabling risk-variable-adjusted-length) dental recalls trial: a multicentre randomised controlled trial investigating the best dental recall interval for optimum, cost-effective maintenance of oral health in dentate adults attending dental primary care. BMC Oral Health 18:135.

[22] Kearns CE et al. (2015) Sugar Industry Influence on the Scientific Agenda of the National Institute of Dental Research's 1971 National Caries Program: A Historical Analysis of Internal Documents. PLOS Med 12:e1001798, https://doi.org/10.1371/journal.pmed.1001798

[23] https://kelleyuustal.com/the-sugar-lobbys-dirtiest-tricks/; http://www.zuckerverbaende.de

guideline committees. But until that becomes a reality, you and your family can start eating less sugar. By doing so, you will not only be doing your teeth good.

Diabetes and the Sugar Scandal

The connection between sugar consumption and diabetes mellitus and its life-threatening cardiovascular complications, which exists in addition to dental health and is even more important, has now been proven beyond doubt. But it took a very long time for this to be accepted by the medical profession. It all began with one of the biggest scientific scandals of all time[24] which also cost many lives. It is closely linked to one of the most prestigious universities in the world, Harvard University in Boston, USA, and again to the sugar industry, which managed to deflect attention from sugar to fat regarding the dietary reasons for the sharp increase in cardiovascular deaths after World War II. The revelations are important because the debate over the relative harm of sugar and saturated fat continues to this day. For decades, medical professionals then exhorted the public to reduce their fat intake, leading many people to consume foods low in fat but—and what many don't know or pay attention to—extremely high in sugar at the same time. These are the root cause of the obesity and diabetes crisis.

But, from the beginning, the scandal was uncovered by a publication in the *Journal of the American Medical Association*[25] and relied on thousands of pages of correspondence and other documents in the archives of Harvard University and other libraries. In the 1950s, coronary heart disease and heart attacks increased, especially in men. This prompted studies into whether dietary components might play an important role in this, including cholesterol, excess calories, amino acids, fats, carbohydrates, vitamins, and minerals. By the 1960s, two prominent physicians had developed conflicting hypotheses about the causes: John Yudkin (author of the visionary book *Pure, White and Deadly*) identified high-sugar diets as causative of high rates of heart disease.[26]

---

[24] YouTube video: https://www.srf.ch/play/tv/redirect/detail/116b34f9-c87a-4819-8058-75b08fd33232

[25] Kearns CE et al. (2016) Sugar Industry and Coronary Heart Disease Research: A Historical Analysis of Internal Industry Documents. JAMA Intern Med 176:1680–1685, https://doi.org/10.1001/jamainternmed.2016.5394

[26] Yudkin J (1957) Diet and coronary thrombosis. Lancet 270:155–162, https://doi.org/10.1016/S0140-6736(57)90614-1; Yudkin J (1964) Dietary fat and dietary sugar in relation to ischaemic heart-disease and diabetes. Lancet 2:4–5, https://doi.org/10.1016/s0140-6736(64)90002-9

In contrast, Ancel Keys postulated that total fat, saturated fat, and cholesterol were responsible.[27]

John Hickson, a sugar industry executive, proposed a plan to other companies in the same industry to counter the alarming findings about sugar with industry-funded research to change public opinion through information and legislative programs. In 1965, Hickson commissioned Harvard researchers D. Mark Hegsted, who later became head of the Division of Nutrition at the US Department of Agriculture, where he helped draft the precursor to the federal government's Dietary Guidelines in 1977, and Fredrick J. Stare, chairman of Harvard's nutrition department, to write a review article that would debunk the anti-sugar studies. It was to be a review paper because these—especially when they appear in such prestigious (so-called "high-impact") medical journals as the *New England Journal of Medicine*—shape the entire scientific debate or define the state of the science. Hickson wired Hegsted and Stare (I won't call them scientists anymore at this point) a total of $6500, which is equivalent to about $50,000 today. The money came from a trade group called the Sugar Research Foundation, now known as the Sugar Association. It was not until 1984, for example, that the *New England Journal of Medicine* began requiring authors to disclose payments to them or their research groups.[28]

Hickson self-selected the publications to be discussed and made it clear that he wanted the outcome to "absolve" sugar. Hegsted reassured sugar industry executives. "We are aware of your special interest", he wrote, "and will report on it as best we can". While working on their article, Hegsted and Stare shared and discussed early drafts with Hickson, who in turn was "pleased with what they wrote". Hegsted and Stare had dismissed the data on sugar as insufficient and inconclusive and the data accusing saturated fat as medically relevant. "Let me assure you that this is exactly what we had in mind, and we look forward to publication in print", Hickson wrote.

After the report was published, Hegsted influenced the government's dietary recommendations to highlight fat as a driver of heart disease, while sugar was largely described merely as empty calories linked to tooth decay. And, after all, brushing your teeth would help against that (see above). So Hickson achieved his goal; the debate about sugar and heart disease died down, while low-fat diets gained the support of many health authorities.

---

[27] Keys A & Grande F (1957) Role of Dietary Fat in Human Nutrition. III Diet and the Epidemiology of Coronary Heart Disease. Am J Public Health Nations Health. 47:1520–1530, https://doi.org/10.2105/ajph.47.12.1520

[28] McGandy et al. (1967) Dietary Fats, Carbohydrates and Atherosclerotic Vascular Disease. N Engl J Med 277:186–192, https://doi.org/10.1056/NEJM196707272770405

Low-fat products that are still marketed today include, for example, skim milk, which is used in pig farming for fattening purposes. Children who drank 1% skim milk had a higher body mass index (BMI), or more fat on their bodies, than children who drank whole milk.[29] Today, warnings about fat, especially saturated fat, remain a cornerstone of dietary recommendations, although in recent years the American Heart Association, the World Health Organization, and other health agencies have also warned that too much added sugar increases the risk of cardiovascular disease. So overall, for 50 years, research on the role of diet and heart disease, including many of today's dietary recommendations, was largely shaped by the sugar industry, and discussion of sugar was nipped in the bud for decades. Instead, low-cholesterol diets with unsaturated rather than saturated fats, i.e. margarine rather than butter, were preached. I still remember the first time I saw Coca-Cola with the label "cholesterol-free" in a US American supermarket.

Is such influence and lobbying history and unthinkable nowadays? No, the food industry continues to influence nutrition science.[30] Coca-Cola, the world's largest producer of sugary drinks, continues to support scientists who downplay the link between sugary drinks and obesity and funds studies that claim children who eat candy tend to weigh less than children who don't eat candy. Whether studies show that extremely sugary drinks like Coca-Cola promote obesity and type 2 diabetes depends on who paid for the study. Between 2001 and 2016, 60 studies were published on the consumption of extremely sugary drinks and their link to obesity and diabetes. When the studies were led by independent researchers, they showed a clear link between sugar consumption and obesity and diabetes, respectively. However, in 26 studies, no such link was found. What was different about these studies? They were all conducted by researchers with financial ties to the beverage industry. The results were published in the *Annals of Internal Medicine*.[31]

The beverage industry also pays nutritionists and so-called health experts to write posts on social media opposing taxes on extremely sugary drinks and, in contrast, encouraging consumers to see them as healthy snacks.[32] As a

---

[29] Scharf RJ et al. (2013) Longitudinal evaluation of milk type consumed and weight status in preschoolers. Archives of Disease in Childhood 98:335–340, https://doi.org/10.1136/archdischild-2012-302941

[30] Bes-Rastrollo M et al. (2013) Financial Conflicts of Interest and Reporting Bias Regarding the Association between Sugar-Sweetened Beverages and Weight Gain: A Systematic Review of Systematic Reviews. PLoS Medicine 10:e1001578, https://doi.org/10.1371/journal.pmed.1001578

[31] Schillinger D et al. (2016) Do Sugar-Sweetened Beverages Cause Obesity and Diabetes? Industry and the Manufacture of Scientific Controversy. Annals of Internal Medicine 165:897–895, https://doi.org/10.7326/L16-0534

[32] O'Connor A 2015 Coca-Cola Funds Scientists Who Shift Blame for Obesity Away From Bad Diets. New York Times https://well.blogs.nytimes.com/2015/08/09/coca-cola-funds-scientists-who-shift-blame-for-obesity-away-from-bad-diets/?mtrref=www.google.com&assetType=REGIWALL

"science-based" solution, Coca-Cola is advocating for defining the obesity crisis as a lack of exercise or energy balance problem, rather than a problem of too many calories and sugar. To this end, the company has endorsed a "non-profit" organization called the Global Energy Balance Network. The network's website (gebn.org) is registered with Coca-Cola's Atlanta headquarters, from where it is also administered. There is no mention of Coca-Cola's financial support. Coke's support of prominent health researchers is reminiscent of the tobacco industry's tactic of confusing science and sowing doubt about the health risks of smoking.

Regular consumption of one sugar-sweetened drink per day increases the risk of diabetes (regardless of an increase in body weight) by 13%. The countries with the highest sugar consumption have the highest type 2 diabetes rates and vice versa.[33] Now, one could argue people who eat a lot of sugar may eat a lot in the first place and therefore be overweight and, as a result, exercise too little, and perhaps obesity and lack of exercise are the real reasons for the correlation between sugar and diabetes. But even if you compare people who are the same weight or overweight, or the same amount of physical activity, the effect of sugar remains.[34] It remains one of the six major lifestyle risks for chronic disease and explains the near tenfold increase in the rate of diabetes in the population since the 1950s (see Fig. 4.2).

The most common form of diabetes was not always called type 2. Originally, this was a form of diabetes that usually only appeared in adulthood. Even into my medical school years in the 1980s, it was therefore called adult-onset diabetes. However, nowadays, it affects more and more younger people, and so the name type 2 was introduced to distinguish it from the rarer autoimmune type 1 diabetes. Poor diet, often coupled with lack of exercise, has thus pushed the stage of the chronic disease well into adolescence. The long-term consequences, heart attacks, strokes, amputations, impaired vision, and kidney damage, can hardly be prevented by the so-called anti-diabetic drugs. Basically,

---

[33] Imamura F et al. (2015) Consumption of sugar sweetened beverages, artificially sweetened beverages, and fruit juice and incidence of type 2 diabetes: systematic review, meta-analysis, and estimation of population attributable fraction. BMJ 351:h3576 https://doi.org/10.1136/bmj.h3576; Weeratunga P et al. (2014) Per capita sugar consumption and prevalence of diabetes mellitus - global and regional associations. BMC Public Health 14:186 (2014). https://doi.org/10.1186/1471-2458-14-186

[34] Basu S et al. (2013) The Relationship of Sugar to Population-Level Diabetes Prevalence: An Econometric Analysis of Repeated Cross-Sectional Data. PLOS One 8:e57873. https://doi.org/10.1371/journal.pone.0057873

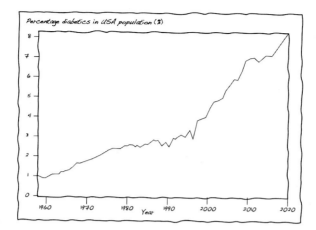

Fig. 4.2 The surge of diabetes in the US population from 1958 to 2020

these are also just drugs that normalize the symptom of elevated blood glucose levels. The reasons why pure symptom treatment cannot be sufficient and why the NNT for the relevant late effects is so high (between 45 and 100) correspond to those in the hypertension example (see Chap. 1).[35]

The evidence-based dietary recommendation is not to cut out sugar but to keep the ball rolling. For example, the WHO recommends that no more than 10% of daily calories be covered by added sugar.[36] Everyone should be able to manage that. Physical activity is also important, of course, and must be balanced with total calorie intake. It should be obvious that those who eat more than they consume will gain weight. Exercise, however, also stimulates the appetite and thus causes people to eat more calories. So, exercise consumes far fewer calories than most people think. A can of Coca-Cola contains ten teaspoons of sugar; to burn these, you would have to walk about 5 km, or 1 h. Who does that? Supplementing a nutrition program with exercise helps, but a change in diet achieves much more effect.[37]

---

[35] Niessner A et al. (2018) Antidiabetic medication of patients with cardiovascular disease-summary of the literature and application in clinical practice. J of Cardiology 25:124–127.

[36] Goran MI et al. (2017) Simplified and age-appropriate recommendations for added sugars in children. Pediatric Obesity 13:269–272, https://doi.org/10.1111/ijpo.12235

[37] McTiernan A et al. (2007) Exercise Effect on Weight and Body Fat in Men and Women. Obesity 15:1496–1512, https://doi.org/10.1038/oby.2007.178

And two more points are also important to know about sugar and nutrition. On many foods, the sugar content is hidden by creative alternative names. These include sucrose, dextrose, raffinose, glucose, fructose-glucose syrup, starch syrup, caramel syrup, lactose, maltose, (barley) malt extract, and maltodextrin but also seemingly healthy honey, grapefruit sweetener, and (agave) thick juices. There are up to 7 g of sugar per serving in salad dressings (French, vinaigrette), 12 g in soups and sauces, and 20 g in alcoholic beverages such as a glass of cider or a double sherry; even in bread and sandwiches, there is sugar, sometimes a teaspoon per two slices. Equally high levels of sugar can be found in breakfast smoothies, breakfast bars, and so-called low-fat fruit yoghurts, which then contain a lot of sugar in return. So, watch out!

A second misconception is that sugar substitutes or sweeteners, which are among the most widely used food additives in the world, are healthier or even beneficial. However, sweeteners cause diabetes just the same, through changes in the composition and function of the gut microbiome, so they are not a solution but rather another problem. So, if a little sugar is to be added, then take sugar and not artificial sweeteners![38]

Diabetes and massive obesity are often referred to as a pandemic, with dramatic consequences for our healthcare system and restrictions on life expectancy and quality of life for millions of people, respectively. However, compared to the COVID-19 pandemic starting in 2019, diabetes is not a fateful, hard-to-prevent pandemic that has swept the world. With the simple, targeted, and sustainable lifestyle measures, it would be possible to return diabetes disease rates to the 1950s levels and without drugs. Then we would also have only adult-onset diabetes again and no more juvenile-onset type 2 diabetes. For adult-onset diabetes, which occurs even in the absence of over-eating and malnutrition, there are probably risk genes about which research and preventive drug development might be useful but not for most of today's diabetics. Their diabetes mellitus is predominantly not a medical problem but rather a political problem: the lack of will to implement and finance genuine prevention. The situation is not much different in other fields of lifestyle risks, where there is also a lack of political or economic will for genuine prevention.

---

[38] Suez J et al. (2014) Artificial sweeteners induce glucose intolerance by altering the gut microbiota. Nature 514:181–186, https://doi.org/10.1038/nature13793

Red Meat

Keeping the ball rolling on sugar without banning it outright, and enforcing this in various ways, would be one of the most important prevention imperatives. The simplest approach would be to impose a sugar tax that pays for all the long-term health damage that sugar causes. Other countries have already done it.[39]

The situation is similarly clear for red meat, the muscle meat of beef, pork, lamb, or game.[40] Sugar and red meat (especially when processed into[41] sausages and other convenience foods) are the foods where reduction has the most significant effect on health. Red meat increases the risk of all-cause mortality, especially cancer. More and more young people, especially those aged 20–29,[42] are getting colorectal cancer, while it is declining in 50-year-olds due to screening colonoscopies. In fact, the screening age should urgently be lowered to 45. The same applies to the mortality risk due to cardiovascular diseases; this also correlates with the consumption of red meat. Trimethylamine N-oxide (TMAO), a substance produced by our gut microbiome from choline, phosphatidylcholine (lecithin), and L-carnitine, appears to be the cause of this. Food high in choline and L-carnitine includes meat, energy drinks, and protein shakes. Red meat also alters the gut flora towards TMAO-producing bacteria; conversely, these are reduced by vegetarian diets or white meat.[43,44]

---

[39] Wissenschaftliche Dienste des Bundestags (2018) Ausgestaltung einer Zuckersteuer in ausgewählten Ländern und ihre Auswirkung auf Kaufverhalten, Preise und Reformulierung. https://www.bundestag.de/resource/blob/561136/48c40ebb6f02c5e1dbc6f0984c45ddbf/wd-5-064-18-pdf-data.pdf

[40] Pan A et al. (2012) Red Meat Consumption and Mortality: Results from 2 Prospective Cohort Studies. Archives of Internal Medicine 172:555–63.

[41] Hall KD et al. (2019) Ultra-Processed Diets Cause Excess Calorie Intake and Weight Gain: An Inpatient Randomized Controlled Trial of Ad Libitum Food Intake. Cell Metabolism, https://doi.org/10.1016/j.cmet.2019.05.008

[42] Vuik FE et al. (2019) Increasing incidence of colorectal cancer in young adults in Europe over the last 25 years. Gut 68:1820–1826; Araghi M et al. (2019) Changes in colorectal cancer incidence in seven high-income countries: a population-based study. The Lancet Gastroenterology & Hepatology 4:511–518, https://doi.org/10.1016/S2468-1253(19)30147-5

[43] Heianza Y (2017) Gut Microbiota Metabolites and Risk of Major Adverse Cardiovascular Disease Events and Death: A Systematic Review and Meta-Analysis of Prospective Studies. Journal of the American Heart Association 6:e004947, https://doi.org/10.1161/JAHA.116.004947

[44] Tang WHW et al. (2014) Gut Microbiota-Dependent Trimethylamine N-Oxide (TMAO) Pathway Contributes to Both Development of Renal Insufficiency and Mortality Risk in Chronic Kidney Disease. Circulation Research 116:448–455, https://doi.org/10.1161/CIRCRESAHA.116.305360

Alcohol

In addition to smoking, which everyone now knows—despite the ban on tobacco advertising and increased tobacco taxes—still causes massive damage to the health of many people, alcohol also appears among the eight major and avoidable health risks. The reader might spontaneously object: But a small consumption of alcohol, the glass of red wine in the evening, is healthy, isn't it? Unfortunately, not. The discussion about alcohol has gone back and forth in recent decades, from "no alcohol" to "as little as possible" and from "which alcohol is the same" to "only red wine is healthy", and again it doesn't matter where the alcohol comes from; the main thing is to drink as little as possible. The current situation results from a gigantic forward-looking study of half a million people over a period of 10 years, i.e. no retrospective correlation: It is now clear that there is no healthy maximum amount of alcohol. Even moderate alcohol consumption has a negative effect on brain structure and function. Higher blood pressure and BMI further increase the risks of alcohol on brain health as shown from the UK Biobank.[45] Moreover, every 25th cancer worldwide is due to the consumption of alcohol, with men being affected in more than three out of four cases. Alcohol consumption can subsequently cause cancers of the lips and oral cavity, pharynx, larynx, oesophagus, colon, rectum, liver, and the female breast.[46] There are also genetic variants, about half of which influence the average alcohol consumption; environmental factors such as stress are additional triggers. Alcohol therefore generally increases the risk of stroke by about a third for every 280 g of alcohol consumed per week. At no amount does light or moderate alcohol consumption have a protective effect. Why should there be? Not everything in life that is fun or brings pleasure must be healthy. Therefore, alcohol should not be banned, but a tax corresponding to the associated health risk, which then has to be borne by the community of solidarity, i.e. all of us, would be appropriate, as is the case with sugar. Cheers![47]

---

[45] Topiwala A et al. (2021) No safe level of alcohol consumption for brain health: observational cohort study of 25,378 UK Biobank participants. medRxiv; https://doi.org/10.1101/2021.05.10.21256931; Evangelou E et al. (2021) Alcohol consumption in the general population is associated with structural changes in multiple organ systems: A population-based study in UK Biobank. eLife https://doi.org/10.7554/elife.65325; Mukamal KJ et al. (2008) Beliefs, motivations, and opinions about moderate drinking: a cross-sectional survey. Family medicine-Kansas City 40:188.

[46] Rumgay H et al. (2021) Global burden of cancer in 2020 attributable to alcohol consumption: a population-based study. Lancet Oncology 22: 1071–1080, https://doi.org/10.1016/S1470-2045(21)00279-5

[47] Millwood IY et al. (2019) Conventional and genetic evidence on alcohol and vascular disease aetiology: a prospective study of 500000 men and women in China. 393:1831–1842; https://doi.org/10.1016/S0140-6736(18)31772-0

Vegetables and Fresh Fruit

After the only three sensible dietary restrictions (sugar, red meat, and alcohol), let me present one more sensible dietary recommendation; this time a positive one. What food is proven to be beneficial to health? A plant-based diet with lots of vegetables and fruit. It's often referred to as the Mediterranean diet, but that's not really accurate. For one thing, not all components of the Mediterranean diet fall under this, and, for another, it is not a diet. The fact is, however, that in Mediterranean countries such as Spain, Greece, and Italy, mortality from cardiovascular disease is lower than in northern European populations or the USA.[48] A healthy diet can be more accurately described by its soluble and insoluble fibre content,[49] and this is best achieved through a plant-based diet (vegetables, fruit, and wholemeal products).[50] Soluble fibre is found mainly in fruit and vegetables; insoluble fibre is found mainly in cereals and pulses.[51] Unfortunately, only a fraction of people eat a healthy, fresh, and balanced diet. It is therefore fatal that only 40% of people still cook for themselves every day; the others eat highly processed industrial products,[52] which cause people to eat even more.[53]

That's it: these two guidelines—lots of plants and little sugar/red meat/alcohol—sufficiently describe the relevant evidence as far as prevention through healthy eating is concerned. That's all you need to know. Nor is there more knowledge. It's a mystery to me how self-proclaimed nutrition gurus can generate religiously held nutrition myths that deviate from this without any scientific evidence or whose disciples can follow them and read several 100-page nutrition compasses. Healthy eating is simple, should be practised in every kindergarten, and should be part of the school curriculum, including self-cooking.

---

[48] Rees K et al. (2019) Mediterranean-style diet for the primary and secondary prevention of cardiovascular disease. Cochrane Database of Systematic Reviews 3:CD009825, https://doi.org/10.1002/14651858.CD009825.pub3

[49] Mann J (2001) Dietary fibre and diabetes revisited. European Journal of Clinical Nutrition 55:919–21.

[50] Reynolds A et al. (2019) Carbohydrate Quality and Human Health: A Series of Systematic Reviews and Meta-Analyses. The Lancet 393:4344–45.

[51] Rubin R (2019) High-Fiber Diet Might Protect Against Range of Conditions. JAMA 321:1653–1655, https://doi.org/10.1001/jama.2019.2539

[52] Germany, as it eats - the BMEL Nutrition Report 2019. https://www.bmel.de/DE/themen/ernaehrung/ernaehrungsreport2019.html

[53] Hall D et al. (2019) Ultra-Processed Diets Cause Excess Calorie Intake and Weight Gain: An Inpatient Randomized Controlled Trial of Ad Libitum Food Intake. Cell Metabolism 30:67–77.e3.

Movement Plus Strength Plus Agility

The next major risk behaviour is too little exercise and poor physical fitness. Sitting is the new smoking, especially in Corona times. To increase the latter, 2½ h of physical activity per week and 10,000 steps daily are recommend by many, a number that has been elevated to dogma, and I'm sure many don't make it on their pedometers every day and get frustrated. But they don't have to make it either. If you take "live longer" as a goal, the benefits stop at 4400 steps per day. So, there's no need for challenging workout plans or workouts that push you to the limit. Just walking briskly for 2½ h a week—that's 21 min a day, every (!) day—reduces three of the main risk factors of chronic disease: blood pressure, cholesterol, and diabetes.[54] Anyone should be able to do that. But that's not all. Aging impairs skeletal muscle growth and leads to decreased muscle mass and strength; two factors are directly linked to mortality rates in older people.[55] Strong, healthy muscle mass leads to improved health, independence, and functionality and counteracts osteoporosis. And as a third component, light flexibility training is still necessary to maintain quality of life and treat or, even better, prevent occasional pain symptoms (back, shoulder). These three simple, easy-to-do fitness principles—endurance, strength, and flexibility—should be known by everyone and taken to heart on a regular basis. They would have a huge impact on physical well-being and avoiding osteoporosis and fragility. Knowledge of the simplest principles of a healthy lifestyle maintains or creates health and well-being. And this too would be important to teach in schools and offer in the workplace and to practise privately.[56]

[54] Abbasi J (2019) For Mortality, Busting the Myth of 10000 Steps per Day. JAMA 322:492–493; Williams PT & Thompson PD (2013) Walking Versus Running for Hypertension, Cholesterol, and Diabetes Mellitus Risk Reduction. Arteriosclerosis, Thrombosis, and Vascular Biology 33:1085–1091, https://doi.org/10.1161/ATVBAHA.112.300878

[55] McLeod M (2016) Live strong and prosper: the importance of skeletal muscle strength for healthy ageing. Biogerontology 17:497–510, https://doi.org/10.1007/s10522-015-9631-7; Kim S (2014) The Association between the Low Muscle Mass and Osteoporosis in Elderly Korean People. J Korean Med Sci. 29:995–1000, https://10.3346/jkms.2014.29.7.995

[56] King AC (2000) Comparative effects of two physical activity programs on measured and perceived physical functioning and other health-related quality of life outcomes in older adults. J Gerontol A Biol Sci Med Sci 55:M74–83, https://doi.org/10.1093/gerona/55.2.m74

Psyche: Sleep Plus Stress

The third pillar of prevention, besides nutrition and physical fitness, is the psyche with sufficient sleep and effective stress prevention or stress management as main elements, again, things that can be learned or that should be taught. Much worse than obesity or diabetes "pandemics" is a chronic lack of restful sleep, for example, by taking a long time to fall asleep, sleeping fitfully at night, waking up and lying awake for a long time, or waking up much too early in the morning and not being able to fall asleep again. During the day, many people then feel tired and worn out. About one in five adults and as many as 30% of all children are affected.[57] However, the normal duration of sleep varies greatly from person to person and is between 5 and 9 h, depending on age. The first 3–4 h of sleep per night is the most restful. Therefore, it's not a disaster if you've only been able to sleep 3–4 h; you'll make it through the day. However, this should not happen on a regular basis, because long-term sleep disorders increase the risk of obesity, diabetes,[58] and Alzheimer's[59] disease. In addition to poor sleep hygiene, unprocessed stress, for example, in a relationship or a workplace with a mismatch between increased psychological demands and lack of control over one's own activities, can impair sleep and likewise increase the incidence and mortality of cardiovascular disease.[60] Outdoor light at night, so-called nocturnal light pollution, and nighttime aircraft noise have recently been added as causes of sleep deprivation and thus as risk factors for sleep and health, in particular coronary heart disease. These cannot be modified by an individual and require regulatory measures.[61]

---

[57] Pinch G (2016) Sleep disorders: Common - and significantly underestimated. Dtsch Arztebl 113:A-234/B-199/C-197, https://www.aerzteblatt.de/archiv/174912/Schlafstoerungen-Haeufig-und-deutlich-unterschaetzt

[58] Shan Z et al. (2015) Sleep Duration and Risk of Type 2 Diabetes: A Meta-analysis of Prospective Studies. Diabetes Care 38:529–537, https://doi.org/10.2337/dc14-2073; Stenvers DJ et al. (2019) Circadian clocks and insulin resistance. Nat Rev Endocrinol 15:75–89, https://doi.org/10.1038/s41574-018-0122-1

[59] Shokri-Kojori E et al. (2018) β-Amyloid accumulation in the human brain after one night of sleep deprivation. Proceedings of the National Academy of Sciences U.S.A. 115:4483–4488, https://doi.org/10.1073/pnas.1721694115

[60] Framke E et al. (2020) Contribution of income and job strain to the association between education and cardiovascular disease in 1.6 million Danish employees. European Heart Journal 41:1164–1178, https://doi.org/10.1093/eurheartj/ehz870

[61] Münzel T (2021) The dark side of nocturnal light pollution. Outdoor light at night increases risk of coronary heart disease, European Heart Journal, 42:831–834, https://doi.org/10.1093/eurheartj/ehaa866; Saucy A et al. (2021) Does night-time aircraft noise trigger mortality? A case-crossover study on 24886 cardiovascular deaths. Eur Heart J 42:835–843.

What to Do?

That brings us to all eight risks and behaviours that contribute to 80% of all chronic diseases worldwide, probably together with risk genes. One of the eight risks, poor medical care, probably does not apply to industrialized countries; rather, we have too many useless check-ups. The risk of not taking advantage of preventive measures such as vaccinations and early detection mainly affects men, if at all. So, what remains is the magic triangle of diet (sugar, red meat, alcohol), body (exercise, strength, and agility), and psyche (sleep and stress). And what is to be done? Remember what was eventually possible with respect to the risk factor, smoking, after decades of fighting the lobby of the tobacco industry.[62] That could mean massively reducing sugar consumption in the face of resistance and misinformation by the sugar industry; massively reducing red meat consumption (also for many other reasons such as animal welfare and the climate gas methane[63]); and education, awareness, and massive coaching to teach healthy and fresh eating, physical fitness, healthy sleep, and stress avoidance. That wouldn't be cheap, but it would be orders of magnitude cheaper than driving the cart into the dirt and then treating symptoms in chronically ill people at great expense for the rest of their lives. High taxes on sugar and alcohol, as well as tobacco, and education and clear labelling of harmful products and highly processed convenience foods. The food traffic lights introduced in 2019 although only on a voluntary basis is a mini step in this direction but a real one.

---

[62] Brandt AM (2012) Inventing Conflicts of Interest: A History of Tobacco Industry Tactics. American Journal of Public Health 102:63–71, https://doi.org/10.2105/AJPH.2011.300292

[63] Saunois M (2016) The global methane budget 2000–2012. Earth Syst. Sci. Data 8:697–751, https://doi.org/10.5194/essd-8-697-2016; Nisbet EG et al. (2019) Very Strong Atmospheric Methane Growth in the 4 Years 2014–2017: Implications for the Paris Agreement. Global Biogeochemical Cycles 33:318–342, https://doi.org/10.1029/2018GB006009

5

Male Plus Low Income = Double Whammy

Check-up success at the GP, check-up success at the dentist, less diabetes, healthier diet, less alcohol consumption, more exercise, better sleep, less stress, and life expectancy all correlate somehow with better education and higher socio-economic status[1] and virtually not at all with the healthcare systems in place in each country. Some of the most different health systems are those in the USA (mostly private) and the UK (state-run), for example. In the USA, people tend to have private health insurance up to 65, often through their employer; in England, healthcare is free and funded by taxes. How education affects health in old age in both countries was investigated in two studies: in the UK "English Longitudinal Study of Ageing (ELSA)"[2] and in the USA "Health and Retirement Study".[3] The result is as follows: Differences in both health systems have little effect on the expected years of life in good health. The situation is different with education and socio-economic status.

Uneducated = Minus 10

People with higher education have up to 6 years longer life expectancy in England and even 9 years in the USA. Of course, income and socio-economic status correlates with education. The wealthiest group of 50-year-olds has a

---

[1] Zaninotto P et al. (2020) Socioeconomic Inequalities in Disability-free Life Expectancy in Older People from England and the United States: A Cross-national Population-Based Study. The Journals of Gerontology: Series A 75:906–913, https://doi.org/10.1093/gerona/glz266

[2] The English Longitudinal Study of Ageing (ELSA), https://www.elsa-project.ac.uk

[3] The Health and Retirement Study, https://hrs.isr.umich.edu/welcome-health-and-retirement-study

© The Author(s), under exclusive license to Springer Nature Switzerland AG 2022
H. H. H. W. Schmidt, *The end of medicine as we know it - and why your health has a future*,
https://doi.org/10.1007/978-3-030-95293-8_5

further life expectancy without chronic diseases of 31 years; in the poorest group, it is only 22 years, i.e. up to 9 years less. The reason is thought to be a healthier lifestyle. The possibility of easier access to medical services falls away as a justification in England.

These data can be transferred one to one to Germany, a country with yet another solidaric, healthcare system.[4] Here, too, the upper income brackets have a life expectancy several years higher than the lower ones, across all age groups and genders. Men with low education and income die 10 years and women 8 years earlier than well-educated men and women. Looking only at healthy life expectancy, that is, years of life spent in very good or good general health, the difference between the lowest and highest income groups accounts for as many as 13 years for women and 14 years for men. And this finding is by no means new. As early as 1847, the poor man's physician, medical reformer, and statistician, Salomon Neumann, described the crux of the problem thus: "Wealth and education express themselves countably—and this is an official fact-in the laws of mortality".[5]

This dependence of health and life expectancy on education begins in childhood. A higher level of education among mothers gives their children a longer life.[6] If a mother had at least a secondary school diploma from the 1940s onwards, her adult children aged 65 and over have an average life expectancy that is 2 years longer than children whose mothers had at most an elementary school diploma at the time. Better educated mothers are likely to pay attention to a healthier lifestyle for their children in terms of a balanced diet, smoking habits, alcohol consumption, and exercise.

However, the focus on and use of the term "education" as an explanation for poorer health and shorter life expectancy has been questioned. Lower education also correlates with lower income and socio-economic status. Social disadvantage and adverse conditions not only produce disproportionate harm because of greater exposure to unhealthy lifestyle factors; socio-economic hardships could make the individuals more susceptible to the harmful impact of environment and lifestyle, associated with accelerated ageing and increased

[4] Lampert T & Kroll LE (2014) Social differences in mortality and life expectancy. Ed. Robert Koch Institute, Berlin. GBE kompakt 5, https://edoc.rki.de/bitstream/handle/176904/3128/2_de. pdf?sequence=1&isAllowed=y; Lampert T et al. (2007) Social inequality in life expectancy in Germany. Aus Politik und Zeitgeschichte 42:11–18, http://www.bpb.de

[5] Neumann S (1847) Die öffentliche Gesundheitspflege und das Eigenthum. Critical and positive aspects with reference to the Prussian medical constitutional question. Adolph Rieß, Berlin 1847, https://books. google.de/books?id=sy0CAAAAcAAJ

[6] Huebener M & Marcus J (2019) People with lower educated mothers have lower life expectancy. German Institute for Economic Research Weekly Report 86:198–204, https://www.diw.de/documents/ publikationen/73/diw_01.c.617294.de/19-12.pdf

mortality and cardiovascular disease risk. Promotion of a healthy lifestyle alone might not be sufficient to reduce the socio-economic inequity in health, such as poverty, education, and access to medical advice and care. The impact of these differences and the complex interplay between socio-economic status and health disparities have become even more evident during the COVID-19 pandemic. Thus, even in industrialized countries, an interdisciplinary dialogue among preventive medicine, economics, and political sciences is needed to define a joint agenda for action.[7]

Male = Minus 5

Besides education, gender alone is also a risk factor. The health and life expectancy of boys and men is considerably worse than that of girls and women.[8] However, this gender inequality has hardly been reflected in health policy and is almost accepted, even by so-called gender scientists, as a given up to self-inflicted (risky behaviour). The Global Burden of Disease Study 2010 on the global burden of disease showed that women had a longer life expectancy than men in the period from 1970 to 2010. During this period, women's life expectancy at birth increased from 61.2 to 73.3 years, while men's life increased from 56.4 to 67.5 years.[9] These figures show that the gap in life expectancy has widened from 4.8 to 5.8 years of life to the disadvantage of men. Eastern Europe shows the largest difference in life expectancy between men and women: 11.6 years.[10] Also this disparity was accentuated during the COVID-19 pandemic. In each age group, about two to three times as many men as women died from COVID-19 per 100,000 men or women. Only because of the high proportion of women in the population group over 80 years of age is the proportion of men among COVID-19 victims nationwide "only" around 55%. To put it simply, men do not die more often from COVID-19 because they have already died from other diseases or in accidents.

[7] Liuzzo G et al. (2021) Unhealthy lifestyles mediate only a small proportion of the socioeconomic inequalities' impact on cardiovascular outcomes in US and UK adults: a call for action for social cardiology, European Heart Journal 42:2420–2421, https://doi.org/10.1093/eurheartj/ehab287; Niedzwiedz CL et al. (2020) Ethnic and socioeconomic differences in SARS-CoV-2 infection: prospective cohort study using UK Biobank. BMC Med 18:1601–1614.

[8] Bulletin of the World Health Organization 2014; 92: 618–620, https://doi.org/10.2471/BLT.13.132795, https://www.who.int/bulletin/volumes/92/8/13-132795/en/

[9] Wang H et al. (2012) Age-specific and sex-specific mortality in 187 countries, 1970–2010: a systematic analysis for the Global Burden of Disease Study 2010. Lancet 380:2071–94.

[10] UCL Institute of Health Equity (2013) Review of social determinants and the health divide in the WHO European Region: final report. Copenhagen: World Health Organization, Regional Office for Europe, http://www.instituteofhealthequity.org/projects/who-european-review

How can this gender gap be explained? In many societies, men generally enjoy more opportunities, privileges, and power than women, but these perceived advantages do not translate into better health. Explanations put forward include:

- More hazardous occupations: Higher levels of occupational exposure to physical and chemical hazards. In 2010, almost eight times more men died from work-related causes than women. In Europe, 95% of fatal accidents and 76% of non-fatal accidents in the workplace occur to men.[11] Occupations with the highest risk of fatal workplace accidents, such as mining, agriculture and fishing, the military, firefighting, and working on construction sites, employ far more men than women,[12] with little aspiration for the introduction of a "women's quota".

- Less preventive care/early detection: Women are ahead in all the early detection examinations offered, such as the general check-up from the age of 35 or skin cancer screening, as well as examinations for bowel cancer by means of a stool sample or colonoscopy. Only one in five men over the age of 45 visits a urologist regularly. The number one reason given by men is lack of time, followed by fear of a bad diagnosis and respect for the prostate examination with a finger. Many men engage in a kind of ostrich tactic: sticking their heads in the sand and not wanting to see or hear anything. Only when something is broken do you get it fixed—in other words, repair medicine rather than preventive medicine. As a result, men die more often and at a younger age from heart disease. One reason could be lower oestrogen levels but also poorly treated high blood pressure or high cholesterol. In addition, and quite contrary to the "man flu" stereotype,[13] when men are sick, they are less likely to see a doctor, and when they do see a doctor, they are less likely to report symptoms of the illness. Women are more likely than men to use health check-ups; although this disparity may be caused by the requirement to see a doctor to prescribe birth control pills,[14] this is also true for dental check-ups.[15]

---

[11] European Commission (2011) The state of men's health in Europe report. Brussels: European Union, http://ec.europa.eu/health/population_groups/docs/men_health_report_en.pdf

[12] Centers for Disease Control and Prevention (2012) Workers Memorial Day. MMWR Morb Mortal Wkly Rep. 61:281.

[13] Actually men suffer more severely from a flu including a higher death rate: Sue K (2017) The science behind "man flu" BMJ 2017:359, https://doi.org/10.1136/bmj.j5560

[14] Hawkes S & Buse K (2013) Gender and global health: evidence, policy, and inconvenient truths. Lancet 381:1783–1787.

[15] Sakalauskienė Ž et al. (2011) Factors related to gender differences in toothbrushing among Lithuanian middle-aged university employees. Medicina (Kaunas) 47:180–186.

- Unhealthy diet/alcohol: According to the National Consumption Study II of the Federal Ministry of Food, Agriculture and Consumer Protection, men eat more meat and sausages, fish, milk (products) and cheese, sweets, and sugary drinks but fewer vegetables and fruit compared to women.[16] Excessive alcohol consumption costs twice as many men as women their lives.[17] For many men, alcohol consumption is associated with ideas of masculinity.[18]

- Suicide: Men are more likely to commit suicide, although depression is considered more common in women and women attempt (non-fatal) suicide more often. Men are less likely to seek help for depression and mental illness.

- Biology: The frontal lobe of the brain—the part that controls judgement and weighing the consequences of an action—develops more slowly in boys and young men than in women. This may contribute to far more boys and men dying in accidents or because of violence, such as drunk driving and homicide. Lack of judgement and consideration of consequences can also contribute to adverse life choices, such as smoking or excessive drinking. Lack of risk competence and displacement mechanisms lead to persistent denial of simple and obvious links between smoking, excessive eating and drinking, lack of exercise, stress, and emerging symptoms of disease.

This gap between men and women in health and life expectancy is grotesquely underreported globally. Although the medical need is clearly on the side of men's health, gender studies on health and life expectancy show a huge bias towards women's health: An online database search of the National Library of Medicine (PubMed) found 152,450 studies on women's health versus only 10,391 on men's health,[19] or just 6%. To date, only three countries in the world—Australia, Brazil, and Ireland—have attempted to address men's disease burden by adopting national male-focused strategies. In Australia, since 2003, women's health research has received more than AUS$833 million from the National Health and Medical Research Council compared to less than $200 million for men. Breast cancer received $60 million more than

---

[16] Max Rubens Institute. National Consumption Survey II, https://www.mri.bund.de/fileadmin/MRI/Institute/EV/NVSII_Abschlussbericht_Teil_2.pdf

[17] Lim S et al. (2012) A comparative risk assessment of burden of disease and injury attributable to 67 risk factors and risk factor clusters in 21 regions, 1990–2010: a systematic analysis for the Global Burden of Disease Study 2010. Lancet 380:2224–60.

[18] Hinote BP & Webber GR (2012) Drinking toward manhood: masculinity and alcohol in the former USSR. Men Masc 15:292–310.

[19] PubMed.gov, https://pubmed.ncbi.nlm.nih.gov/?term=women%27s+health, https://pubmed.ncbi.nlm.nih.gov/?term=men%27s+health, retrieved 2020-12-28.

prostate cancer and ovarian cancer $64 million more than testicular cancer. The smaller funding for men's health research is a paradox given their shorter average life expectancy and the fact that one in two Australian men will be diagnosed with cancer by the age of 85 compared to only one in three Australian women.[20]

This neglect by policymakers is reinforced by negative stereotypes about men. For example, some assume that men are largely disinterested in their health—an attitude that in turn can discourage men from engaging with health services.[21] Health programmes often view men as oppressive, self-centred, disinterested, or violent.[22] Addressing men's health will be especially important to combat the "pandemic" of non-communicable chronic diseases that affect more men than women and men at younger ages. And this is not just a gender equity issue. It is also a question of economic efficiency, because ultimately expensive hospital services must be used.[23] Public and political measures to improve men's health, i.e. men's health, should have three objectives:[24]

1. Schools where stereotypes about masculinity are challenged.
2. Promoting men's health and well-being in the workplace.
3. Targeting health services and health promotion to marginalized men, minority men, men in prison, and men who have sex with men—all of whom have a higher burden of disease and more frequent early death than other men.

Interventions in high-income countries (e.g. Australia, the USA, and Western European countries) generally involved outreach to men in pubs and bars, sports clubs, barbershops, schools, and workplaces, with a focus on weight loss, smoking cessation, and other lifestyle changes. One example among overweight or obese male football fans in Scottish professional football clubs shows that this works.[25] Men and women can also be supported to

---

[20] Prostate News, Men die earlier but women's health gets four times more funding, Prostate Cancer Foundation NZ, https://prostate.org.nz/2014/01/men-die-earlier-womens-health-gets-four-times-funding/

[21] McKinlay E et al. (2009) New Zealand men's health care: are we meeting the needs of men in general practice? J Primary Health Care 1:302–310.

[22] Barker G et al. (2010) Questioning gender norms with men to improve health outcomes: evidence of impact. Glob Public Health 5:539–553.

[23] Juel K & Christensen K (2008) Are men seeking medical advice too late? Contacts to general practitioners and hospital admissions in Denmark 2005. J Public Health (Oxf) 30:111–113.

[24] White A et al. (2011) Europe's men need their own health strategy. BMJ 343:d739.

[25] Hunt K et al. (2014) A gender-sensitive weight loss and healthy living programme for overweight and obese men delivered by Scottish Premier League football clubs (FFIT): a pragmatic randomised controlled trial. Lancet. 383:1211–21, http://do.org/10.1016/S0140-6736(13)62420-4

reshape traditional gender roles to create more equitable relationships in terms of sexual behaviour, intimate partner violence, and prevention of sexually transmitted diseases.[26]

So, what is needed is a global men's health movement. A Google search for the term "Department—Institute—women's health" yields pages and pages of entries; the same search for "Department—Institute—men's health" yields a single institute, the world's first Institute for men's health, situated in Germany[27] at the University Medical Center Hamburg the world's first professor of men's health. The approach is very broad in terms of content, ranging from sports, anti-aging, and lifestyle medicine, to diabetes, depression, and hormone deficiency, to sexual dysfunction. The last point, as far as erectile dysfunction (i.e. lack of penile erectile function) is concerned, is extremely important as it can be the first sign of serious cardiovascular disease.[28] Given the dramatic gap in men's health and the mounting evidence on how to close it, the next step is to put the issue on the agenda of all national governments and global health institutions without compromising efforts to improve women's health. A new organization, Global Action on men's health, was recently formed to advocate for national, regional, and global health policies. It is time to recognize not only the benefits of such policies for men but also the potential benefits for women, children, and society.[29] Men's physical illness, for example, can affect the mental health of their partners. When men are ill, are injured, or die, households and female partners suffer a loss of income.[30] Closing the men's health gap (Fig. 5.1) would therefore benefit men, women, and their children.

Uneducated + Male = Minus 15

After the previous considerations on the aspects "uneducated" and "man", you might ask yourself how it is with uneducated men or educated women. And you would be right in your assumption: Men at risk of poverty in Germany have an average life expectancy of 70.1 years; rich women, on the other hand,

[26] Dworkin SL et al. (2013) Gender-transformative interventions to reduce HIV risks and violence with heterosexually active men: a review of the global evidence. AIDS Behav 17:2845–63.

[27] https://www.uke-io.de/medical-services/medical-treatment/mens-health.html

[28] de Kretser DM (2010) Determinants of male health: the interaction of biological and social factors. Asian J Androl 12:291–297, https://doi.org/10.1038/aja.2010.15

[29] https://gamh.org

[30] Hagedoorn M et al. (2001) Chronic disease in elderly couples: are women more responsive to their spouses' health condition than men? J Psychosom Res 51:693–696.

Fig. 5.1 Difference in total (below) and post-retirement (above) life expectancy for poor (black bar) and rich (open bar) males and females

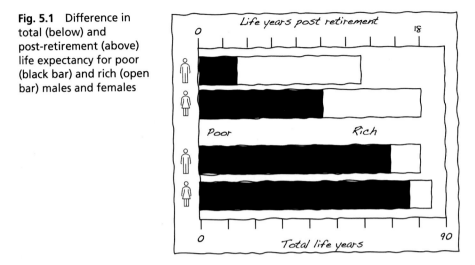

have an average life expectancy of 85 years, which is exactly 15-year difference! In between, women at risk of poverty have a life expectancy of just under 77 years and rich men 81 years. According to a study by Zürich Life Insurance, many poor people therefore live such short lives that a general extension of the retirement age to 71 or even 73 is hardly possible. Poor people would then have no prospect of retirement. According to statistics, rich people are those who have more than 150% of the average income; citizens who have less than 60% of the average income at their disposal are considered at risk of poverty.

From a medical point of view, one could conclude that there is just a lack of education in the population—especially among men—regarding healthcare and health risks. Is the solution only to be found in school or vocational school education about health? Should the cause (and solution) of these dramatic differences in life expectancy really be so trivial? Education is a problematic concept with at least three meanings: firstly, as socially relevant competence capital, secondly in the Humboldtian sense as the shaping and refinement of an individual self-image, and thirdly as the link between society and the individual in the habitus concept of the French sociologist Pierre Bourdieu, in which personal networks and origins guarantee renown, prestige, and success. In the latter concept of education in particular, social integration and financial security are two essential health-promoting factors. For social inequalities, however, education can be both poison and medicine in one: both a way to escape social inequality and a main criterion to define social inequality.[31] Because of this dual character, it is difficult to correlate a

---

[31] El-Mafaalani A (2020) Education Myth: The unjust society, its education system and its future. 320 p., Kiepenheuer & Witsch, Cologne, ISBN-10: 346205368X.

notion of education that is not further defined with health. In this respect, the term health education should not be overused as an explanation here: Education is just education. Education is neither a health concept nor a magic bullet.

The aim of a prevention-oriented health system should therefore be to equalize life expectancy between the educated and the uneducated, the poor and the rich, and men and women. A recent exciting observation was that the difference in life expectancy is a recent development of the twentieth century. Until then, the life expectancy of both sexes was similar. Since then, the lifespan of both sexes increased with the decline in dangerous infections, but this trend was decisively slowed down in men as the influence of chronic diseases, which usually only become important after middle age, increased. The increase begins from an age of 40; is most prevalent between 50 and 70, highest at 60 years; and only levels out again for 90-year-olds. With respect to causality, both lifestyle, in particular smoking, and a mechanistically unknown higher tendency to cardiovascular diseases contribute. Moreover, maternal mortality decreased, while men often have unhealthy or even dangerous occupations.[32]

Thus, also these observations point to the close interplay between health and socio-economic conditions. Moreover, we see that as soon as infections are eliminated and other diseases appear, we are not able to handle them with sufficient impact, and they become chronic, apparently affecting more men than women. This confirms that we have an (unprecise) disease system rather than a health system. One must wonder: Are the incentives for all healthcare providers (i.e. doctors, hospitals, and so on) consistent with the noble goal of enabling health? Probably not. But where exactly is the sticking point? Therefore, dear reader, we must—willy-nilly—take a trip into our healthcare system and our healthcare policy in addition to the previous scientific analysis.

---

[32] Beltrán-Sánchez H et al. (2015) Twentieth century surge of excess male mortality. Proceedings of the National Academy of Sciences 112:8993–8998; https://doi.org/10.1073/pnas.1421942112

6

False Incentives

No two countries are alike when it comes to organizing and delivering healthcare for their people. When the Prussian government sent Rudolf Virchow to Upper Silesia in 1848 to investigate the epidemic of typhus there, he identified hunger, poverty, and poor hygiene as the main causes. Virchow saw the state and the church as responsible. And his prescription? Not medicine, but political and social reforms: "Medicine is a social science, and politics is nothing more than medicine on a large scale".[1] So, Virchow became politically active in the Reichstag, the German parliament, and a constant proverbial thorn in the German chancellor Bismarck's side culminating in the infamous Sausage Duel over a debate on the funding for the navy. Bismarck challenged Virchow the next day to a duel, but as the one challenged Virchow was allowed to choose the weapons, and he chose two seemingly alike sausages, one filled with trichinae (a worm which causes a deadly zoonotic disease) and the other a normal sausage. Virchow then asked Bismarck to choose his weapon and eat it, and then he will do the same. Bismarck's representatives refused, and thus no duel was fought. In December 1884, Otto von Bismarck introduced the first large-scale compulsory insurance to establish universal healthcare. However, Bismarck's original intentions were not genuinely social. His health insurance was a reluctant reaction to upheavals among the working class in the wake of the Industrial Revolution, and a way to secure a political advantage against the Socialist Workers Party. Thus, health = politics, and, notwithstanding the desire and goal to help a patient, an important and legitimate

---

[1] Baasch A. (2019) Rudolf Virchow: politics as medicine on a grand scale. Stories of Democracy; https://www.demokratiegeschichten.de/rudolf-virchow-politik-als-medizin-im-grossen/

H. H. H. W. Schmidt, *The end of medicine as we know it - and why your health has a future*, https://doi.org/10.1007/978-3-030-95293-8_6

incentive for healthcare providers and organizations is money and profit provided the patient comes first. So, it is worth looking at the political and financial incentives in different healthcare systems.

Universal Health Coverage

Among all industrialized countries in the world, universal health coverage is the standard and defined by the WHO as "all people and communities can use the promotive, preventive, curative, rehabilitative and palliative health services they need, of sufficient quality to be effective, while also ensuring that the use of these services does not expose the user to financial hardship". There are at least four ways to reach this goal:

- Single payer systems
- Socialized medicine
- Insurance mandates
- Hybrid systems

True and fully single payer systems are only very few in the world. In Canada and Taiwan, the government pays for medical care and restricts alternative payment mechanisms. In the USA, Medicare is an example. In socialized medicine, such as the UK, the government not only pays for healthcare but also owns the facilities and employs the professionals. In the USA, the Veterans Health Administration is socialized as the government owns all hospitals and all healthcare providers are government employees. In UK's "National Health Service" (NHS), every citizen is treated in the same way. There is no health insurance, and NHS is instead paid for through a small extra tax. Information on patients is readily shared between medical establishments as electronic healthcare records. Income does not matter; cost-benefit considerations of procedures do. For example, expensive "life-extending" drugs or procedures are not available when the cost outweighs the benefit (remember the NNT) but can be "purchased" outside the NHS if a patient insists. These standards and controls are set by the National Institute for Health and Care Excellence (NICE). This prevents pharma companies, for example, taking advantage of the system. NICE is considered a world leader in this. On the downside, universal healthcare has many regulations and leaves no option for patients to choose the physician or treatment that they want, and waiting times can be long, e.g. in NHS dentistry patients must wait up to 3 years for an appointment, and appointments may be cancelled, sometimes even in between the different steps of a root canal treatment. Those who pay privately for their dental treatment, on the other hand, receive appointments, but co-payments for this are high.[2] Being government employees, many nurses and doctors feel understaffed compared to many high-income countries and are not satisfied with their financial packages or incentives. They may work, however, also in private healthcare to top up their salary, and pensions are generous.

In hybrid systems, single payer elements are combined with insurance mandates. For example, in Australia, France, Singapore, Sweden, and the UK, the government provides a standard set of care for all citizens, with options to supplement this with private insurance. Finally, in insurance mandate systems, such as Japan, the Netherlands, and Switzerland, the government does not pay for healthcare but mandates that all citizens purchase health insurance from private or public insurers. This may include a lowest minimum standard coverage, subsidies for low-income citizens, and opt-outs for high-income citizens. But how do different systems perform?

The Loser Is…

The World Economic Forum criticizes that we have mainly volume- or input-based healthcare without systematic assessments of the quality of services, i.e. its output or value for each individual patient. When 11 high-income countries were analysed for performance measures across five domains—access to care, care process, administrative efficiency, equity, and healthcare outcomes—the top-performing countries overall were Norway, the Netherlands, and Australia. USA ranked last (Fig. 6.1), despite spending far more of its gross domestic product on healthcare; it ranked last on access to care, last on administrative efficiency, last on equity, and last on healthcare outcomes.[3]

Another dichotomy that can easily be drawn up is the ratio of money invested in prevention, i.e. true healthcare versus sick care.

---

[2] Healthwatch (2021) Twin crisis of access and affordability calls for a radical rethink of NHS dentistry, https://www.healthwatch.co.uk/news/2021-05-24/twin-crisis-access-and-affordability-calls-radical-rethink-nhs-dentistry

[3] Schneider EC et al., Mirror, Mirror 2021—Reflecting Poorly: Health Care in the U.S. Compared to Other High-Income Countries, Commonwealth Fund, https://doi.org/10.26099/01DV-H208

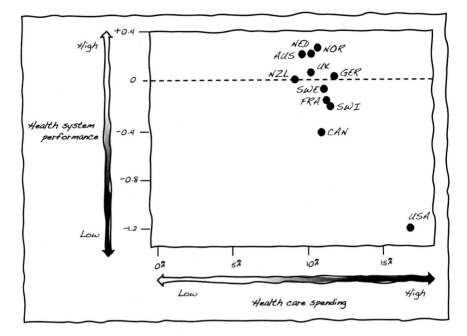

Fig. 6.1 Healthcare system performance compared to spending (as a per cent of GDP)

Only 1% for Prevention

Looking into the details how healthcare costs distribute in the different sectors and purposes, expenditures of the German statutory health insurance were, for example, analysed in detail. Of the total 252 billion euros in 2019, pure benefit expenditure amounted to around 240 billion euros. The rest of 5% were administrative costs. The hospital sector represents the largest share of expenditure (Fig. 6.2) (80 billion euros, 34%). This is surprising and does not correlate with where we have the most contact with the healthcare system in our lifetime, namely, with outpatient medical care, through all general practitioners and specialists combined. These account for only half of what is spent on hospitals (41 billion euros, 17%). The third largest expenditure is the pharmaceutical sector (also 41 billion euros and a share of 17%).[4] Considering the high *Number Needed to Treat* and the low success rate of currently prescribed drugs, there is an obvious savings potential here. Finally, the fourth position with all dental services is also surprising, which at 15

---

[4] Health Care Data: Expenditure (2020) Verband der Ersatzkassen; https://www.vdek.com/presse/daten/d_versorgung_leistungsausgaben.html

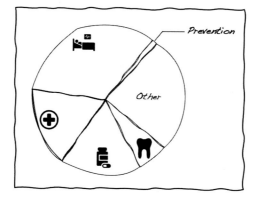

Fig. 6.2 Ratio of German Statutory Health Insurance expenditures, according to input into hospitals (top), outpatient physicians (left), pharmaceuticals and dentists (bottom), and an almost negligible expenditure on prevention (narrow black striped segment top right). Not labelled are other miscellaneous benefits for remedies and aids, sickness benefits, and others

billion still account for 6% and thus more than one-third of the 17% of all other general practitioner and specialist costs—and the 52% privately payable costs that are not covered by the health insurance funds are not even included.[5]

Shockingly low is the expenditure on the most cost-effective medical intervention, i.e. prevention. Only 2.7 billion, or 1%, of all health expenditure is invested here. It could not be clearer that the incentives lie predominantly in the care of diseases rather than in the preservation of health and that we have a disease system but no health system. Taking a closer look where the most money is spent, in the hospitals, one can observe what happens when cost-effectiveness is not monitored or controlled.

Why Germany Was So Well "Prepared" for COVID-19

Germany has a gigantic overcapacity in hospitals and ranks number one in the frequency of X-rays and back, knee, hip, and shoulder surgeries and heart catheters. The resulting overcapacity in intensive care beds turned out to be Germany's advantage in the COVID-19 pandemic. German hospitals are engaged in a gigantic arms race of commercialization of unnecessary health services that create an irrational demand for more intensive care beds. Since

---

[5] Jahns T. Turnover of a dental practice, https://www.praxisgruendungen.de/umsatz-einer-zahnarztpraxis/

many of these health services were non-essential to say the least, they could be shifted with ease during the COVID-19 pandemic. By postponing elective—and probably many unnecessary—surgeries, an extremely large number of ventilation beds, at least per capita much more than any other European country, became available, and unlike in many other countries, Germany's ventilation capacities hardly ever reached their limits during the COVID-19 pandemic.[6] In other countries, triage, i.e. prioritization of medical assistance when resources were insufficient, became necessary because their planning was only done for what was necessary and sensible. There was none of Germany's unnecessary overcapacity and much less to no leeway to postpone any surgeries. How did Germany end up in this situation? In 2003, the previous cost recovery principle was replaced with the Australian Diagnosis Related Groups (DRG) system. Of note though, shortly after its introduction in Germany, the Australians abolished the system again. They had noticed that the number of diagnoses had more than doubled, because each new or secondary diagnosis brought additional money into a DRG system. Economically astute German clinics—especially chains—could now make enormous profits, but municipal or state clinics, if they were not careful, could also make extreme losses. During the principle of self-cost recovery, hospitals were not allowed to make a profit. Any surplus was deducted in the following year. In the opinion of some health economists, self-cost recovery principle led to a self-service mentality in hospitals and to longer hospital stays for patients, since they were billed per day and per bed. However, the total length of stay had already fallen by 1985 from 18 to 14 days, i.e. by 24% when DRGs were introduced. There were excesses though, for example, the private income of chief physicians, which could amount to several million Deutschmarks per year, and thus an unequal treatment of privately and statutorily insured patients. In addition to their fixed salary, chief physicians had the so-called liquidation right for optional medical services for private patients. The chief physicians paid part of the income to the hospital operator, who provided the entire infrastructure including staff; another part was paid to the subordinate physicians, in particular the senior physicians, who assisted in the treatment of private patients (pool participation). The rest was the chief physician's private income. However, instead of correcting the few weaknesses of cost recovery, the entire hospital financing was reformed according to market economy principles, and hospitals became a branch of industry for private capital investors. The ban on making profits was lifted, and the new per-case flat-rate

---

[6] Zieglmeier M (2020) The concealed reason. Deutsche Apotheker Zeitung 25:42, https://www.deutsche-apotheker-zeitung.de/daz-az/2020/daz-25-2020/der-verschwiegene-grund

system set many economically rational but medically and ethically wrong
incentives:

- Squeeze staff costs, leading to time pressures on staff and poorer care
  for patients.
- Select patients with the most favourable cost-revenue ratio.
- Increase the number and severity of cases, resulting in overtreatment and
  mishandling and making patients sicker than they are.

None of this existed in the case of cost recovery since this form of financing
did not contain such economic incentives. Now in the DRG system, staff
positions that were cut converted into investment fund revenues. And contrary to its goals—and as could have been anticipated from the Australian
experience—total hospital expenditure has risen more steeply than before
(Fig. 6.3), as has the number of cases.

Thus, DRGs must be regarded as a failure. However, this is only the case if
the actual purpose was to reduce costs. The counterhypothesis would be as
follows: Lobbyists have abolished the welfare state principle of cost-covering
in order to convert the hospital sector into a lucrative business field for private
investors. Listed hospital chains emerged that cherry-picked so-called good

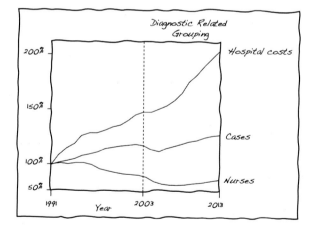

Fig. 6.3 Misguided developments in the German hospital system since the introduction of flat rates per case (1991 = 100%): Hospital costs and cases increase, and non-
medical staff (nurses) decreases because profits can be increased. (Source Federal
Statistical Office: Inventory of Hospital Planning and Investment Financing in the
Federal States of the German Hospital Association)

risks, such as hip replacement patients without significant concomitant diseases and with a low risk of complications. Patients with multiple concomitant diseases and a high risk of becoming "long-stayers" who could not be treated at anything approaching cost recovery were left to community hospitals with their mandate to provide care. Conversely, experienced physicians, especially surgeons, who specialized in certain operations and performed them with minimal complication rates, were lured away from these municipal clinics to the corporations. Thus, although the average length of stay of patients fell from 14 to 7 days, the number of cases increased at the same time.

Many municipal clinics and district hospitals were first renovated by the county with tax money and then sold to a corporation for a symbolic euro. To fill the large number of beds, older and older patients with concomitant illnesses were persuaded to undergo therapies that would have been discouraged a few years earlier because the risks were too great. Now 90-year-olds were being fitted with hip joint prostheses instead of being advised to put up with a little pain and use physiotherapy. Thanks to improved surgical techniques and elaborate intensive care, this also works surprisingly well and without complications, at least in the short and medium term.

And then medical tourism began, bringing patients willing and able to pay any sum demanded. At the big health fairs in Dubai and Riyadh, the German health system was praised. Arabs with multiple illnesses, later Russians, and other nations with superrich came with their families, resided in the most expensive hotels, and shopped to pass the time. An undesirable side effect was that many Arab patients did not simply pay for a service rendered but only for its success. And it is just not that easy to simply fix a person who has spent a lifetime on a diet of fatty meats and sweets, resulting in severe diabetes and massive organ damage. That's exactly the kind of unrealistic promises of salvation that had been advertised at health fairs. Lessons were learned. Not by keeping a distance from medical tourism in the future, but by requiring every "foreign self-payer" to deposit large sums of money in cash. Delicious in this context is the legendary "money exchange" action at the university hospital of the University Clinics of Aachen, Germany.[7] In May 2010, a man with an Arabic name contacted the commercial director of the hospital and claimed to be the contact person of a man from the Libyan upper class. This wealthy patient wanted to be treated in the Aachen clinic. Shortly afterwards, in June, a meeting took place at which the director was asked to exchange the 60,000 euros in cash for smaller notes, as they themselves only had large ones with

---

[7] Aachener Zeitung (2010) Fraud: University hospital now has 60,000 euros in play money, https://www.aachener-zeitung.de/nrw-region/betrug-uniklinikum-hat-jetzt-60000-euro-spielgeld_aid-27210397

them and this was very impractical. With the smaller notes, one wanted to settle smaller bills. The director himself agreed and got the sum in smaller notes. The swindlers exchanged the suitcases unnoticed. What remained was a suitcase full of play money. When this was noticed, the perpetrators were long gone.

However, the Arab customers brought with them not only money but also germs that are resistant to almost all antibiotics.[8] Arab countries are, in fact, world leaders in the misuse of ultrawide spectrum and reserve antibiotics and thus also in the development of resistance. As mentioned before, both the treatment of critically ill but wealthy patients and the risk of infection resulted in two reactions that gave Germany the advantage during the COVID-19 pandemic: Intensive care and hygiene and microbiology capacities were massively expanded, while in countries such as Italy capacities were insufficient, and many COVID-19 patients died because of bacterial superinfections with multi-resistant hospital germs. The marketing value of the globally perceived low COVID-19 mortality in German hospitals will allow medical tourism to climb to new heights after the COVID-19 pandemic.

So, while other EU countries have a leaner healthcare system that merely ensures that the population is provided with sensible medical services, and southern EU countries have been cut to the bone by the banking and euro crises, Germany has taken a different path. The introduction of DRGs allowed investors to introduce "maximum medicine" where it was financially lucrative, rather than limiting themselves to the optimal or value-based medicine. The COVID-19 pandemic was one of the few conceivable scenarios in which such an oversized system was a benefit to a country.

But it didn't stop there; even on top of the already bloated system, there was further "tweaking" to make even more gains and not even always by legal means. The motives for the methods are not just greed but also financial need, as the state-run, other than private hospitals have been unable to meet their investment obligations for years resulting in backlog of at least 30 billion euros.[9] Hospital operators and especially the hospital chains have come up with various strategies of "optimization". One rather brazen method works quite independently of the patient: the increasing phenomenon of exaggerated hospital bills—on average by about 2000 euros for every second bill. The first inspection service of statutory health insurers to go public recovered 307

[8] Fuchs F (2010) Dangerous germ in the hospital. Süddeutsche Zeitung, https://www.sueddeutsche.de/muenchen/patienten-mit-erreger-infiziert-gefaehrlicher-keim-im-klinikum-1.149298
[9] Deutsche Krankenhaus-Gesellschaft (2019) Bestandsaufnahme zur Krankenhausplanung und Investitionsfinanzierung in den Bundesländern, https://www.dkgev.de/fileadmin/default/Mediapool/3_Service/3.4._Publikationen/2019_DKG_Bestandsaufnahme_KH-Planung_Investitionsfinanzierung.pdf

million euros from conspicuous invoices from hospitals. Extrapolated to all 2000 hospitals in Germany, this means approximately 3 billion euros in incorrect billing every year. Despite the ever-increasing clear-up rate, the methodology tends to spread with 20% more complaints in 2018 compared to 2017, or 40% more than in 2016. The more is checked, the more is found. The rate of complaints remains the same, with no trend toward a reversal toward more correct billing behaviour. Hospitals are training optimizers for the creation of cases and the subsequent billing of flat rates per case, hiring them specifically for that purpose and simply taking their chances of getting caught. If they are caught, the hospitals usually cut their bills without any objection. In return, the medical service of the health insurance is now upgrading.

What are the tricks of the clinics? Since a hospital stay is more profitable than an outpatient therapy, clinics charge for a hospital stay even though the treatment could have been done on an outpatient basis, for example, for a gastroscopy as a control examination after a cancer operation. Or a rheumatism patient who is to have an MRI is wrongly admitted as an inpatient for 2 days. In many cases, the patient is in the hospital longer than necessary, for example, patients are already admitted 1 or 2 days before a planned operation. However, most of the money can be made by choosing the right principal diagnosis. For example, the remuneration for a ventilator patient in intensive care increases by more than 9800 euros if he or she is ventilated for more than 24 h. Dying has never been as difficult and expensive as it is today.

Even Dying Isn't Easy

Unfortunately, there can be disastrous misguided incentives for hospitals to prolong dying by a few pointless hours or days of artificial respiration for thousands of euros, even if the prognosis is hopeless.[10] In Germany, artificial respiration is thus expanding in an almost grotesque way to intensive care in the private home. Whereas in 2003 only 500 patients were ventilated at home, this figure has now risen to around 30,000 patients, i.e. 60 times more. With costs of up to 27,000 EUR per month, this is a very profitable business. However, ventilation is dangerous for the patient, so the rule should be: The shorter, the better. However, in up to 70% of patients, the discharge from intensive care is delayed beyond the medically reasonable duration. Discretion?

---

[10] Thöns M (2018) Patient ohne Verfügung - Das Geschäft mit dem Lebensende, Piper, 336pp; https://www.piper.de/buecher/patient-ohne-verfuegung-isbn-978-3-492-31219-6

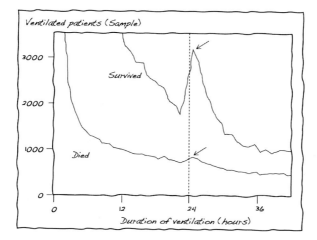

Fig. 6.4 Duration of ventilation within a sample of surviving and deceased patients. The peak shortly after the 24-h mark is conspicuous, as from here onwards billing becomes possible or a second day can be calculated. (Thöns M (2018) Overtherapy in intensive care: the medicine problem of this century. Pflege Professionell, https://pflege-professionell.at/uebertherapie-in-der-intensivmedizin-das-medizinproblem-dieses-jahrhunderts#_edn30)

I can only assume this is done to secure a revenue stream a little longer.[11] Hospitals are also ventilating older and sicker patients for long periods of time. There is an absurd peculiarity in the fee schedule in this regard: Ventilation started in the operating room is only to be coded if the ventilation interval lasts longer than 24 h.[12] Ventilations lasting less than 24 h are not reimbursed, the so-called ventilation hurdle. However, if ventilated 1 min longer, up to EUR 23,426 can be charged, depending on the diagnosis. However, there is a striking accumulation of ventilation, just beyond 24 h (Fig. 6.4). Thousands of patients are therefore quite obviously being ventilated for longer in an "optimized" manner in terms of billing, possibly even deceased patients even beyond the hour of death. Perverse, I can't call it anything else!

Only about 40% of patients survive ventilation for more than 2 weeks,[13] and of these, only about 12% of the elderly make it back to their former lives.

[11] DIGAB (2017) Outpatient intensive care after tracheostomy. Deutsche Medizinische Wochenschrift 142:909–911, https://doi.org/10.1055/s-0043-109101

[12] Spierling J (2019) Coding guidelines for critical care contexts. Medtronic, https://medinfoweb.de/data/CMM_Multicontents/files/PM/20190731_medtronic_kodierhilfe_intensivmedizin.pdf

[13] Damuth E et al. (2015) Long-term survival of critically ill patients treated with prolonged mechanical ventilation. A systematic review and meta-analysis. Lancet Respiratory Medicine 3:544–553, https://www.thelancet.com/journals/lanres/article/PIIS2213-2600(15)00150-2/fulltext

Most of them remain severely physically and mentally disabled. I can only strongly advise you to write a legally effective living will today—preferably notarized and deposited—that excludes senseless maximum therapy. However, do not use any template but address your current health situation and mention very specifically measures that you do not want in their nature or duration. For this, however, you absolutely need the advice of your attending physician to assess which measures these might be.[14] And even if you already have a living will, regularly adapt it to your current and personal health situation and your individual risks. For example, in the case of acute illnesses and the prospect of recovery, you will naturally want the maximum medical help. But in the case of a long course of illness and no realistic prospect of reaching a state of consciousness, you will want restrictions, for example, the exclusion of force-feeding and unnecessary medication.

The Surgery Boom

Since hospitals were paid according to cases and no longer according to beds, a second strategy for revenue "optimization" emerged, namely, to increase the severity per case primarily by increasing the number of predictable and expensive operations. Especially for bypass operations of the coronary vessels, high returns were thus quickly achieved, and cardiologists became the new stars of the clinics. They even entered the domain of cardiovascular surgery by using cardiac catheters not only for diagnosis and imaging of coronary vessels but also—if they were narrowed—widened them in the same operation and a few years later even inserted stents that kept the coronary vessels open even more permanently. Initially, heart and vascular surgeons were still left with heart valve operations, but cardiologists can now also insert these safely and quickly using modern blood vessel catheters. Cardiac catheter examinations (with or without stent) raise the reputation of a hospital and were performed three times as often in Germany than in other countries. Do Germans have sicker hearts than people in other countries? Certainly not. This high number of interventions can therefore not only have medical reasons. Germany's dense supply of cardiac catheterization laboratories is certainly an advantage in life-threatening emergencies. But there are not so many acute cases that all catheter places would be used to capacity. Moreover, it makes sense that a physician

---

[14] Langer S et al. (2013) Dealing with living wills: Problems caused by blanket formulations. Dtsch Arztebl110:A-2186/B-1924/C-1870,https://www.aerzteblatt.de/archiv/149204/Umgang-mit-Patientenverfuegungen-Probleme-durch-pauschale-Formulierungen

who performs this risky procedure does so relatively often to stay in practice. A hospital without a cardiac catheter lab is considered second class and on the hit list. So, it's also about reputation and securing the future of a hospital. The guidelines for cardiac catheter examinations are clear, but not all doctors adhere to them. A cardiac catheter examination is only appropriate for patients who have severe angina pectoris symptoms or a heart attack despite drug therapy. The grey area begins when a disease of the coronary vessels is present, but the patient has no acute symptoms. Some doctors like to just "check it out". However, this is in no way covered by the treatment guidelines. The German Institute for Quality Assurance and Transparency in Health Care found that, in 2017, 45% of patients with stable coronary heart disease covered by statutory health insurance who underwent cardiac catheterization did not follow the guidelines.

After cardiology, shoulder, hip, knee, and back complaints were discovered by the clinic "optimizers". With these orthopaedic and neurological complaints, respectively, your therapy depends a lot on whom you consult, a surgeon, an internist, or a physiotherapist. So, you can either end up on the operating table, take painkillers permanently, or do regular gymnastics. As far as orthopaedic surgery is concerned, Germany is far in the lead in an international comparison of industrialized countries. Every year, 400,000 artificial joints are implanted in Germany. Half of these operations are hip prosthesis operations, of which at least one in five is considered unnecessary.[15] Because the indications are becoming broader and broader to be able to operate on more patients, the complication rates are also increasing. Many patients are dissatisfied with their new joint afterwards, and 35,000 artificial joints are therefore replaced prematurely every year.

The most common cause of hip problems is wear and tear (osteoarthritis). The protective layer of cartilage that covers the femoral head is worn away. This leads to pain and inflammation. But only when the cartilage layer is completely gone and bone rubs on bone is joint replacement the only option. In at least half of the cases operated on, the affected leg was normally mobile,

---

[15] German Society for Orthopaedics and Trauma Surgery (2015) Fallpauschalen liefern falsche Anreize, https://dgou.de/presse/pressemitteilungen/detailansicht-pressemitteilungen/artikel/dkou-2015-fallpauschalen-liefern-falsche-anreize/; Deutsche Krankenhaus-Gesellschaft (2019) Bestandsaufnahme zur Krankenhausplanung und Investitionsfinanzierung in den Bundesländern, https://www.dkgev.de/fileadmin/default/Mediapool/3_Service/3.4._Publikationen/2019_DKG_Bestandsaufnahme_KH-Planung_Investitionsfinanzierung.pdf; Habit S (2013) Falsche Anreize, überflüssige Operationen. OVB Online, https://www.ovb-online.de/weltspiegel/wirtschaft/falsche-anreize-ueberfluessige-operationen-2992387.html; Editorial (2012) Techniker Krankenkasse criticizes superfluous back surgeries. Dtsch Arztebl, https://www.aerzteblatt.de/nachrichten/49679/Techniker-Krankenkasse-kritisiert-ueberfluessige-Ruecken-OPs

just with pain. Here the causes can be muscular problems, for example, muscle weakness, tension, and fascia hardening due to lack of movement and a lot of sitting. And perhaps it is also due to being overweight that the joints are slowly giving up. Who would constantly overload their beautiful car with concrete blocks until the axles and steering are finally gone? Probably nobody! So instead of surgery, lifestyle changes, weight loss, regular stretching and coordination exercises, and muscle building and strengthening would have helped just as much, if not better. These are all exercises that you can even do yourself—perhaps after a brief period of instruction—very well at home and even for free.

Disc surgeries are also increasing rapidly. Occasional back pain can become chronic, affecting one-third of all 18–59-year-olds. Back pain costs approximately 11 billion euros per year. Surgery is suggested to one in ten back pain patients. However, when a team of experts including physiotherapists, pain specialists, and psychotherapists look at the X-rays and findings for a second opinion before surgery, 85% of surgery recommendations are rejected, and alternatives to surgery, such as physiotherapy or pain management, are recommended.

So, patients are clearly receiving medically unnecessary operations. This is simply because operations and inpatient admissions are more lucrative for hospitals than treating patients as outpatients and sending them home. And beds are better utilized, which are considerations that fit more with a hotel industry than a healthcare industry. But many patients also contribute, seeming strangely disinterested in their own bodies. The doctor said yes, and the insurance company is paying. Who would have a new door installed in their car by the first garage that came along if a door jammed or didn't close properly? Probably nobody. With the new hip or the new knee, we see it apparently differently.

The vast majority of all back, shoulder, and knee operations are unnecessary, no more effective than placebo interventions—and yet they happen. In a study on shoulder surgery that could not be described as anything other than spectacular, only placebo or sham interventions were performed on some of the patients.[16] Of course, the patients were informed about this possibility beforehand and agreed to it, although even the placebo patients received anaesthesia and could not say afterwards whether they had also been operated on during the arthroscopy or not. Ethically, this was a bit problematic, since

---

[16] Beard DJ et al. (2018) Arthroscopic subacromial decompression for subacromial shoulder pain (CSAW): a multicentre, pragmatic, parallel group, placebo-controlled, three-group, randomised surgical trial. Lancet 391:329–338, https://doi.org/10.1016/S0140-6736(17)32457-1

it could not be assumed that patients whose joints were only mirrored but not operated on would benefit from this; they were deprived of normal treatment, so to speak. But then came the surprise: The arthroscopy with surgery did not show significantly better results than the sham procedure (only arthroscopy without surgery), or rather it was unnecessary in most cases. The results generally questioned the value of this surgery for these indications. I can say from personal experience that I trained away a shoulder tightness or impingement syndrome that recurred over a period of weeks by doing a very specific exercise at my gym. And whenever these symptoms occur, I quickly get them under control with it.

Surgeons are therefore put under pressure by their clinics via bonus and malus regulations to "sell" operations to fill existing operation capacities or are seduced by attractive bonuses and personal monetary interests to operate more frequently. Another reason may be that surgeons must have performed a certain number of specific operations as part of their specialist training, as laid down in the so-called compulsory catalogue.

In one case, the nonsensical nature of the intervention was proven to be so great that action was taken. In 2015, arthroscopy for knee joint osteoarthritis was removed from the benefits catalogue of the statutory health insurance funds. Studies showed that people with knee joint osteoarthritis who received arthroscopy suffered as much and as frequently from pain afterwards as those without the procedure. The measure is completely ineffective for this diagnosis.

Passive consumption of more and more medical services therefore does not necessarily always mean an improvement but often even a deterioration for you as a patient. Some may shy away from asking questions or even questioning a diagnosis and therapy or even obtaining a so-called second opinion from another specialist out of misunderstood respect for the doctor who used to be called "God in White". It is highly recommended to seek a second opinion before any elective surgery. For example, if your doctor says you have incipient knee osteoarthritis and magnetic resonance imaging showed a meniscus tear, you shouldn't blindly follow a surgery recommendation. Joints are made to move regularly. For example, it can help a lot to choose the right sport that is easy on the knee, i.e. cycling and swimming, instead of knee-straining jogging, tennis, or golf. Other so-called conservative methods, the possibilities of which are rarely exhausted, include the injection of hyaluronic acid. This biotechnologically produced substance smoothes, albeit temporarily, the remaining, roughened cartilage mass in the joint.

However, the mentality of clinics to focus on high throughput with "surgeries instead of beds" carries another risk for you. Not only were many operations in themselves unnecessary, for reasons of cost or optimization, clinics are discharging their patients earlier and earlier after surgery to so-called rehabilitation (rehab) clinics. Every third rehabilitation measure relates to pain after back, shoulder, hip, or knee surgery. Older patients with new hip or knee joints are particularly problematic. Since the introduction of flat rates per case, their length of stay in hospital has fallen by around 5 days and is continuing to fall. Rehab clinics are increasingly taking on tasks for which they are not actually responsible and which used to take place in the hospital, for example, wound care and pain relief. However, the rehabilitation clinics are not fully reimbursed for these increased medical and nursing expenses, which amount to a one-time charge of approximately 4000 euros. And it is not surprising that in case of complications many patients must be sent back to the clinics—one more reason to think twice and three times whether one really wants to get involved in such an operation or whether it would not be better to try non-surgical methods and one's own initiative instead of letting oneself fall into the role of the patient in need of an operation. This is also appropriate in the case of cardiac catheter examinations, which seem to be so undoubtedly sensible.

Up to now, it has been almost exclusively about the biggest cost factor, the clinics. However, very few of us have been to hospital, but we have been to a general practitioner, specialist, or dentist more often or regularly. And what do we experience there? Usually closely timed consultations and sometimes months of waiting time for appointments unless you are a private patient. And one reads that most medical practices would have to close without private patients. Some health politicians vehemently contradict this and demand 100% equal treatment of patients with statutory and—in those countries where possible—private insurance.

USA: The Extreme Case

Is the USA the only industrialized country in the world that does not have universal health coverage for all citizens? The USA has some of the best doctors and hospitals in the world, for those who can afford them. Even those who are sceptical of the claim that medical costs cause most bankruptcies concede that they are a significant contributor.[17] In the rest of the developed world, medical costs are hardly ever cited as a driver behind personal bankruptcy and covered through a system of societal solidarity (Fig. 6.5).

---

[17] https://www.bloomberg.com/view/articles/2017-01-17/the-myth-of-the-medical-bankruptcy

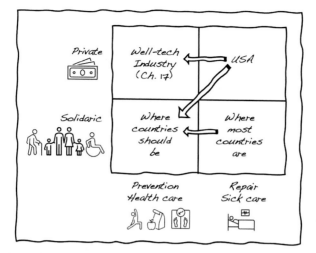

Fig. 6.5 Status of health coverage in most countries with respect to solidaric and private financing and focus on sick care versus prevention, where they should develop towards, and how the USA appears to be an exemption to both (see also Chap. 17)

As a trade-off, patients in the UK, Canada, and the Netherlands often face far longer wait times for care, particularly "elective" care, than those in the USA or private payers in Germany. Providers are generally much better paid in the USA, which has the lowest life expectancy and highest infant mortality rate. This is a major driver behind the higher costs, in addition to higher costs to plan, regulate, and manage health systems and services and higher per capita pharmaceutical costs, resulting in 17.8% of its gross domestic product spent on health, while other countries range from 9.6% to 12.4%.

Speaking of higher pharmaceutical costs, the pharmaceutical industry is the third largest cost component in the healthcare system, besides hospitals and physicians in private practice. Since the pharmaceutical industry not only supplies drugs but also researches diseases, it is deeply involved in the crisis of medicine. Therefore, this is worth a chapter of its own, especially since the end is coming as well for the pharmaceutical industry as we know it.

7

The End of Big Pharma

Not only are the costs of medicines high, which is why prescription medicines alone account for the third largest cost factor in the healthcare system, but the costs and risks for the pharmaceutical industry have also exploded. At the same time, the industry seems to be running out of ideas, which I see as one of the key symptoms of the crisis in medicine. This is where the concept of defining symptoms as disease and the treatment of symptoms as therapy was the first to suffer shipwreck. At least at the level of drug approval or negotiations with health insurance companies, every new drug is compared with existing drugs for every indication. If no real advantage is apparent, then such new developments fail or at least do not generate the sales revenues they would have to generate to recoup the previous costs and the costs of all failed projects of the same company.

It is also less and less sufficient to alleviate a symptom such as high blood pressure or to correct blood parameters such as cholesterol or blood sugar. Instead, what is relevant is whether fewer patient-relevant events such as heart attacks or strokes occur or whether life is prolonged. And here you already know the Number-Needed-to-Treat problem. If a concept has weaknesses, it doesn't get better by trying it the same way again and again. Unfortunately, on top of all the failures, some Big Pharma companies are lately trying to use semi-legal or illegal tricks to gain advantages. If Big Pharma continues in this manner, these companies will no longer exist in a few years or at least not in their present form and economic power.

H. H. H. W. Schmidt, *The end of medicine as we know it - and why your health has a future*, https://doi.org/10.1007/978-3-030-95293-8_7

The Costs Explode

The average cost of bringing a drug to market has risen exponentially for the pharmaceutical industry since the 1980s and has remained roughly constant since 2010 at an extremely high level of around USD 1.8 billion per successfully developed and approved drug.[1] Other studies calculate even higher costs of USD 2.8 billion. At the same time, the number of drugs approved per year has hardly increased since the 1960s (see Fig. 7.1). If one also considers the fact that two-thirds of newly approved drugs subsequently turn out to offer no advantage at all over the previous standard therapy, these are clear indicators of a crisis in the entire pharmaceutical industry.

The rise in costs between the 1990s and 2000s can be explained in part by more costly screening and development technologies but in large part by the cost of unsuccessful development trials. These failures are multiplying and must be indirectly co-funded by the fewer successful launches. Another cost driver is that the time from synthesis of a drug through preclinical optimization and clinical testing (usually in three phases) to market launch has increased to an average of 12 years, with 90% of drugs failing only in the final phase of clinical testing, i.e. when most of the costs have already been incurred.

Hardly Any Innovations

In addition, the few innovations still taking place are not evenly distributed across all indication areas in medicine, nor do they follow the mortality figures for different diseases and thus the medical need. Figure 7.2 divides the drug innovation pattern into 15 disease areas. In some medically highly relevant areas such as neurology (Alzheimer's disease, stroke) and cardiovascular diseases (hypertension), the pharmaceutical industry has experienced a series of failures and in some cases has withdrawn completely. In almost all indication areas, there is relative innovative silence. In some medically important areas, such as agents to combat parasitic infections, it is clear how generally sparse or non-existent innovations are and have been. One example is Chagas disease, a zoonosis caused by a parasite (transmitted from animals to humans by bloodsucking insects) endemic to South America, which remains one of the most neglected tropical diseases more than a century after its discovery. Approximately eight million people are affected with over 10,000 deaths

---

[1] Wouters OJ et al. (2020) Estimated research and development investment needed to bring a new medicine to market, 2009–2018. JAMA 323:844–853, https://doi.org/10.1001/jama.2020.1166

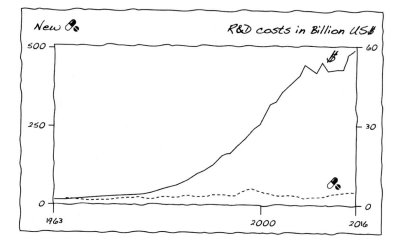

Fig. 7.1 The number of new drug approvals per year is not keeping pace with the rising research and development costs (in billions of US $). (Tufts Center for the Study of Drug Development (2017) Cost of Developing a New Drug/Tufts CSDD Cost Study, https://csdd.tufts.edu/tufts-csdd-cost-study; DiMasi JA et al. (2016) Innovation in the pharmaceutical industry: new estimates of R&D costs. Journal of Health Economics 47:20–33)

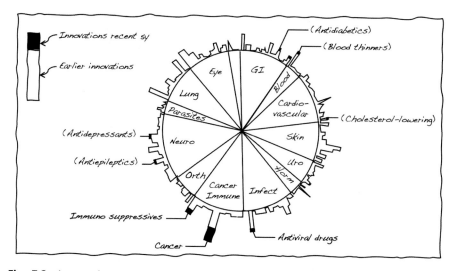

Fig. 7.2 Innovation patterns according to 15 therapeutic areas (WHO Anatomical Therapeutic Chemical Classification System): gastrointestinal and metabolic, blood, cardiovascular, skin, urology, hormones, infectious diseases, cancer and immune system, orthopaedics and muscle diseases, neurology, parasitic infections, lung, eye and other sense organs, and others. The outer columns represent sub-indications of these areas, and their height shows the number of approved drugs. Shown in black are the current innovations, which are essentially limited to immunosuppressants, tumour drugs, and antiviral drugs, i.e. only 2 of 15 therapeutic areas. (Santos R et al. (2016) A comprehensive map of molecular drug targets. Nature Reviews Drug Discovery. 16:19–34, https://doi.org/10.1038/nrd.2016.230)

annually. Due to population migration and tourism, Chagas disease has now also been reported in the USA, Canada, and many European countries.

In recent times (shown as a black bar), innovations have taken place almost mainly in the fields of cancer, immunology, and to some extent in infectious diseases (hepatitis C virus). The so-called immunosuppressants, i.e., drugs which suppress the immune system, have meant great progress and a blessing for patients, for example, in the treatment of psoriasis with up to complete freedom from symptoms and so far without relevant side effects. Hepatitis C treatment also cures a large proportion of patients. However, the seemingly most innovative area of cancer therapeutics, in which virtually every pharmaceutical company is currently researching, contains many pseudo-innovations.

Approximately half of the studies that led to the new approval of cancer drugs in Europe between 2014 and 2016 were so flawed that the extent of efficacy was either overestimated or not certain.[2] The errors are related to the design, conduct, analysis, and reporting of the trials. During this period, only ten trials (26%) had overall patient survival as a key measure. All other studies measured surrogate parameters, such as "time without further tumour enlargement" or "tumour response rates to therapy", which did not allow conclusions about prolonged life or improved quality of life.

Limited Growth and Terminal Decline

Not only have the costs of drug development exploded and innovation yields recently been poor, but Big Pharma is facing a conceptual crisis that began back in the 1950s. Since then, the number of newly approved drugs per billion dollars spent on research and development has halved every 9 years and has fallen 80-fold when adjusted for inflation (Fig. 7.3). This trend has been slightly cynically referred to as Eroom's law, as a play on words and a twist on the established Moore's law. Gordon Earle Moore is the co-founder of the computer chip company Intel. His Moore's law describes the exponential increase in the number of transistors that could be placed on an integrated circuit. This number doubled every 2 years from the 1970s to 2010 and was the basis for the information technology and accompanying socioeconomic

---

[2] Huseyin N et al. (2019) Design characteristics, risk of bias, and reporting of randomised controlled trials supporting approvals of cancer drugs by European Medicines Agency, 2014–16: cross sectional analysis. BMJ 366:l5221, https://www.bmj.com/content/366/bmj.l5221

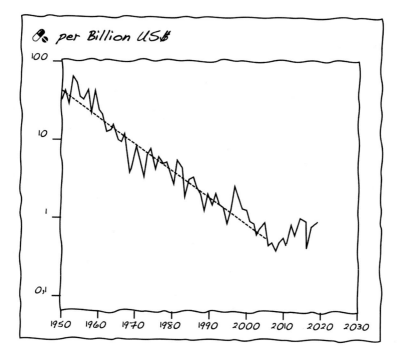

Fig. 7.3 Eroom's law of pharmaceutical research and development (Scannell JW et al. (2012) Diagnosing the decline in pharmaceutical R&D efficiency. Nature Reviews Drug Discovery 11:191–200, https://doi.org/10.1038/nrd3681). Shown is the decrease in approved drugs per billion dollars invested from 1950 to 2010 and a projection for the 2020s. Note that the left axis is logarithmic. Thus, it is not a linear but exponential efficiency deterioration

revolution we have seen over the last 40 years. In the pharmaceutical industry, the reverse is true.

This loss of efficiency in the pharmaceutical industry is therefore not a recent event. It already started in the 1950s. Efficiency did not worsen because legislation on the approval of drugs was tightened worldwide in the 1970s as a result of the thalidomide scandal caused by the German company, Grünenthal. It also did not improve with the introduction of so-called biological drugs, such as those used so successfully for psoriasis (see above). The hoped-for breakthrough in the understanding of diseases through the sequencing of the entire human genome also failed to materialize in large part because the twenty-first-century technology still clashes with eighteenth- and nineteenth-century definitions of disease.

Therefore, a constant, unremitting logarithmic loss of efficiency over several decades leads to only one conclusion: The whole concept of how drugs are developed, and thus how we recognize disease, is fundamentally flawed. Obviously, in the beginning, there were still "low-hanging fruit", that is, it was still relatively easy to get a drug to a market that relieved only one symptom, especially when there was no competition yet. Now, however, this approach is becoming more and more difficult, failing more and more often, and becoming more and more costly. Big Pharma is virtually running into the wall, even though in recent years the loss of efficacy seems to have been stopped[3] but still at very high costs per successful drug development. It doesn't take a prophet to see that this will hardly be financially viable if the development of a drug (including all failures) will cost on average one billion US dollars or more.

Here, everything we have already discussed so far comes together logically: Hardly any disease is understood mechanistically, so we usually label it according to its symptoms and/or an organ; hence, we are then left with treating only symptoms because treating causes is not possible. It is no wonder that this approach is highly inefficient for patients, and they hardly benefit from their medicine. And so, it is no surprise that it is impossible to develop precisely effective drugs in this scenario. After all, how do you expect to make something better than its predecessor if the new approach has the same weaknesses as the old one. I hope the crisis in medicine is now becoming clearer to you and you realize that I am not exaggerating.

However, Big Pharma is the most vulnerable part within the crisis because, unlike Small Pharma, it is based on constant innovation. Only innovative drugs receive patent protection, and only for patent-protected, quasi-unique drugs can high prices be charged. Patent protection usually expires after 20 years. Of this time, development has taken about 14 years. Pharmaceutical companies patent new substances or substance families relatively early so that the subsequent costly development is already largely under patent protection. They could also do this without patent protection and keep their project secret. However, this is risky because another pharmaceutical company might write a competing patent during this time, which in the worst case would prevent the first company from marketing the product. So, it's always a balancing act between not too early and not too late. As a rule, once all clinical studies have been completed and the approval process has been concluded, there are about 6 years left for patent protection, and thus exclusive use and marketing, to recoup all previous costs (including those of all other parallel projects which failed during the same period) and, ideally, to make a profit.

After patent protection expires, however, any other company can also market the same drug for the same indication. The prices for such imitation preparations (generics) are on average two-thirds cheaper than for the corresponding

---

[3] Ringel MS et al. (2020) Breaking Eroom's Law. Nat Rev Drug Discov. 19:833–834, https://doi.org/10.1038/d41573-020-00059-3. PMID: 32300238.

initial supplier preparation. Many generics are even cheaper. It is still possible to make money with them but not to the extent of a Big Pharma company.

Investments are necessary for innovations. Sustainable business growth and value creation depend on constant research and development productivity with a positive return on investment that generates revenues that can be reinvested in new research and development projects. But productivity is falling. Both investment and returns for each drug are also staggered over many years. Most products fail to reach the market and fail at different points in development with different costs accumulated up to that point. Late failure costs disproportionately more than early failure.

Whoever of the big management consultancies analyses this situation economically, for example, Deloitte or Boston Consulting,[4] comes to the same conclusion: The return on investment in pharmaceutical R&D is rapidly declining. The most frightening thing about this analysis is how robust, consistent, and rapid the downward trend in return on investment is over a period of more than 20 years and that it is already below the cost of capital and will fall to zero within just a few years.

I've already mentioned a few possible reasons for this: rising costs, burdensome clinical trial timelines, declining success rates in development, a stricter regulatory environment, and increasing pressure from payers to look more closely at whether a new drug really offers patients an advantage over standard therapy. According to business analysts, there is also a fundamental business problem that brings all these factors together: Unlike other industries, the product line is finite. There are only so many human conditions that can be treated, although it sometimes feels as if new conditions are quite creatively invented out of sensitivities, for example, social anxiety disorder instead of shyness.[5] As each new drug improves the current standard of care (or at least it should), the bar is raised for the next drug, making it more expensive, more difficult, and less likely to achieve such improvement while reducing the potential room for improvement. Thus, more and more investment must be made to achieve a smaller and smaller increase in value for patients, which must lead to a diminishing return on investment: This is where the law of diminishing returns proves itself. All this must continue if we do not make

---

[4] Stott K (2017) Pharma's broken business model: An industry on the brink of terminal decline. EndpointNews; https://endpts.com/pharmas-broken-business-model-an-industry-on-the-brink-of-terminal-decline/; Stott K (2018) Pharma's broken business model - Part 2: Scraping the barrel in drug discovery. EndpointNews; https://endpts.com/pharmas-broken-business-model-part-2-scraping-the-barrel-in-drug-discovery/

[5] Flintrop J (2003) The "disease inventors": the honest doctor is the stupid one. Dtsch Arztebl 100:A-3352/B-2791/C-2611; https://www.aerzteblatt.de/archiv/39864/Die-Krankheitserfinder-Der-ehrliche-Arzt--ist-der-Dumme; Blech J (2005) Die Krankheitserfinder: Wie wir zu Patienten gemacht werden, Fischer.

conceptual progress and continue to treat symptoms ineffectively instead of causes of disease.

Since drug development can easily consume the entire initial R&D investment, and since this is the rule rather than the exception, since most drugs ultimately fail at some point in development without generating a return, the return on investment may well become systematically negative up to 100%. As a result of many failures, the simplified 15 indication areas of drug development (see Fig. 7.2) have now obviously turned into a minefield for Big Pharma, with large areas being avoided. This is the only way to understand the focus on cancer and immune diseases, two of the few areas in which major progress can be made (see psoriasis) and small ones can still be marketed (cancer).

Basically, drug research and development are like drilling for oil, where the largest, cheapest, and easiest deposits with the highest expected returns are prioritized and exploited first and less attractive deposits that are smaller and more expensive and promise lower returns are left for later. Here, too, there is an increasing danger of spending more than can be extracted afterwards. Interestingly, both the pharmaceutical and oil industries, both of which were stock market giants, have long since been replaced by platform technology giants like Apple, Amazon, and Alphabet. And the decline continues, mirrored exactly in the ups and downs of Merck and Pfizer's enterprise values, which have now disappeared from the world's top ten industrials, just as Shell, Gazprom, and PetroChina apply. Only Exxon just made it into the top ten in 2018 (Fig. 7.4).

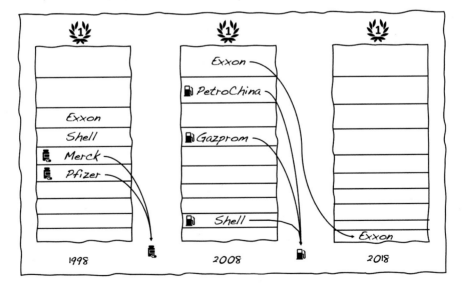

Fig. 7.4 The world's ten most valuable companies in 1998, 2008, and 2018. (https://milfordasset.com/insights/largest-companies-2008-vs-2018-lot-changed; https://www.bloomberg.com/news/articles/2019-01-07/amazon-becomes-most-valuable-company-inching-past-microsoft)

How will Big Pharma develop now? Declining research and development productivity and declining return on investment will lead to declining sales growth until growth becomes negative and sales shrink. The decline in sales then reduces the financial scope for R&D investment, causing sales growth to decline even further—and so on until the industry, at least in its current form, will be gone.

The pharmaceutical industry itself also emerged from the decline of the chemical and dye industries when chemicals and dyes slowly became commodities. Out of the ashes grows the new. And therein lies the only real hope for the pharmaceutical industry, or rather for the hundreds of thousands of people who work in it. Just as the pharmaceutical industry evolved from the chemical industry and the biopharmaceutical industry evolved from the pharmaceutical industry, the pharmaceutical and biopharmaceutical industries will evolve into something quite different—but more on that in the second part of the book. Darwin's theory of evolution applies to businesses and industries as it does to species of life: It is not the strongest of the species that survives, nor the most intelligent, but the one that is most adaptable to change. The alternative is: adapt or die!

Big Pharma in Court

Such a fundamental crisis of an entire industry not only results in productive change management but also opens the bag of tricks to still be profitable with the old methods for as long as possible, up to and including fraud. Major drug companies such as Pfizer, GlaxoSmithKline, Eli Lilly, and Johnson & Johnson regularly pay large sums to settle lawsuits for fraud. In 2009, Roche sold the supposed flu drug Tamiflu worldwide for several billion euros but published only part of the studies on its efficacy and disclosed only after great public pressure that the drug is even less useful than feared but can cause the most serious side effects. In any case, the flu virus-specific mechanism of action proposed by the manufacturers does not match the clinical data.[6]

Other examples include the supposedly stomach-friendly painkiller Vioxx from MSD and the antipsychotic Zyprexa from Eli Lilly. Vioxx was marketed without sufficient clinical documentation, even though it was known at the time to cause fatal heart attacks. In the first 4 months of 2000, MSD spent $67 million advertising Vioxx, which was more than any company had ever spent

---

[6] Jefferson T et al. (2014) Neuraminidase inhibitors for preventing and treating influenza in healthy adults and children. Cochrane Database of Systematic Reviews:CD008965, https://10.1002/14651858. CD008965.pub4

advertising any other drug at that time. In terms of sales, Vioxx became Merck's second best-selling drug. Merck dismissed the studies that Vioxx increased the risk of heart attack compared to other painkillers, claiming instead that other painkillers reduced the risk of heart attack and that this only appeared to result in an increase in risk from Vioxx. In 2004, under pressure from the US Food and Drug Administration, Merck withdrew approval for Vioxx and in 2011 agreed to pay €700 million in damages and penalties.[7] By then, Vioxx had caused at least 140,000 heart attacks with an estimated 60,000 deaths.[8]

Pfizer paid $2.3 billion in the USA in 2009 in what the largest healthcare fraud trial was then ever for illegally marketing the painkiller Bextra,[9] the largest fine ever for a pharmaceutical company. The company GlaxoSmithKline topped that in 2011, agreeing to pay $3 billion to settle a drug fraud lawsuit, the marketing of the diabetes drug Avandia for unapproved indications.[10] For Abbott, Eli Lilly, and Johnson & Johnson, it was 1.5, 1.4, and 1.1 billion, respectively, and for other Big Pharmas, sums in the double and triple digits. In each case, the charges involved crimes such as fraud, deception, bribery, or illegal marketing. Pfizer was fined $141 million in 2010 for improperly marketing the anti-epileptic drug Neurontin, specifically finding that Pfizer had violated the Racketeer Influenced and Corrupt Organizations (RICO) racketeering statute over a 10-year period. Other examples include slimming pills and appetite suppressants—which are generally not recommended—such as Redux and Pondimin,[11] which caused fatal pulmonary hypertension and were withdrawn by Wyeth-Ayerst after scientific pressure. In the case of the epilepsy drug Neurontin, it was Pfizer again, whose Warner-Lambert subcompany admitted to aggressively marketing the drug for unapproved conditions such as bipolar disorder, pain, migraine headaches, and drug and alcohol withdrawal.[12]

---

[7] Wilson D (2011) Merck to Pay $950 Million Over Vioxx. New York Times, https://www.nytimes.com/2011/11/23/business/merck-agrees-to-pay-950-million-in-vioxx-case.html

[8] Krumholz H et al. (2007) What have we learnt from Vioxx? BMJ 334:120, https://doi.org/10.1136/bmj.39024.487720.68

[9] Harris G (2009) Pfizer Pays $2.3 Billion to Settle Marketing Case. New York Times, https://www.nytimes.com/2009/09/03/business/03health.html?_r=0&auth=redirect-apple

[10] Serafino P & Kitamura M (2011) Glaxo to Pay $3 Billion to Settle U.S. Sales, Avandia Cases. Bloomberg, https://www.bloomberg.com/news/articles/2011-11-03/glaxo-agrees-to-pay-3-billion-to-settle-u-s-probe-into-sales-marketing

[11] Curfman GD (1997) Diet Pills Redux. N Engl J Med 337:629–630, http://www.nejm.org/doi/full/10.1056/NEJM199708283370909; Mark EJ et al. (1997) Fatal pulmonary hypertension associated with short-term use of fenfluramine and phentermine. N Engl J Med 337:602–606.

[12] Tansey B (2004) Huge penalty in drug fraud/Pfizer settles felony case in Neurontin off-label promotion. SFGATE, https://www.sfgate.com/business/article/Huge-penalty-in-drug-fraud-Pfizer-settles-2759293.php; Reuters Editorial (2010) US jury's Neurontin ruling to cost Pfizer $141 mln. Reuters, https://de.reuters.com/article/pfizer-neurontin/us-jurys-neurontin-ruling-to-cost-pfizer-141-mln-idUSN259778920100325

Another example: Sanofi-Aventis' antibiotic Ketek was no more effective than existing antibiotics in its class, but it had specific side effects that other antibiotics did not have and that were already detectable in the first studies and were confirmed again and again over time: eye disorders, unconsciousness, cardiac arrhythmias, and severe and sometimes fatal liver damage. Drug regulators reviewed the harm-benefit ratio and acknowledged that patients were at greater risk of serious adverse side effects than from other antibiotics and issued a warning to that effect but otherwise took no action to withdraw the drug from the market. Eventually, Sanofi-Aventis withdrew the drug from the market "for economic reasons".[13]

And in 2021 in a rare legal defeat, Bristol Myers Squibb and Sanofi were fined US$834M for "deceptive marketing" on the best-selling blood thinner Plavix. Hawaii first sued the pharma giants in 2014 for failing to warn that the drug had poor effects on people who can't metabolize it. Bristol Myers Squibb and Sanofi could have pointed to a simple genetic test, and by failing to do so, the companies put patients at "grave risk of serious injury or death in order to substantially increase their profits".[14]

Of course, these are just excesses, and there are excellent scientists and decent people working in the pharmaceutical industry who are certainly critical of such occasional practices. It is only at the decision-making levels that some obviously take the risk of being caught and sued, even if it costs human lives.

Besides, you may think, surely there are independent scientists outside the pharmaceutical industry who are making sure that there is a counterweight to Big Pharma in research. But is that really the case? Unfortunately, no. Here, too, an innovation block and, again, false incentives prevail worldwide.

---

[13] Editor (2018) Telithromycin: a welcome market withdrawal. Prescrire Int 27:210, https://english.prescrire.org/en/81/168/55234/0/NewsDetails.aspx; Ross DB (2007) The FDA and the Case of Ketek. N Engl J Med 356:1601–1604, https://doi.org/10.1056/NEJMp078032

[14] Tong A (2021) In a rare legal defeat, Bristol Myers Squibb and Sanofi fined $834M for 'deceptive marketing' on best-selling blood thinner Plavix. Endpoint News, https://endpts.com/in-a-rare-legal-defeat-bristol-myers-squibb-and-sanofi-fined-834m-for-deceptive-marketing-on-best-selling-blood-thinner-plavix/

8

Research Not for Patients

To clarify the causes of diseases and to develop new therapies is not only the task of the pharmaceutical industry, which we dealt with in the previous chapter, but above all basic biomedical research. Pharmaceutical companies also draw their ideas for drug development from the findings of all biomedical scientists worldwide.

First, research not only needs bright ideas, but it also needs to be financed. Although most university departments, unlike many international universities, have basic equipment, staff, and research funds, these are usually not sufficient for ambitious projects. So additional so-called third-party funds must be raised. Fortunately, in this respect, most industrialized countries are richly blessed with funding sources.

However, when comparing different countries, major differences with respect to the commitment to research become apparent (Fig. 8.1). This cannot be explained by less resources as Fig. 8.1 normalizes research funding as per cent of gross domestic product (GDP). Thus, it is no surprise that many talented young researchers from Southern Europe are forced to migrate north to the richer or more research-oriented Scandinavian countries, Belgium, and Germany, a brain drain from which those countries will be suffering for decades.

© The Author(s), under exclusive license to Springer Nature Switzerland AG 2022
H. H. H. W. Schmidt, *The end of medicine as we know it - and why your health has a future*,
https://doi.org/10.1007/978-3-030-95293-8_8

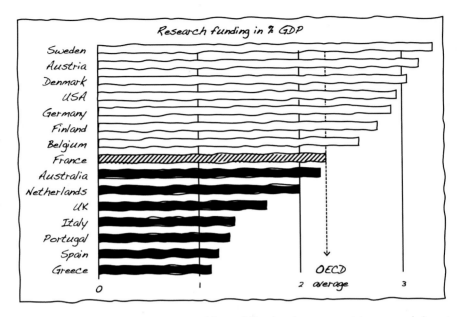

Fig. 8.1 Research output (measured by publications) compared to research input, each in relation to the gross domestic product of 13 different European countries. (Schulz F (2019) Effects of tax incentives for research in neighbouring Austria. Finance Market & Opinion, http://www.fmm-magazin.de/effekte-der-steuerlichen-forschungsfoerderung-im-nachbarland-oesterreich-finanzen-mm_kat8_id9033.html#; King D (2004) The scientific impact of nations. Nature 430:311–316, https://doi.org/10.1038/430311a)

Research Output = Paper

But what's coming out of biomedical research? Mainly publications but shockingly almost nothing of clinical relevance. Innovation in medicine and the research-based pharmaceutical industry results from scientific translation. This is what biomedical research calls it when basic and preclinical research results in clinical studies whose new findings can be translated into patient benefit. But this does not happen. Most basic and preclinical scientists find themselves in a self-sustaining bubble with the goal of generating publications, preferably in prestigious scientific journals, and then to use this reputation and collegial recognition, even admiration, to attract new research funding. And then? Then publications are generated and published again, and so on (Fig. 8.2).

For example, and in probably the most thorough study of its kind,[1] 25,190 scientific publications were identified from the 5-year period from 1979 to

---

[1] Contopoulos-Ioannidis DG et al. (2003) Translation of highly promising basic science research into clinical applications. The American Journal of Medicine 114:477–484, https://doi.org/10.1016/S0002-9343(03)00013-5

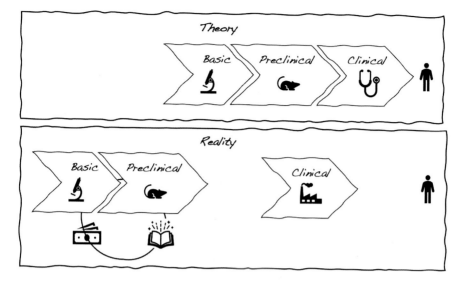

Fig. 8.2 Theory and reality of biomedical research. Above, basic, preclinical, and clinical research are often portrayed as being intertwined for the direct benefit of patients. Below, basic and preclinical researchers raise money to write publications to apply for more funding to write more publications. And clinical research is mainly industry-sponsored and designed for registration trials generating another income stream for university hospitals. Hardly any academic research results in patient benefit

1983 in the six most cited and highly respected journals for basic medical sciences, which were *Science, Nature, Cell, Journal of Experimental Medicine, Journal of Clinical Investigation,* and *Journal of Biological Chemistry.* They had to contain at least one of the following words: "therapy", "therapeutic", "preventive", "vaccine", or "clinical". Of these, in turn, only 101 publications were filtered out that clearly postulated that the technology reported in them could be used clinically—therapeutically or preventively—in the future.

Then it was examined which of these basic research results had now actually been translated into a clinical application or at least clinical research in 2003, i.e. some 20 years after publication—for which 20 years should normally be sufficient. The sobering result: only 27 of the promising technologies had led to at least one published clinical trial within 20 years, 19 of them with positive results. However, it got worse: Only five of these results were licensed for clinical use, and only one was used clinically for the licensed indications! Some form of industry involvement, ideally an industry co-author on the original basic science publication, was most likely to ensure that at least clinical trials took place later, even if they were positive enough to result in a license in only one case.

Generalizing this elaborately studied sample, only 1 in 250 biomedical publications is clinically promising (101 out of 25,190). However, only a quarter of these are then actually clinically tested (27 out of 101). And less than one in ten of those clinically tested then actually find clinical application (1 in 27). This is not to say that basic research must always and constantly be expected to lead to an application. There must certainly also be high-risk research in which a wonderfully simple, logically convincing theory turns out to be wrong in the end or at least has no application at all. But I find it unacceptable that 25,189 of 25,190 research results ultimately have no clinical relevance whatsoever. This no longer has anything to do with biomedical research, at least not with patient-oriented medical research.

At least from clinical university professors, one would expect that they initiate independent research addressing unmet patient needs or optimizing treatment guidelines. However, they as well publish virtually no relevant innovation of their own in the sense that they design a patient study, submit a research proposal to acquire the necessary funding, and then plan and organize the study, ideally multicentric to avoid a local bias, and subsequently analyse the data and publish them. This hardly happens in practice. The vast majority of published clinical trials are industry-funded pivotal studies that are planned and evaluated entirely outside the clinic, for which clinicians merely recruit patients and for which the clinic administration charges not inconsiderable per capita fees.

As I am a scientist myself, I am by no means accusing all my colleagues here. For me, the fault lies primarily in the wrong incentives. If scientists are evaluated solely based on publications (preferably in high-impact journals) and the amount of third-party funding they have acquired, then those who evaluate these scientists and provide them with professorships, rooms, staff, and funding will receive exactly that in return, namely, many (high-impact) publications and third-party funding.

If, however, universities, non-university research institutions and third-party funding bodies were to award careers and funding in biomedicine solely based on clinical and patient-relevant successes, regardless of the journal where these are ultimately published and regardless of whether they were achieved with one or ten million dollars (or pounds), then the entire system (rather like the universe in The Little Prince) would start to move. And then suddenly the patients would also have something from biomedical research, and the innovations would just bubble up. How about research at the patient bed conducted by clinical university professors? Is this at least patient relevant? Unfortunately, not; it is mainly an alternative income stream for hospitals, not more.

Fee for Service

Clinical researches, i.e. studies with and for patients, that are designed, planned, financed, managed, and subsequently published in a high-quality manner by professors at university hospitals are virtually non-existent. There are clinical studies being conducted at university hospitals, but the vast majority are so-called paid registration studies by industry for a new drug or a medical device such as a new pacemaker or hip replacement. These studies are completely designed, planned, financed, and managed by these companies. However, on the subsequent publications, the clinicians are typically first author. This helps the professor's scientific reputation, and the industry likes to promote their product with these "key opinion leaders". In addition, the university hospitals hold out their hands, typically a fixed amount per patient enrolled, and these revenues add to those from health insurance reimbursements and payments from the state for the training of medical students and research.

Commercial clinical studies are often biased by including those patients for whom a positive effect is very likely or by concealing negative results. Studies that are independent of a manufacturer should be necessary here as an important corrective. In addition, companies would understandably never work on questions that do not promise commercial gain, even if they are relevant to patient care, for example, by comparing two or more therapies or drugs with each other, by demonstrating the efficacy of a therapy in a real-world study as opposed to the artificial situation in a commercial registration study with many exclusion criteria, or by developing new therapies that are not financially lucrative. All this should be the primary task of university clinical professors and the research goal of clinical departments. Only about a third of all clinical studies fall into this category of so-called investigator-initiated trials, i.e. without industry funding.[2]

An additional important quality criterion for a clinical study is that it is not only carried out at one clinic, i.e. mono-centric, but ideally at several sites at the same time so that the data are more representative and independent of local factors. Only half of non-commercial studies meet this essential quality criterion. However, even the best study is of no use if it is not published, and discipline here is generally poor. Of all studies, half of them do not comply with this, the majority of which are non-commercial ones. Only one in ten is

---

[2] Bührlen B et al. (2010) Status and conditions of clinical research in Germany and in comparison to other countries with special regard to non-commercial studies. TAB Reports to the German Bundestag 135, https://www.tab-beim-bundestag.de/de/pdf/publikationen/berichte/TAB-Arbeitsbericht-ab135.pdf

published.[3] Incredible, since all the work and data are lost (the drawer effect; see below). Taken together by multiplying all three percentages that only a third are investigator-initiated and non-commercial, of which only half are multicentre, of which only one in ten is published, this suggests that only 1.5% of all clinical studies meet all three criteria (non-commercial + multi-centre + published)—shocking. This is an absolute indictment of clinical research with hospitals obviously viewing clinical trials primarily as an addi-tional source of income but not as an academic obligation of clinical univer-sity professors. But the problems in biomedical research run deeper than just a lack of patient or clinical focus in biomedical research.

Not Reproducible

It all started with a publication from a Bayer Healthcare research department.[4] When a drug company such as Bayer decides on an expensive drug discovery and development programme, it draws the necessary ideas and data largely from the published biomedical literature. Most of this literature comes from academic laboratories, i.e. universities or research institutes. A positive deci-sion has far-reaching consequences and is expensive. The cost of carrying out a comprehensive programme to discover and develop a particular compound, including clinical trials, can total hundreds of millions of euros. Even in the early stages, the investment is substantial. It is therefore essential that the data on which such a decision is based are reliable. To mitigate the risk that such an investment would ultimately be wasted, most pharmaceutical companies perform internal validations of literature data. This involves repeating pub-lished experiments exactly to see if they produce the same results. After the researchers at Bayer Healthcare had the uneasy feeling that this was often not the case, all validation experiments conducted over a period of 4 years were evaluated. The result was sobering. Most of the published data could not be reproduced. The US biotech company Amgen reported that they were only able to reproduce 66 of 53 highly publicized cancer studies, resulting in 89% non-reproducible publications.[5] Within a few years, three more studies were

[3] Goldacre B et al. (2018) Compliance with requirement to report results on the EU Clinical Trials Register: cohort study and web resource. BMJ 362:k3218, https://doi.org/10.1136/bmj.k3218

[4] Prinz F et al. (2011) Believe it or not: how much can we rely on published data on potential drug tar-gets? Nature Reviews Drug Discovery 10:712–713, http://www.nature.com/nrd/journal/v10/n9/full/nrd3439-c1.html

[5] Begley C & Ellis L (2012) Raise standards for preclinical cancer research. Nature 483:531–533, https://doi.org/10.1038/483531a

published, all of which came to the same conclusions.[6] The extent of non-reproducibility ranged from 51% to 89%. Although the exact percentage is not relevant, it is clear and shocking that in any case over half of the biomedical literature is not reproducible.

This points to systemic and costly inefficiencies in the way biomedical research is designed, conducted, and reported. In addition, they represent a gigantic waste of—usually—taxpayer funds, ultimately leading to worthless statements and publications. In the USA, for example, approximately 114.8 billion US dollars is spent annually on life science research, with the pharmaceutical industry being the largest funder (61.8%), followed by government funding programmes and universities (34.5%) and non-profit organizations (3.8%). Of this amount, approximately half is spent on preclinical and basic research and the other half on clinical trials. Assuming a conservative rate of 50% non-reproducible studies, this means that about 28 billion US dollars per year are spent on research that cannot be reproduced. If such data form the starting point for further studies or pharmaceutical developments that are then based on false assumptions, the damage is multiplied.

In an anonymous online survey of 1576 scientists, more than 70% of researchers said they had tried unsuccessfully to reproduce another scientist's experiments.[7] But researchers don't usually approach other researchers about such problems, and so they remain undiscovered or, at best, talking points in the hallways of congresses. Hardly any scientists publish a replicate study, and even most scientific journals, I can confirm from my own experience, dismiss such studies as being too "uninteresting" or "too specific", even if the paper referred to was published in the same journal. Only 13% of failed replicates were published. When asked about the possible causes of non-reproducibility, most stated that there is a high pressure to publish data and to selectively choose only a part of the data for this purpose. Other issues include fierce competition for grants and research positions and growing burdens of bureaucracy that cut into the time that can be spent planning and conducting research.

In my opinion, these comments still scratch only the surface, at least as far as biomedical research is concerned. The goal of biomedical research must be to discover and develop new therapies, better diagnostics, and better prevention for patients. This, and only this, should then be measured as research

---

[6] Freedman LP et al. (2015) The Economics of Reproducibility in Preclinical Research. PLOS Biology 13:e1002165, https://doi.org/10.1371/journal.pbio.1002165

[7] Baker M (2016) 1500 scientists lift the lid on reproducibility: survey sheds light on the 'crisis' rocking research. Nature 533:452–454, https://www.nature.com/news/1-500-scientists-lift-the-lid-on-reproducibility-1.19970

output and form the basis for the allocation of research funding and university careers. What is being measured instead? As described earlier: on the one hand, the number of publications and where they were published and, on the other hand, the amount of third-party funding acquired. In other words, spending money—mostly provided by public, state, or foundation sources—is already considered an achievement. And achievement promotes careers. There it is again, the self-satisfied cycle of biomedical science: money, publications, more money, more publications. The patient plays no role herein. But it is worth taking a closer look at where exactly the weaknesses lie in obviously more than half of all biomedical publications. Why are they not reproducible?

Significant!?

Although misconduct is more common in biomedical research than in other disciplines,[8] the majority of these are not fraud but systematic qualitative and technical errors. But what exactly is going wrong?

Every biomedical research project determines beforehand—or at least should do so—what exactly is to be measured at the end. The most essential measurement is called the primary endpoint. Such a study "hypothesis" might be that drug A prevents death from heart attack or stroke. The opposite result, i.e. that the drug doesn't work, is called the "null hypothesis". At the end of the study, a statistical test is employed as to whether the "null hypothesis" is so unlikely that it can be rejected. In turn, it can then be assumed—for the moment—that the "hypothesis" was probably correct, i.e. drug A indeed prevents death from heart attack or stroke. The statistical test to make this decision is called "significance". "Significance" is thus the absolute magic word in any biomedical research project. After all, it means that a finding is likely to be publishable. The cut-off between a result being significant and not is pure convention and still only a probability. It could still be false. That's why ideally single studies are repeated several times by different researchers and then combined into one meta-analysis. The results of meta-analyses have a much higher reliability than any single study. One will always find a poorly conducted study that shows the most obscure finding, but will it hold up when reproduced and meta-analysed?

[8] Fanelli D (2009) How many scientists fabricate and falsify research? A systematic review and meta-analysis of survey data. PlOS One 4:e5738, https://doi.org/10.1371/journal.pone.0005738

Moreover, the statistical term "significance" is almost always used with a different meaning of the word when used colloquially in the sense of "important", e.g. this is a "significant" study or a "significant" finding. Also, terms such as "proof" and "evidence" are frequently used. This is not the case. As I said before, the rejection of the "null hypothesis" may still have been wrong. Without going too much into the detail of statistics, the value that is calculated to determine statistical "significance" is named the "*p*-value". Its cut-off point is—by convention—0.05. And because it is so important and usually determines whether a dataset can be published, this *p*-value is hunted. Hunted? Yes!

One thousand one hundred and seventy-seven completed biomedical publications were examined, in which a total of 19,584 *p*-values were calculated and published. Of the *p*-values, 20% referred to the main hypothesis to be tested and 80% to the secondary endpoints that were also checked but not relevant for the publication. While the *p*-value frequency for these latter secondary endpoints was evenly distributed over all publications, the distribution of the *p*-values for primary endpoints showed a clear anomaly. There was an accumulation of *p*-values that were just below the 0.05 cut-off, making the endpoints just significant and publishable (Fig. 8.3). However, such a clustering is mathematically completely impossible, and since the data of the different *p*-values frequency came from the same studies, no bias can have arisen from the fact that apples were compared with pears, etc. This makes it very likely that *p*-values have been systematically chased.

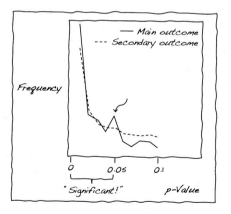

Fig. 8.3 *p*-Value hacking. The lower axis shows the *p*-values and the left axis the relative frequency of these *p*-values. For secondary endpoints (not relevant for publication), the distribution is uniform; for the main endpoint, an anomaly peaks just below 0.05, followed by an underrepresentation of the subsequent *p*-values just above 0.05

p-Values can be hacked,[9] for example, by stopping a study as soon as the *p*-value is just less than 0.05 and not doing any further experiments. The less repetitions an experimenter does, the smaller a sample is, and the larger the random swings become, and coincidentally a *p*-value can become smaller than 0.05. In general, the larger the studies are, the more meaningful they are as such coincidental fluctuations are prevented. Thus, depending on the sample size or the repetitions in a study, true, false positives and false negative findings will be made. This is normal and the reason why only meta-analyses bring us really close to the truth.

The Drawer Effect

Suppose three biomedical research groups perform the same experiment to test whether drug A works in disease B. Now let's assume we know the truth, which is that the drug doesn't work. One group finds indeed the true result, namely, "no effect"; the second, a significant (remember the magic word) improvement of the disease; and the third, the opposite, i.e. the drug makes things even worse (significantly!). The first and last group think to themselves, who cares about a drug that doesn't work or makes a disease even worse, respectively, and put the data in a drawer or paper bin. The second group, however, publishes the exciting data together with a press release from their university that they have probably found a new drug and promising new therapy for disease B. The high-impact factor journal is delighted about an exciting header and gladly accepts the manuscript for publication, after a peer review of course. The first and last group see this paper and are incensed. They no longer understand the world. They also tested this drug, and it doesn't help in this disease at all. They dig out the data from the drawer, write a manuscript, and submit it, sometimes even to the same journal that published the first paper or another to prevent misinformation that circulates in the scientific world. However, the manuscript is rejected without even having been reviewed. The editor felt it was "too specialized" and suggests the authors to submit to another, more specialized journal. But the next journal also declines. Not interested. In the meantime, a whole year has passed, the manuscript has been rejected twice more, and the working group has other projects as well. So, this manuscript ends up in the drawer of oblivion. An isolated case? No.

---

[9] Belas N et al. (2017) P-Hacking in clinical trials: A meta-analytical approach. Working Paper Series 19. Otto von Guericke University Magdeburg Faculty of Economics, https://www.fww.ovgu.de/fww_media/femm/femm_2017/2017_19-p-8998.pdf

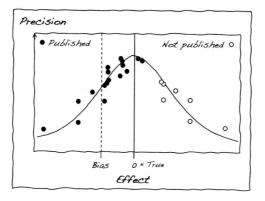

Fig. 8.4 Publication bias favouring studies that show a positive effect (those to the left with black symbols). Neutral or negative studies remain unpublished (open symbols). The lower the precision of a study is (left axis), the higher is the chance to find a result that deviates from the true result = 0. All publicly available data suggest a (false) positive effect

Rather the rule: the drawer problem.[10] And the result? Over the years, in all biomedical research fields, more and more false positive results accumulate, and the neutral or negative ones end up in the drawers because journals find positive results more attractive than negative ones. This publication bias is well studied and described (see Fig. 8.4).[11]

It is therefore no wonder that pharmaceutical R&D programmes or clinical studies which rely on biased data will subsequently fail. They worked on a pseudo project. In addition to the statistical deficiencies and often too small sample sizes, there are also real quality deficiencies.

Quality Defects

The quality of a biomedical study is difficult to measure. Opinions can easily be divided about the design and the data that were collected in a study. One scientist would have done it this way and the other that way. However, there is at least one type of biomedical data whose quality can be accurately

---

[10] Rosenthal R (1979) The file drawer problem and tolerance for null results. Psychological bulletin, 86:638–641, https://doi.org/10.1037/0033-2909.86.3.638

[11] Sena ES (2010) Publication Bias in Reports of Animal Stroke Studies Leads to Major Overstatement of Efficacy. PLOS Biology 8:e1000344, https://doi.org/10.1371/journal.pbio.1000344

measured: the crystal structure of proteins. You don't need to know what they exactly are. It is enough that you know that there is a precise physical value for the quality or resolution of such a crystal that exactly defines the quality or precision of the derived structural information. When the crystal structures were divided according to the journals in which they were published, the surprising finding is that the data of the lowest quality appeared in the highest ranking, so-called high-impact journals such as *Nature, Science,* and *Cell.*[12] Publishing in these journals fosters every biomedical scientist's career and opens up the money bags of funding organizations.

Is it a problem for these journals to publish lower quality or even irreproducible data? Not at all. Surprisingly, they are even rewarded for this. So-called high-impact journals are all about getting cited as often as possible. That's the number from which their "impact" is calculated. Every journal advertises its so-called impact factor. However, controversial papers are cited more often because they are controversial. A 10-year retrospective analysis of non-reproducible papers showed that after publication a reproducible paper was cited an average of 13 times and a non-reproducible one 169 times, 13 times more. It is[13] therefore worthwhile for a journal to take the risk. A higher impact factor means more manuscript subscriptions. And the more attractive a journal is, the higher its price for subscribers, mostly university libraries. The combined sales of major publishers such as *Wiley, Springer Nature,* and *Elsevier* amount to around 6 billion euros per year, not a bad deal for the fact that others do the bulk of the work, i.e. attracting the funding, conducting the experiments, writing the paper, and reviewing the paper. No wonder that scientific publishers generate returns on sales of 30–40%. But with these quality deficiencies, we are still not at the end of the causes of irreproducibility.

Withdrawn!

With so many problems concerning reproducibility and statistical and qualitative deficiencies, it is not surprising that more and more publications must be completely retracted afterwards even by the publishers, i.e. a journal must declare an already published paper null and void. This is the ultimate

[12] Brembs B (2018) Prestigious Science Journals Struggle to Reach Even Average Reliability. Frontiers in Human Neuroscience 12:1–7, https://doi.org/10.3389/fnhum.2018.00037; Brown EN & Ramaswamy S (2007) Quality of protein crystal structures. Acta Crystallogr. D Biol. Crystallogr, 63:941–950, https://doi.org/10.1107/S0907444907033847

[13] Begley CG & Ellis LM (2012) Raise standards for preclinical cancer research. Nature 483:531–533, https://doi.org/10.1038/483531a

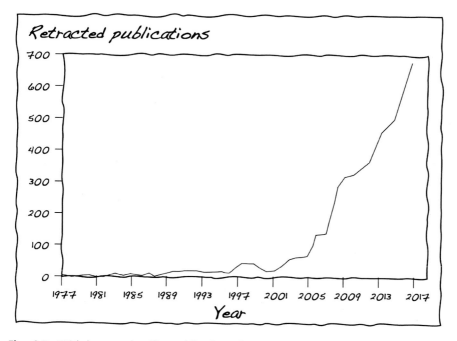

Fig. 8.5 Withdrawn scientific publications from 1977 to 2017. (Retraction Watch: Tracking retractions as a window into the scientific process, https://retractionwatch.com)

punishment that post-publication science can receive: an official declaration that a paper is so flawed or, significantly less often, simply falsified that it must be withdrawn from the literature. This phenomenon has been addressed by Retraction Watch, a blog founded by the Center for Scientific Integrity that researches and reports on publication retractions. While publications from all fields are listed here—how could it be otherwise—the top spots of the most cited publications that had to be retracted are again occupied by high-impact medical journals: No. 1 the *New England Journal of Medicine*, next to *The Lancet, Blood, EMBO Journal,* and *Cancer Research*. The disturbing thing about the *Retraction Watch* data is that the number of retractions is increasing exponentially (see Fig. 8.5).

Every week, about 27,000 research articles are freshly published and registered by *Web of Science*, a huge online database of scientific publications from Thomson Reuters. But about 200 will eventually be marked with a change notice, such as a correction.[14] About 700 are currently retracted each year. Of course, this increase may also be since more and more scientists are taking a closer look at publications, reporting errors and insisting that erroneous papers are actually retracted.

---

[14] Van Noorden R (2011) Science publishing: The trouble with retractions - A surge in withdrawn papers is highlighting weaknesses in the system for handling them. Nature 478:26–28, https://doi. org/10.1038/478026a

If we now add up all that has been found so far about biomedical research—the lack of applicability, the lack of reproducibility, the statistical and quality deficiencies, the almost complete failure of academic-clinical research, and the lack of openness, as well as the exponentially increasing number of withdrawn publications—we arrive at up to 85% of research that is a pure waste of money and time and at best serves to promote one's own career by extending the publication list.[15] Mind you, this does not mean the methodically clean research of a hypothesis, which may turn out to be wrong, but the kind of research that engages in *p*-value hacking, poor design, and poor reporting.

COVID-19 Research

And as if further proof were needed, the COVID-19 crisis accentuates everything said above about the lack of research quality as if in a burning glass. Of course, it was commendable that, given the magnitude of this pandemic crisis, as many scientists as possible wanted to contribute to its solution, be it to research virulence mechanisms, therapies, or vaccines. On the other hand, it was also obviously an opportunity for many groups to publish in one of the most highly ranked journals, or at all. Conversely, of course, each of these journals wanted to be the first to announce or give timely warning of a possible new therapy or vaccine.

Since the beginning of the pandemic, an extraordinary number of COVID-19 studies have been registered. The clinicaltrials.gov registry of the US *National Library of Medicine* quickly listed well over 1000 COVID-19 clinical trials. To be sure, a few of them provided useful information. But the vast majority were too small and poorly designed in the first place to ever become relevant.[16] For example, of 145 registered trials of hydroxychloroquine, an antimalarial drug once so "hyped" *by* Donald Trump, only one provided a protocol. This flood of studies, therefore, merely generated a massive COVID-19 background noise. Many of these studies were only preprints. These are manuscripts that are archived and made publicly available by the authors themselves before they are submitted to a journal and peer-reviewed. MedRxiv, for example, is a forum for such publications. In principle, such forums can provide potentially valuable early access to study results, as the

---

[15] Chalmers I & Glasziou P (2009) Avoidable waste in the production and reporting of research evidence. Lancet 374:86–9, https://doi.org/10.1016/S0140-6736(09)60329-9

[16] Glasziou P et al. (2020) Waste in covid-19 research. BMJ 369:m1847, https://doi.org/10.1136/bmj.m1847

review process for scientific journals can easily take a year or more. However, media outlets picked up on these archived manuscripts as if they were real publications and disseminated them on par with peer-reviewed publications—a veritable "infodemic" on the pandemic!

For example, the preprint of the first reported study of hydroxychloroquine on March 20, 2020—a poorly designed, non-randomized French study of 46 patients[17]—was cited 520 times, including repeatedly by Donald Trump, while a larger, randomized, and therefore much better study of hydroxychloroquine published barely a month later April 14, 2020, showing no benefits of hydroxychloroquine, received far less attention. This unbalanced attention to the first, seemingly positive study triggered a wave of 135 largely unnecessary hydroxychloroquine studies. Moreover, research on non-drug interventions such as distancing, hand hygiene, masks, tracing, and so on, on the other hand, was completely neglected—a shortcoming that made evidence-based decisions on this almost impossible in the months that followed.

And the issue of publication retraction was not absent from the COVID-19 issue[18] either, affecting the two absolute top medical journals, the *New England Journal of Medicine* from the USA and the UK's *The Lancet*.[19] It was the biggest research scandal of the COVID-19 era after a company refused to make the underlying data for both papers available for independent review—something that should be done during a peer review and before publication. *The Lancet* paper was again about the malaria drug. It was claimed to cause serious harm without helping patients, after which the World Health Organization temporarily halted all studies on it worldwide.

There was even a third study posted online only as a preprint on the preprint server SSRN. It claimed that the anthelmintic drug ivermectin dramatically reduced mortality in COVID-19 patients, which led to untested government approval of the drug in several Latin American countries. Shortly thereafter, the preprint on ivermectin disappeared online but had been previously secured by the *Barcelona Institute for Global Health* and was archived on its website along with earlier versions. There is no retraction, as the study was never published. Treatments with this drug continued.

---

[17] Gautret P et al. (2020) Hydroxychloroquine and azithromycin as a treatment of COVID-19: results of an open-label non-randomized clinical trial. Int J Antimicrob Agents 105949, https://doi.org/10.1016/j.ijantimicag.2020.105949

[18] Retractionwatch COVID-19, https://retractionwatch.com/retracted-coronavirus-covid-19-papers/

[19] Piller C & Servick K (2020) Two elite medical journals retract coronavirus papers over data integrity questions. Science, https://doi.org/10.1126/science.abd1697

Predatory Journals, Nonsense Papers, and the Eightfold Publication

And as the icing on the cake of what must have already seemed to you, the reader, to be a rather peculiar scientific publication market, let's take a brief look at the latest perversion, the phenomenon of *predatory* journals and publishers. This somewhat stilted official consensus definition is: "Institutions that prioritize self-interest at the expense of science and are characterized by false or misleading information, deviation from best editorial and publishing practices, lack of transparency, and/or the use of aggressive and indiscriminate solicitation practices".[20] In practice, these are "scholarly" journals that publish—for a fee—anything that looks like a scholarly publication. De facto, you can buy a publication there. It is not checked or peer-reviewed; on the contrary, not even a plausibility check is done. For example, they are collected in Beall's list (https://beallslist.net). A serious scientist should avoid ever publishing in such a journal, even by mistake.

The number of daily emails inviting me to submit a paper to the most absurd journals, to serve as an editor, or to give a talk in Barbados has increased significantly. 99.9% come from predatory publishers, predatory journals, and predatory conferences. Meanwhile, the first court rulings on the matter are finally available. The Indian OMICS group, for example, was fined approximately 50 million US dollars in the USA, and its activities in the USA were largely banned.[21]

For example, articles have been published that quote what appear to be scientific articles by Michael Jackson or contain Pokémon as illustrations.[22] Also almost unbelievable is a case in which the same manuscript was published eight times in different journals, each time with slight variations and different authors. In that case, the publications were probably produced by a Chinese company selling fake manuscripts in English to doctors in China who need a publication for their job applications. Each of the papers even

---

[20] Grudniewicz A (2019) Predatory journals: no definition, no defense. Nature 576:210–212, https://doi.org/10.1038/d41586-019-03759-y

[21] Navarro GM (2019) United States District Court - District of Nevada, https://www.courthousenews.com/wp-content/uploads/2019/04/Publishing.pdf

[22] Ferro S (2013) Nonsense Paper That Cites Michael Jackson And Ron Jeremy Actually Gets Published. Popular Science, https://www.popsci.com/article/science/nonsense-paper-cites-michael-jackson-and-ron-jeremy-actually-gets-published/; Shelomi M (2020) Opinion: Using Pokémon to Detect Scientific Misinformation. The Scientist, https://www.the-scientist.com/critic-at-large/opinion-using-pokmon-to-detect-scientific-misinformation-68098

looks legitimate at first glance; only small parts are ever exchanged or changed.[23]

Sure, these are curious but, unfortunately, not uncommon excesses. A seasoned scientist ignores such journals and publishers, even though they now number in the thousands and more, but the Internet is full of them. They represent the pinnacle of what a misguided fixation on publications rather than patient welfare to promote careers in medicine has now wrought in perversions. But before I conclude this first, negative, crisis-ridden part of this book, I must come to the cardinal problem of medicine with you, namely, the fundamental impasse into which even the best biomedical researcher and best researching clinician falls. The good thing is there is a way out of this impasse, in part II.

---

[23] Forster V (2020) Eight Fraudulent Cancer Research Studies Contained The Same Copied Results. How Does This Happen? Forbes, https://www.forbes.com/sites/victoriaforster/2020/06/09/eight-fraudulent-cancer-research-studies-contained-same-copied-results-how-does-this-happen/

9

Organ-Based Medicine

The core problem of both medicine and all biomedical research, which would also exist if all research had become reproducible, statistically correct, and exclusively patient-oriented, is the division of the human body organ by organ. Apart from you GP, for each organ, there is a specialist in charge (Fig. 9.1) and a clinical department. This is similar for the definition of diseases. For example, all diseases are classified using the *International Statistical Classification of Diseases* (ICD) for diagnoses in outpatient and inpatient care in Germany, both for diagnosis and for billing purposes with the health insurance funds. The[1] ICD-10 is a mono-hierarchically structured classification for diagnoses with up to five hierarchical levels. The core area is formed by the organ-specific chapters. Within the ICD chapters, diseases are then named after a symptom in this organ (e.g. heart failure, heart attack, kidney failure, chronic obstructive pulmonary disease, gastritis, colitis, osteoporosis, myalgia, hearing loss, breast cancer, dermatitis) or—even slightly more weird— after the name of a doctor who first described the disease (e.g. Alzheimer's, Parkinson's, Crohn's, Creutzfeldt-Jakob's, Huntington's, Meniére's, Pfeiffer's, Dupuytren's, Wilson's, etc.).

To some degree, this is even understandable. It is impossible for a single person to have all medical knowledge of all organ-based disciplines at hand. So, some way had to be found to divide up the medical knowledge and areas of responsibility. The seemingly most logical or obvious way was to proceed

---

[1] Structure of the four-digit detailed classification of ICD-10-GM. Federal Institute for Drugs and Medical Devices, https://www.dimdi.de/dynamic/de/klassifikationen/icd/icd-10-gm/systematik/systematik/

© The Author(s), under exclusive license to Springer Nature Switzerland AG 2022
H. H. H. W. Schmidt, *The end of medicine as we know it - and why your health has a future*,
https://doi.org/10.1007/978-3-030-95293-8_9

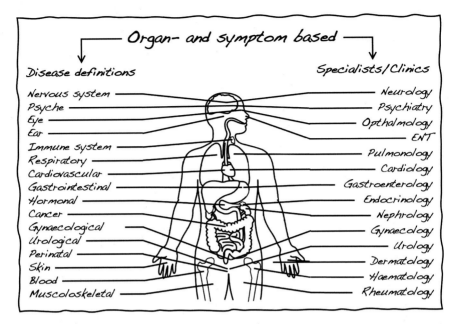

Fig. 9.1 Organ- and symptom-based classification of diseases and medical disciplines

organ by organ. There are only very few medical fields left that at least attempt to look at the whole human body, surgery (although now also often specialized by organ), pathology, forensic medicine, pharmacology, or physiology.[2]

You might ask: "But why is this a problem?" Remember the beginning of the first part of this book. You now know that we do not understand the causes of most diseases. Therefore, we must wait—while that cause works in hiding and unrecognized—until eventually symptoms appear. Only then we notice that there is a disease. But since we still do not know the cause, we just name the disease after this symptom. And then we are left with nothing more than somehow treating the symptoms, with the consequences that are clear to you by now. Such symptomatic therapies can only be very imprecise, so that hardly any patient really benefits from them when it comes to relevant long-term outcomes and cure is impossible. From a certain age on, most have one or more chronic diseases.

But what could a cause of a disease look like? What would it be in concrete terms and how would we then describe and treat or better heal a disease differently? Surprisingly, we don't have to investigate the future at all, because

---

[2] List of specialist titles, DocCheckFlexikon, https://flexikon.doccheck.com/de/Liste_der_Facharztbezeichnungen

there is one group of diseases for which we do indeed know the causes and have a precise definition and name, and no one would consider renaming this disease after one or more of its symptoms, the affected organ(s), or the doctor who discovered it. I am talking about rare diseases.

Rare Diseases as a Model

By the way, rare diseases are not that rare. Each disease is rare, of course, but there are more than 10,000 rare diseases,[3] and approximately 6–8% of humans are affected by a rare disease.[4] In terms of the world population of 7.7 billion, that is 539 million people who are likely to have a rare disease. Together, they could form—after China and India—in terms of population the third largest country on Earth. Because most clinicians are unlikely to have experience in identifying or treating most rare diseases, diagnosis is often missed, delayed, or wrong, and optimal clinical management rarely achieved. Therapy ultimately fails because a clinician simply cannot know all 10,000 rare diseases.

The fundamental difference between rare and what we call common diseases is that the former are caused by a few specific genetic variants, usually only at a single gene, whereas the latter are usually associated with variants at a very large number of different genes, all of which have only a very small effect on their own, and often additional environmental and lifestyle factors are important for symptoms to erupt or at least to modify disease severity. In this way, rare diseases can be precisely defined by a gene or the protein encoded by this gene. And so these diseases are named after a gene or its protein product, e.g. beginning with "A":

- Aceruloplasminemia
- Acetyl-CoA acetyltransferase-2 deficiency
- Acetyl-carnitine deficiency
- ACTH deficiency
- ACTH resistance
- Acyl-CoA oxidase deficiency
- Adenine phosphoribosyltransferase deficiency
- Adenosine monophosphate deaminase-1 deficiency

---

[3] Haendel M (2020) How many rare diseases are there? Nature Reviews Drug Discovery, 19:77–78, https://doi.org/10.1038/d41573-019-00180-y

[4] European Organisation for Rare Diseases (2005) Rare Diseases: Understanding This Public Health Priority, Paris, https://www.eurordis.org/IMG/pdf/princeps_document-EN.pdf

- Adenosylhomocysteine hydrolase deficiency
- Adenylosuccinase deficiency
- And so on

Such precisely defined diseases are almost unpronounceable, not only for laymen. And most doctors will have no idea what these genes or proteins are for. However, the big advantage is the exact cause of the disease is identified, and thus—if a treatment is available—it can not only be treated in a precise manner, but it can also possibly even be cured. Precise means close to a *Number Needed to Treat* of 1, which means that every diagnosed patient would also benefit from the treatment.

Taking a closer look at a rare disease, another major problem becomes apparent with our current approach to name a disease after a symptom. For example, in aceruloplasminemia, adult patients can suffer from the following nine symptoms:

- Unsteadiness of gait
- Involuntary movements
- Grimacing
- Parkinson's-like symptoms
- Depression
- Memory disorders
- Retinal symptoms
- Diabetes mellitus
- Anaemia

Or let's take adenylosuccinase deficiency: Here the four symptoms are:

- Mental developmental delay
- Motor developmental delay
- Epileptic seizures
- Autistic behaviour

If we did not know the cause of these two rare diseases—as is the case with most non-rare diseases—we would have named them according to symptoms and organs. Patients with aceruloplasminemia could easily be confronted with up to nine different diseases, and those with adenylosuccinase deficiency, with four. Doctors would have tried to somehow alleviate the symptoms with multiple drugs, which would probably have drug-drug interactions and cause multiple side effects, further adding to the symptoms.

This is exactly what happens with what we call now complex and chronic diseases. Most likely also here the unknown gene variants plus lifestyle will cause symptoms in different organs with a high probability that a patient will be diagnosed for each symptom with a different disease. No one realizes that—as far as the cause is concerned—it is the same underlying disease, just with different symptoms in different organs. Just a single disease has been artificially complicated into several diseases, so-called comorbidities, i.e. disease that often occur together.

And it gets even worse. There may be different genetic variants that—together with lifestyle components—lead to different symptoms, e.g. disease 1 causing depression and coronary artery disease; 2, depression and migraine; 3, depression and diabetes; 4, depression and stroke; 5, depression and Parkinson's disease; and 6, depression and cancer. With some simplification, these six forms of depression will be all lumped together into one disease named "depression", treated with some symptomatic antidepressants that mostly do not really work. Doctors cannot and do not realize that they are dealing with six different diseases that coincidentally all share this one symptom, depression. However, since the six causes are different, the therapies should be completely different.

This organ- and symptom-based disease dilemma extends 1:1 deep into biomedical research and genetics. For example, neuroscience has its own journals, congresses, and animal models for preclinical research, as does cardiology and cardiovascular research, as does dermatological research, immunological research, gastroenterological and nephrological research, and so on. Thus, biomedical research is exactly split up according to the same principle, separated organ by organ. Therefore, we make no progress. If we continue like this, 100 years from now, we will still be defining symptoms as disease and treating symptoms chronically. But there are the first, albeit still very tentative, signs that throughout medicine a rethink is slowly beginning.

The Organ Boundaries Are Falling

When I was a medical student in the 1980s, each specialist treated his "own" tumour patients, i.e. the neurologist treated brain tumours, the gynaecologist treated breast and uterine tumours, the gastroenterologist treated colon and stomach tumours, and so on. This is almost non-existent anymore, at least in modern hospitals. Nowadays, all tumour patients are discussed in a so-called tumour board—completely independent of the organ in which the tumour occurs. Oncologists acknowledge that—with respect to the selection of therapeutic drugs—it does not matter in which organ a tumour grows or how it looks histologically. The drug therapy must be based on the mutations in the specific tumour cell. Two tumours in different organs may have the set of mutations and require identical therapies; two tumours in the same organ may look histologically completely identical, but the mutations are different and thus require different therapies. Nevertheless, treatment outcomes by and large have still not improved significantly, but this is due to the sort of anti-cancer drugs that we still have. They essentially fall into three categories:

- Non-specific cytotoxins
- Targeted drugs acting on partially cancer-specific mechanisms
- Few drugs that target already highly specific cancer-driving gene variants[5]

Slowly, similar centres and interdisciplinary boards are emerging also for autoimmune diseases, similarly completely organ-agnostic. And there is also movement in research. Also, basic biomedical scientists are slowly discovering that dividing the human body by organs may not have been such a good idea after all. It was a way to cope with the flood of knowledge but is now obviously hampering medical progress. For example, we are increasingly recognizing the fundamental interactions between the intestine and the brain, which often involve the same messenger substances, e.g. the Leuven *Laboratory for Brain-Gut Axis Studies* (*LaBGAS*) in Belgium. In addition, the interaction of the cardiovascular system with the brain, for example, the reciprocal relationship between heart failure and depression, is supported by the Dutch *hartstichting*. In Germany, the Max Planck Society has founded the Institute for Heart and Lung Research in Bad Nauheim; the German Research Foundation is funding an inter-university collaborative research centre on heart and kidney. There is therefore hope that the deficiencies in medicine, which are increasingly being recognized by *out-of-the-box* thinking clinicians, will—or indeed must—lead to comprehensive changes. One researcher, for example, is already calling for a way out of the crisis in cardiology towards a more holistic and personalized medicine[6] and for us to stop continuing to lump together symptoms such as atherosclerosis or hypertension as if they were one disease.

---

[5] Santos R et al. (2017) A comprehensive map of molecular drug targets. Nature Reviews Drug Discovery, 16:19–34, https://doi.org/10.1038/nrd.2016.230

[6] Niroomand F (2013) Cardiology: a way out of the crisis. Dtsch Arztebl, 110:A-1946/B-1721/C-1685, https://www.aerzteblatt.de/archiv/147784/Kardiologie-Ein-Weg-aus-der-Krise

Redefining Autoimmune Diseases

Many chronic inflammatory diseases are now recognized as autoimmune diseases, in which our immune system, instead of eliminating bacteria, viruses, and cancer cells, turns against us and our healthy cells. The more common forms of these diseases include:

- Rheumatoid arthritis
- Graves' disease
- Hashimoto's thyroiditis
- Sjøgren's syndrome

Each of these affects about 1% of the world's population. In addition, there are numerous other autoimmune diseases that are less common: type 1 diabetes, multiple sclerosis, Crohn's disease, vitiligo, a form of anaemia, a form of liver cirrhosis, systemic lupus erythematosus, and ankylosing spondylitis. In total, over 80 autoimmune diseases have been identified. These are currently still differentiated according to the organ in which symptoms occur, i.e. joints, skin, brain and nervous system, intestine, and pancreas, and they are treated accordingly by different specialists.[7]

However, within each of these diseases, there are profound differences with respect to additional symptoms and severity. For example, in rheumatoid arthritis, there is a wide variation in age of onset and, with age, in the number of joints affected and their distribution. In some more severe cases, people develop complications outside the joints, for example, pulmonary fibrosis. So most likely, rheumatoid arthritis is not one disease but only a similar symptom of several genetically different diseases with different additional symptoms. Moreover, some patients have more than one autoimmune symptom, e.g. rheumatoid arthritis plus gastrointestinal Crohn's disease or psoriasis of the skin, or all three. This was found after the initial success in some—but not all—patients with rheumatoid arthritis treated by injecting antibodies that dampen the immune system (anti-TNF therapy/TNF, tumour necrosis factor, is a signalling substance of the immune system involved in local and systemic inflammation). Surprisingly, Crohn's disease and psoriasis also responded to this treatment. Thus, most likely there is a subtype of rheumatoid arthritis caused by TNF, also having gastrointestinal and skin symptoms, like Crohn's or psoriasis, and this cause is treated. All these subtypes have in common that

---

[7] Cho J & Feldman M (2015) Heterogeneity of autoimmune diseases: pathophysiologic insights from genetics and implications for new therapies. Nat Med 21:730–738, https://doi.org/10.1038/nm.3897

the measured TNF levels are an important predictor of subsequent therapeutic success.

However, in other autoimmune diseases such as multiple sclerosis, this anti-TNF therapy is not effective at all and may even worsen the disease. Another example is a signalling pathway (IL-23) which can also be effectively used therapeutically in various immune diseases such as the chronic inflammatory bowel diseases ulcerative colitis and Crohn's disease, in psoriasis with and without joint involvement, or in ankylosing spondylitis. This means one can begin to subtype and group classical autoimmune diseases with symptoms in different organs via the drugs that work—again an argument against organ-based disease definitions and a wind of change that is gently beginning to breeze through our clinics. Let me present a third example, besides tumour and autoimmune diseases: asthma, another disease label that is no longer tenable.

Asthma ≠ Asthma

An editorial in one of the most prestigious medical journals, *The Lancet*, entitled "After asthma: *airways diseases need a new name and a revolution*" caused quite a stir.[8] The conclusion was that asthma can no longer serve as an adequate disease definition. Asthma denotes only a symptom. From its Greek root, the word "asthma" can be translated as "shortness of breath" or "breathlessness", i.e. merely a description of a symptom, however, in Greek. That doesn't make it more precise. As early as 2006, *The Lancet* noted that settling for such a merely descriptive term or label for a family of respiratory diseases had hindered rather than helped progress.[9] Doctors had probably realized that asthma was not so uniform after all and had come up with many subdivisions over the years, such as allergic asthma, adult-onset asthma, exercise-induced asthma, and occupational asthma. However, all of these are still ultimately not causative distinctions and have no bearing on treatment or treatment success. Subsequently, subtypes—also termed endotypes—were proposed,[10] which no longer describe the symptom but measurable biomarkers or response to treatment. With this the deconstruction of the diagnosis of asthma began, but the

---

[8] Kleinert S & Horton R (2018) After asthma: airways diseases need a new name and a revolution. The Lancet, 391:292–294, https://doi.org/10.1016/S0140-6736(17)32205-5

[9] Editors (2006) A plea to abandon asthma as a disease concept. The Lancet, 368:705, https://doi.org/10.1016/S0140-6736(06)69257-X

[10] Anderson GP (2008) Endotyping asthma: new insights into key pathogenic mechanisms in a complex, heterogeneous disease. Lancet 372:1107–19, https://doi.org/10.1016/S0140-6736(08)61452-X

mills grind slowly in medicine. *The Lancet* convened a committee taking the position that even focusing exclusively on the lung to explore the causes of asthmatic symptoms was counterproductive and plain wrong. Instead, it would be necessary to look more closely at what other diseases occur in other organs (comorbidities) and whether lifestyle and environmental factors play a role. In addition, one should not wait until symptoms appear but be more involved in primary prevention and more focused on cure. There should no longer be a separation between paediatric lung specialists (paediatric pulmonologists) and adult lung specialists (pulmonologists), as the growth and development of the lungs is influenced by environmental factors such as indoor and outdoor air pollution, smoking, and other hazardous inhaled substances even before birth in all age groups. According to this Lancet Commission, research must also change. In studies and epidemiological research, the question must be asked: What respiratory disease is being studied? The diagnosis of "asthma" as it is now used is an arbitrary term and anachronism. Patients would also need to be involved in this rethinking. So, from now on, every patient diagnosed with asthma should ask their doctor: "What asthma do I have?" Or, better yet, "What chronic respiratory disease do I have?" Researchers and clinicians have been invited by *The Lancet* to join the revolutionary rethinking of chronic respiratory disease.

It's about nothing less than a revolution. With this Part I on the crisis is done. Then, let's get the revolution started. In doing so, a quick summary of the main conclusions, which will all be resolved in Part II of the book, is presented:

- Our organ-centric view of medicine has led to an impasse.
- Prevention is neglected.
- Since diseases can neither be prevented nor cured, many become chronic.
- Life expectancy is stagnating and, in some countries, declining.
- Men and people with lower socioeconomic status live shorter.
- Biomedical research is highly irreproducible, of poor quality, and not patient-focused.
- Healthcare providers are given false incentives to commercialize against patient welfare.
- Very few patients benefit from their medicines and therapies.
- Big Pharma is not sustainable in its current form.

At the end of Part II, we will take another look at these theses and contrast them with the core theses on the medicine of the future. In Part III, I will show you that this is not a phantasy book about organs growing in a Petri dish or cyborg-like human enhancements in a distant future but that the future that I describe has begun and that you can benefit from it already today. But let us pause for a moment and consider where exactly we want to go with a better medicine.

10

Interjection 1: How Healthy Do You Want to Be?

Before we take off into the new medicine and move from Part I to Part II, I would like to pause with you for a moment and reflect on two aspects that the German physician and psychiatrist Klaus Dörner[1] and the philosopher Byung-Chul Han[2] have thrown into the spokes, so to speak, like a little stick. Dörner writes: "One can do an infinite amount for one's health. But that doesn't have much, often nothing, to do with whether and to what extent one feels healthy—and it's the latter that counts". And Han observes, "Today there is a … fear of pain everywhere. Any painful condition is avoided. … Pain tolerance is rapidly declining". What both warn about is to strive for a state of complete well-being, or suspiciously observing and constantly optimizing oneself—whereby the slightest disturbance in well-being becomes an illness, or at least a symptom that must be treated.

Health is hard to define. Is it a feeling? We feel healthy even though a tumour is already slowly growing inside us. So it can't be that. Is it the complete absence of disease or risk of disease? Tumour cells are created in our body every day, and our immune system removes them. We all carry risks and will die one day from it or from an accident. So, it can't be the absence of risk either. Neither can the World Health Organization's definition of health as "a state of complete physical, mental and social well-being and not merely the absence of disease or infirmity", for we always carry within us genetically defined risks of disease that produce symptoms without or only with lifestyle

[1] Dörner K (2002) Health care system: in the progress trap. Dtsch Arztebl 99:A-2462-2466/B-2104/C-1970, https://www.aerzteblatt.de/archiv/32976/Gesundheitssystem-In-der-Fortschrittsfalle

[2] Han B-C (2020) Palliative Society - Pain Today. Happy Science 169, MSB Matthes & Seitz, Berlin, https://www.matthes-seitz-berlin.de/buch/palliativgesellschaft.html?lid=2

© The Author(s), under exclusive license to Springer Nature Switzerland AG 2022
H. H. H. W. Schmidt, *The end of medicine as we know it - and why your health has a future*,
https://doi.org/10.1007/978-3-030-95293-8_10

errors. Complete freedom from disease will not exist, not even in the future. Even worse, if we constantly ask ourselves whether we are healthy and constantly listen to ourselves, this will most likely negatively affect our well-being. Paradoxically, you can always do more for your health but feel less and less healthy. I would most likely follow Hans-Georg Gadamer's definition that health only exists as a state in which one forgets that one is healthy.[3]

What about the opposite, the definition of illness? According to the insurance law of the statutory health insurers, illness is an "objectively tangible, abnormal physical or mental condition that is contrary to the rules, requires the need for curative treatment and can lead to incapacity for work". So here the need for treatment defines the disease and that is highly subjective. Han picks up on this with the concept of pain. It is already clear from the use of painkillers that pain is perceived exclusively as something to get rid of. But we cannot make it disappear; it always comes back, because it is not a disease but a signal from our body. Pain research has put a lot of effort into standardizing pain. Nevertheless, two people will perceive the identical pain stimulus differently; even the same person will feel it differently on different days in different moods. Thus, a signal can easily turn into a disease. Up to 15% of people report suffering from migraine. On average, people take painkillers 52 times a year.[4] It should be borne in mind that the placebo effect of painkillers can be as high as 60%. The typical sequence—dissolve the effervescent headache tablet, drink it, and after 10 min the headache already feels much better—is pharmacologically completely impossible. If a patient feels this way, it must have been a placebo effect. In the USA, the unconditional will to eliminate pain to the maximum and with the heaviest guns has ended in an opiate crisis of historic proportions. Tens of thousands of people have fallen victim to it, partly due to the criminal machinations of Purdue, Johnson & Johnson, and other pharmaceutical companies for which penalties of 572 million dollars have been imposed.

The risk is therefore that everyday disturbances of well-being, which are part of normal life, are increasingly defined as an illness, bordering on hypochondria, in need of treatment. Even the cure of a disease or a successful prevention, which objectively promotes health, can cause a perceived deterioration of health, for example, through over-attention to oneself including permanent self-optimization. If health becomes an end in life instead of taking

---

[3] Gadamer H-G (2010) Über die Verborgenheit der Gesundheit. Aufsätze und Vorträge. medizinHuman 10, Edt. Hontschik B, 215p, Suhrkamp

[4] Diener H-C et al. (2008) Per capita consumption of analgesics. A survey of nine countries over 20 years (1985 to 2005). Pharmaceutical Journal, https://www.pharmazeutische-zeitung.de/ausgabe-372008/pro-kopf-verbrauch-von-schmerzmitteln/

health as an occasion to fill one's life with meaning, if everyone exploits the health system to the maximum with the claim to have an enforceable right to health, then health becomes a product of which—if one can afford it—one always wants more. Through the redefinition of mild disorders of well-being such as exhaustion, nervousness, stress, flatulence and constipation, agitation, or problems with diet and time change as requiring therapy,[5] the definition of what is pathological has been extended further and further.

Conversely, we have almost completely excluded important areas of life such as growing old and dying. Whereas in the past people went home from hospital to die, today they generally die in hospital, in a home, or in a hospice. The need for care outside the family has increased a 100-fold in just a few decades. Since today one dies almost only in old age, dying and death have become invisible and no longer belong to the world of life experienced as normal and "healthy". The healthy can thus participate optimally in the work process without being "distracted", but the old and those in need of care are isolated, which ultimately harms both. We will not be able to revive the old extended family, but we will be able to revive multigenerational residential communities, houses, or other forms of living.[6]

Another aspect we will have to learn to deal with is as follows: How do we behave when a risk of disease or a disease process has been clearly demonstrated for us by new technology, but we are not sick yet? It makes sense if we see this as an opportunity to react preventively and adjust our lifestyle accordingly. It would be bad, however, if we were to go through our whole lives with a burden because of this now known risk. Many of us will not be able to develop this attitude on our own but will need advice and psychological coaching.

All these trends harbour a potential that becomes more destructive the more it is marketed and left to competition with fatal effects on the social sector and healthcare. A reasonable level of health, prevention, and therapy should, like water, air, and a basic income, be part of the solidaric provision of public services in every society from which a meaningful individual life can develop. However, the essential prerequisites for health should not become a service or a commodity. Medical facilities such as clinics should not serve the profit maximization of *shareholder value*. Competition as to who is the best doctor or surgeon should lead to high quality but not to an expansion of quantity. Germany, for example, has about as many beds in

---

[5] Hennrich D, Initiative "Homeopathy helps!", https://www.homoeopathiehilft.at

[6] https://www.wohnen-im-alter-nrw.de/wohnformen/gemeinschaftliche-wohnformen/praxisbeispiel-alt-und-jung, https://www.wg-gesucht.de/artikel/mehrgenerationen-wg-miteinander-von-jung-und-alt-statt-allein, https://www.forschungsinformationssystem.de/servlet/is/217216/

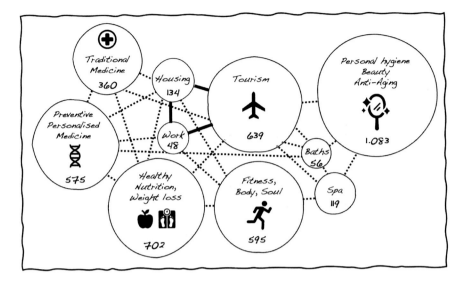

Fig. 10.1 The future well-being industry, which goes far beyond traditional medicine. Sales figures in billions of US dollars refer only to the USA

rehabilitation and spa clinics as the rest of the world. Rehabilitation should, however, be directed as quickly as possible to where people live, i.e. not to rehabilitation centres.

There is no doubt that other healthcare providers will emerge beyond traditional medicine, and that is good and necessary simply because prevention is currently shockingly underused and medical doctors are simply not trained for it. Thus, different healthcare providers need to take over this role. For example, the components of fitness and wellness, which currently still have the aura of a fitness studio or a bathing complex with sauna area, are already forming a market in the USA estimated at approximately 4 trillion US dollars, which is referred to as *well-being*, not wellness (Fig. 10.1).[7] These free markets would be well advised not to promote the conversion of all healthy people into sick people but to promote health maintenance.

Although in principle the human being is at the centre of all this, he or she must not become the permanent purchaser of products and services without which he or she would not feel optimal. According to Dörner, such a health or wellness industry could run the risk of becoming a "vitality destruction machine". In a vital society, living healthily must not only mean the one-sided relief of burdens but the simultaneous constant balancing with strain. This means, for example, not to fight every pain with a painkiller.

---

[7] Global Wellness Economy Monitor (2018) Global Wellness Institute, https://globalwellnessinstitute.org/industry-research/2018-global-wellness-economy-monitor/

Relief must not be maximized but optimized—physically, psychologically, and socially. Surprisingly, people with grave fates are usually strong enough to bear them.

In the future, we will be able to enjoy amazing progresses in medicine and prevention, which I will now describe in Part II of this book, but we will always have to provide for strain as well. If, for example, the relief provided by cars, escalators, and lifts ultimately leads to or exacerbates muscular atrophy, osteoporosis, diabetes, and cardiovascular disease, it has achieved nothing, or the contrary. For example, I never use escalators, and I only use a lift when I'm carrying luggage up to the fifth floor. Why don't you try that too if you're not already doing it? If stress is stressful and makes you sick, then it's not stress that needs to be avoided, because even occasional stress is natural and part of our lives, but rather we need to improve our stress management and resilience or be coached to learn this.[8] These are just two facets of the future of health, and both are important.

So, the question is: How healthy do you want to be? Mindful of this little interjection inspired by three wise men—Klaus Dörner, Byung-Chul Han, and Hans-Georg Gadamer—I look forward with them to the end of medicine as we know it and to a future that, as I will then show you quite concretely in Part III, has already begun.

---

[8] Wulff T, Stressism, https://www.stressismus.de

Part II

The Medicine of the Future

11

Re-discover the Whole Patient

The innovations required to eliminate the undesirable developments described in the first part of this book are tantamount to a revolution. It is no longer a matter of optimizing a candle, but of inventing something completely new with an electric light bulb. It is not a matter of somehow improving sailboats, making them bigger or faster, but of replacing them—because their optimum has been exhausted—with something completely new, such as steam-powered ships, which are not only faster, but offer completely different possibilities for mechanical work on board. We are not only digitalizing medicine and optimizing some workflows, but we are also entering a new era of medicine, health, and prevention.

Wave #6

Let's think back to the five Kondratieff waves from the first chapter. One wave did not always build exactly on the other, but it is very likely that the IT revolution of the fifth wave will also have a significant impact on the sixth. What could this wave be? There is currently a lot of talk about Industry 4.0 and online retail, or about renewable energies and electric cars.

Are these really all revolutions, or is it not more a case of carrying on as before, just a bit more digital or more digital than before? Are electric cars really the big revolution, when the first electric cars were built in Hungary, the Netherlands, and the USA in 1882[1] and innovative engineers are already

---

[1] Timeline: History of the Electric Car, https://www.energy.gov/timeline/timeline-history-electric-car

© The Author(s), under exclusive license to Springer Nature Switzerland AG 2022
H. H. H. W. Schmidt, *The end of medicine as we know it - and why your health has a future*,
https://doi.org/10.1007/978-3-030-95293-8_11

working on the next step, the hydrogen car, an electric car with a hydrogen fuel cell that combines all the advantages and makes the electric car look obsolete?[2] Or is it really a revolution if the essential processes in various industries 3.0 basically remain the same and only through digitization to industry 4.0 less paper is created or some ordering and manufacturing processes are optimized or made more efficient? Or is the replacement of fossil fuels by renewable energies to mitigate global warming really the great revolution, when these technologies have been around for a long time and only we and our elected politicians were not able to manage and implement this technology in a consistent and socially acceptable manner? Hydropower has been used since the Middle Ages, and since the end of the nineteenth century to generate electricity. The first silicon photovoltaic cell was developed in 1954, and in 1955 solar cells were technically applied for the first time in the power supply of telephone amplifiers. And as early as 1891, there was the first wind turbine for electricity generation. In my eyes, all of these—Industry 4.0, online commerce, and renewable energies—are not the sixth wave. These are not real revolutions, but gradual developments, and what they bring to the individual is unclear. A real revolution always means that major industries and concepts disappear, and in their place other new ones that we never thought possible before come into being, so that afterwards nothing is the same as before. And above all, the added value is clear to everyone in genuine revolutions. Much of the alleged Industry 4.0 deserves at most the label 3.5. Continuous optimization of automation within a company has little to do with disruption. Only when better value creation is achieved, for example, by sharing information across companies, would a genuine disruptive innovation effect be conceivable.[3]

Although digitization is a technology that can no longer be ignored in many areas, it alone will not be the bearer of the sixth wave,[4] not least because, according to futurologist Leo A. Nefiodow, it does not fulfil three of the main criteria for such a new wave in the Kondratieff sense: New Market, Full Employment, and Life Cycle. Digitization itself does not constitute a new market, because a Kondratieff cycle gives rise to entirely new markets and with them many entirely new jobs. Nor does digitization ensure full

[2] Stegmaier G (2020) The truth about the fuel cell. Auto Motor Sport, https://www.auto-motor-und-sport.de/tech-zukunft/alternative-antriebe/wasserstoffauto-brennstoffzelle-co2-neutral-batterie-lithium/

[3] https://de.cloudflight.io/presse/industrie-4-0-hype-blockiert-iot-innovationen-und-digitale-produkte-24582/

[4] Nefiodow LA (1996) The Sixth Kondratieff-Ways to Productivity and Full Employment in the Age of Information, Rhein-Sieg-Verlag, St. Augustin, 223 p., https://www.kondratieff.net/der-sechste-kondratieff; Händeler E (1997) The Sixth Kondratieff: Health becomes an economic power. Dtsch Arztebl 94:A-1116/B-948/C-891.

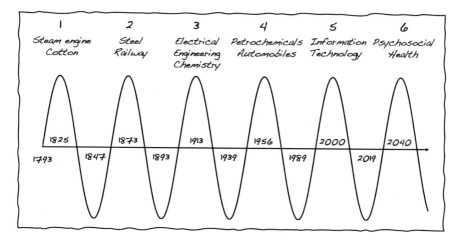

Fig. 11.1 The sixth Kondratieff wave redefines psychosocial health

employment, because it will save more old jobs than it will generate new ones. After all, it is about increasing efficiency and simplification.

Finally, the life cycle aspect states that a truly innovative technology or concept has three phases: basic innovation, dynamic growth, and a new "normal". After that, a technology may still be needed, but it is no longer a driver of innovation. For example, the railroad was certainly such a revolutionary innovation, but no longer drives innovation and yet continues to be used. And so, the sixth Kondratieff wave will also certainly use the tools of the fifth wave, the IT revolution, but it will, I am convinced, involve something quite different from Industry 4.0 or renewable energy (which are coming anyway because they are overdue), namely, a complete redefinition of psychosocial health (Fig. 11.1).

After 200 years and five Kondratieff waves, decreasing life expectancy, chronic diseases, exploding health costs, and environmental damage limit the further development of our societies to the detriment of national economies. The gigantic financial damage to several generations caused by COVID-19 is just one example of the consequences if we do not prioritize health and prevention high enough. We must and will have to completely rethink how we preserve or restore health and prevention, and how we finance this in a broad social, indeed global consensus. And we need to answer why all this will not cause any costs that hinder economic growth, but—on the contrary—will be essential to be able to grow sustainably at all. The result must be classless medicine without distinction between so-called industrialized nations, emerging economies, and developing countries. It must be fully democratic, without false incentives that create obstructive cost barriers.

A key issue will be socioeconomic safety, education, and access to knowledge, the lack of which can currently cost up to 10 years of life and a great deal of quality of life. Unequal life chances never remain individual, but in their consequences always create problems for society. I agree with Leo A. Nefiodow, who formulated that "without efforts to make people healthy [it will not be possible to] place the economy on a future-oriented foundation".

By solving these problems, the many economic aspects of the sixth Kondratieff wave will make it a real job engine and a genuine new market. It will also cushion the decline in employment due to digitization via new jobs in healthcare. The sixth Kondratieff wave of psychosocial health will not only be able to cure diseases like hypertension and prevent its dramatic consequential risks, which will be a blessing for every single patient. Via a fundamental holistic recovery of every individual—at least the chance to do so—it will enable the next dominant economic epoch with completely new industries and value creation, but also become the guarantor of all subsequent waves and innovations.

IT Platforms Join in

A previous Kondratieff wave does not necessarily influence the next one, but it will be the case with the sixth. If we want to overcome the arbitrary split-up of the human body into organ-based disciplines and rather capture the complexity of the entire human body and have this knowledge up to date at our fingertips, then Big Data and artificial intelligence will be needed. No human brain can store and analyse this amount of data. We no longer do a clinical trial with 4000 patients but analyse the data of hundreds of thousands to millions of people and patients. This way we eliminate any bias in selecting patients for a clinical trial and can identify correlations independent of limited organ-based disciplines and diseases. In Scandinavia and the UK, where healthcare is free and patient data have been stored anonymously for decades, we can do cross-sectional snapshots but also virtual in silico trials over time. This is essential to discover cause and effect relations over 20–30 years apart. None of the current clinical trials lasts this long and can do this.

And because Big Data is so technology-intensive and there are so many IT platforms among the current top ten industries that can do everything and are not fixated on one product and one distribution channel, it is also no surprise when Apple, Amazon, and Alphabet vehemently engage in the health revolution. For instance, one of Google's main business models is to cure age-related diseases. Yes, to cure! Not about collecting data for patients or about patients, no, Google wants to cure diseases. That means they're going to have to get into the biotech market. Google or its holding, Alphabet, has already recruited one of the directors of the US *National Institute of Health*, founded or bought Verily and Calico, respectively, and another 350+ biotech companies. Google has become a health company, stealthily, quietly. Calico, for example, stands for *Calico Life Sciences LLC* (https://www.calicolabs.com) and researches topics related to aging and associated diseases. The company focuses largely on age-related diseases such as Alzheimer's, cancer, and cardio-vascular disease. Google believes it can improve millions of lives by taking a long-term, comprehensive view of healthcare and biotechnology. Of course, Calico is taking a Big Data approach to healthcare and will collect and analyse massive amounts of information from patients to at least accelerate, if not revolutionize, healthcare innovation. According to Calico, the best way to fight aging is to focus on disease prevention, that is, preventing and curing rather than treating. Three of Calico's four founders previously worked in genetic engineering, which clearly defines its approach. Since 2014, Calico has entered a strategic alliance with the US pharmaceutical company AbbVie to focus its research more on the aging process and age-related diseases.[5] Although we often associate diseases with genes, drugs are usually developed against the protein molecules encoded by these genes. For this purpose, it is at least helpful, sometimes essential, to know the 3D structure of these protein molecules to optimally model drugs to perfectly fit into a binding pocket of the protein molecule. Until now, the elucidation of such a 3D structure has been an extremely laborious and not always successful process and has repre-sented one of the greatest challenges in biology. Posed! That's because an arti-ficial intelligence network developed by Google offshoot DeepMind took a giant leap in 2020. DeepMind's AlphaFold programme outperformed about 100 other research teams in predicting protein structures in a biennial com-petition. Google's DeepMind has always been better than all the other teams, but since 2020 they've been in a league of their own and have basically solved the problem. And a few months later in 2021 AlphaFold resolved the

---

[5] Petri A (2013) Google to banish death with new company, Calico. The Washington Post, https://www.washingtonpost.com/blogs/compost/wp/2013/09/18/google-to-banish-death-with-new-company-calico/; Dougherty C (2014) Calico, Google's Anti-Aging Company, Announces New Research Facility. New York Times, https://bits.blogs.nytimes.com/2014/09/03/googles-anti-aging-company-announces--new-research-facility/?_php=true&_type=blogs&_r=0; Callaway E (2020) 'It will change everything': DeepMind's AI makes gigantic leap in solving protein structures. Nature, https://www.nature.com/articles/d41586-020-03348-4

structures of all human proteins, an incredible powerful asset in developing new—or optimizing old—drugs.[6]

Amazon, on the other hand, first bought PillPack, an online drug delivery service, in 2018 and, in 2020, renamed it Amazon Pharmacy. Between the drug manufacturer and the patient, there are several intermediaries: in the USA, different wholesalers plus usually pharmacy chains; in other countries at least two, i.e. the individual pharmacist plus in most cases a wholesaler. Amazon does not need these middlemen, which allows for higher discounts or lower prices. This is especially beneficial for self-pay patients in the USA, where drug companies charge some of the highest drug prices in the world. In addition to the existing PillPack on-site pharmacies, Amazon will establish further ones. However, such chain pharmacies are (still) prohibited in some countries. Quite obviously, Amazon plans to take over the entire pharmaceutical market in the USA and probably further. The only gap on this path so far is the lack of a cold chain to ship temperature-sensitive drugs, which is essential for insulin and vaccines, for example. Thus, Amazon Pharmacy is currently limited. However, one special feature that Amazon can offer thanks to PillPack is so-called blistering for medicines taken on a long-term basis. For this purpose, the tablets are removed from their packaging and repackaged in a patient-friendly manner, i.e. one blister set per day, if necessary, even separately for morning, noon, and evening. This has been proven to increase patient compliance, i.e. regularity of intake and preventing dosage errors. In an initial test phase limited to its Seattle employees, Amazon created a virtual health clinic called "Amazon Care". Without having to make an appointment, Amazon employees get quick access to healthcare, at their convenience in terms of time and space (at home, in the office, or virtually). In terms of data security, Oasis Medical is an intermediary company to prevent Amazon, as an employer, from obtaining sensitive employee data. However, Oasis Medical is a subsidiary of Amazon, albeit standalone. With no travel or wait times, Amazon Care connects Amazon employees or their family members with a doctor or nurse practitioner via live or video chat. For an in-person appointment, a nurse practitioner can also drop by their home or work. In addition, Amazon Care doctors can also prescribe medications and have them delivered within a few hours or set them up for pickup at a pharmacy of choice. Additionally, Amazon bought Health Navigator, a start-up that provides programming interfaces for the medical sector. With this, Amazon plans to

---

[6] Jumper J et al. (2021) Highly accurate protein structure prediction with AlphaFold. Nature 596:583–589, https://doi.org/10.1038/s41586-021-03819-2; Tunyasuvunakool K et al. (2021) Highly accurate protein structure prediction for the human proteome. Nature 596:590–596, https://doi.org/10.1038/s41586-021-03828-1

integrate its Amazon Care clinics and into its existing PillPack/Amazon Pharmacy services. Amazon is also building with several developers and healthcare companies to further develop its artificial intelligence assistant Alexa to use it to care for chronically ill patients, schedule drug prescriptions, and deliver medications as needed.

Finally, Apple, as the third IT platform, has become active on a completely different terrain: the personal patient or health record on the smartphone. The Health app uses machine learning to individually display the most important data such as minutes of exercise, vital signs, and the chronological course of cholesterol or blood pressure values. For this purpose, the HealthKit interface was programmed to allow other developers to interact with their apps with the Health app. In this way, extensive data is accumulated, enabling therapy control, or monitoring of disease prevention (nutrition, sleep, and exercise) or demanding fitness goals, or facilitating family planning. Health entries allow patients, doctors, and therapists to view patient records—clearly displayed from the smartphone—without having to rely on paper documents. Further, the ResearchKit app allows patients to give consent to make their health data available in anonymized form for medical research (asthma, Parkinson's, and diabetes mellitus). Other similar offerings include Google Health, Microsoft's HealthVault, or Swisscom's Evita.

All these are not yet the revolutionary breakthroughs we will need for future medicine, but they will be certainly most helpful on this journey. They also underline once again that the real next socioeconomic revolution indeed concerns health. There is no other explanation for the fact that the three largest IT industry companies have entered the market at the same time and on such a massive scale. Moreover, coincidentally or in concert, they have, for now, perfectly divided up the digital health market: Google the therapeutics, Amazon the logistics, and Apple the personal health record. There is hardly any overlap and a lot of synergy.

There are differences between electronic health and patient records. The latter is a collection of a person's medical data, like the electronic medical record in a hospital (if it is digitized and not still on paper) or the practice EDP system of the attending physician. The current disadvantage is that all this data is distributed among different doctors and clinics where a patient has received treatment, and the data is often incompatible with each other. An electronic *health record* (*personal health record*) goes one step further and contains non-medical information (nutrition, fitness, sleep). With all apps, the patient should have exclusive data sovereignty, but not a doctor or health insurer. However, a patient can then grant them full or partial read or write access. The Apple Health app is more on the side of an electronic health record, but with the goal of evolving towards a full electronic patient record as well.

In contrast, many countries copy these apps more badly than well. Germany has introduced a mandatory electronic patient record, Austria the "Elga" health record paired with an "e-card", and Switzerland is to introduce an electronic patient dossier. In the USA, Medicare and Medicaid have an EHR Incentive Program. In the UK, NHS Connecting for Health project launched GP2GP which enables GPs to transfer a patient's electronic medical record to another practice when the patient moves making the UK probably one of the world leaders in this. There are very few General Practices in the UK which are not computerized. Unlike in the USA, GPs have not had to deal with billing and have been able to concentrate on clinical care. Given the free *Exposure Notifications Express technology* available from Google and Apple, further national programme development seems slightly redundant or should at least join forces and have one European or even global WHO solution. The main conclusion, however, remains that if the world's three largest platform technology companies are pivoting to health, then there's a good chance that this is where the greater innovation and—in their view—market potential lies. Whether the market and health are so compatible is something we will come back to later.

How Big Data Is Helping to Redefine Diseases

Not only in health management (therapeutics by Google, logistics by Amazon, and the personal health record by Apple), but also in biomedical research, the use of Big Data has entered and is changing everything. In the early days, especially after the sequencing of the human genome, involved the identification of genes being associated with certain diseases. For rare but often severe to early fatal diseases, one gene defect is often sufficient. This is then termed a monogenetic disease. Other gene variants are less severe, more common and many of these are associated with chronic diseases, but each gene has very little predictive value on its own. This approach did not take us much further, also because these gene-association studies were still conducted on classical organ- or symptom-based disease definitions, such as hypertension. They assumed hypertension was one disease. But if we assume now that hypertension is not a disease but rather a symptom of several disease causes, then it becomes clear that when all the genetic information on several diseases was lumped together an impenetrable data salad is generated which in the end tells us nothing. On top of that, many genes would require different lifestyle errors to eventually trigger disease symptom, i.e. hypertension plus a risk for stroke or heart attack. But better step by step and let's ignore lifestyle for the moment and look at genetic causes; otherwise it would get too complicated too quickly.

Let's assume a set 1 of genetic variants causes several symptoms including hypertension and—importantly—also the risk for a heart attack. Let's also assume that there is a second set of genetic variants that causes several other symptoms but also hypertension and—importantly—also the risk for a stroke. And let's further assume that there is a third and a fourth set of genetic variants that cause yet other symptoms including in both cases hypertension but—importantly—no risk for a heart attack, a stroke, or any other serious health risk. Currently, we know none of these genetics risks and simply treat all patients with drugs that lower blood pressure. But we know that simply doing this will hardly help any patient because the causal mechanism keeps boiling underneath and the risk for a heart attack or stroke with gene sets or causes 1 and 2 will not simply disappear by taking away the symptom hypertension. Obviously, one would like to know and treat only causes 1 and 2. Instead, patients with causes 3 and 4 would not need to be treated at all, since they may have higher blood pressure than the average person, but no medical risk associated with it. It would be a waste to treat those patients and rather pit them at risk of experiencing some of the drug side effects. However, a genetic association study on all patients with high blood pressure, assuming that this is a single disease, will eventually find all these genes that are somehow associated with high blood pressure or blood pressure regulation leading to a hundred or more genes[7] and ultimately no progress. In the end, after all these genome-wide association (GWAS) studies, 95% of all patients with hypertension are still diagnosed with primary hypertension and treated symptomatically. Nothing has changed, apart from lots and lots of papers in high "impact" journals. However, no "impact" for patients. Not that this genetic

---

[7] Padmanabhan S et al. (2012) Genetic basis of blood pressure and hypertension. Trends in Genetics 28:397–408, http://linkinghub.elsevier.com/retrieve/pii/S0168952512000546; Ehret GB et al. (2011) Genetic variants in novel pathways influence blood pressure and cardiovascular disease risk. Nature, 478:103–109, http://www.nature.com/doifinder/10.1038/nature10405; Oikonen M (2011) Genetic variants and blood pressure in a population-based cohort: the Cardiovascular Risk in Young Finns study. Hypertension 58:1079–1085, https://hyper.ahajournals.org/content/58/6/1079.full; Miyaki K et al. (2012) The combined impact of 12 common variants on hypertension in Japanese men, considering GWAS results. Journal of Human Hypertension, 26:430–436, https://doi.org/10.1038/jhh.2011.50; Warren HR et al. (2017) Genome-wide association analysis identifies novel blood pressure loci and offers biological insights into cardiovascular risk. Nat Genet 49:403–415 https://doi.org/10.1038/ng.3768

information is completely useless, but the main conceptual breakthrough has been initiated by Albert-László Barabási, a Hungarian physicist and network scientist.

Barabási works on different types of networks from huge data sets to extract surprising new information from them through pattern or cluster recognition. Barabási mathematized network research and discovered so-called scale-free networks, social networks, networks of fake news, networks of pandemics, networks of art, tennis, books, food, etc. So fascinating to look at that his lab even opened an art section.[8] In these scale-free networks, dots (or nodes as they are called in network science) are connected through lines (called edges). However, the nodes are not of equal rank. Some nodes have much more connections than others and are called hubs. Some other nodes have very few connections, perhaps only one, locate to the periphery, and are not very important for the stability of the network. Most other nodes are in between, not dispensable but also not a hub. We too are, for example, a social network: some of us have lots of friends and colleagues and are very influential, others not very connected, almost lonely. Moreover, we stick together with people we like (our friends), we work with (colleagues), or our family. All these groups are called clusters in network science. So far so clear, I hope. Now let's take one more step towards medicine.

Our body also functions as a network, i.e. a network of organs; within these organs, a network of cells; and within each cell, a network of proteins encoded by the DNA in the nucleus, all of this immersed in small molecules such as glucose, metabolites, fatty acids, hormones, messenger molecules, and so on, all interconnected and surrounded by a cell membrane. A complex multi-organ, multi-cellular network like that of our body must be highly resistant to the failure of as many nodes or connections as possible. If the slightest disturbance or failure would lead to a collapse of our body, we would not have made it through evolution. Probably a lot of trial and error was necessary until the machine homo sapiens was fully functional and resilient to stressors. However, if one of the *hubs* in our system fails, severe network disruptions occur. This can range from death, e.g. in a heart attack or stroke, to milder dysfunctions, e.g. we lose one eye but can still see, or lose one foot but can still walk (with a prosthesis). Translated to the cellular level, if a not-so-important protein is affected, the cell will do just fine; if an essential protein is affected, e.g. to utilize oxygen or glucose as energy sources, the cell will die. In between are lot of other proteins which—when damaged, possibly together with a couple of

---

[8] Weibel P et al. (2021) Hidden Patterns: Visualizing Networks at Barabasi Lab; https://www.artbook.com/9783775748629.html

other proteins nearby also being damaged—may cause symptoms, e.g. slow down the cell or make it less stable, but will not kill it. An analogous example is the failure of only a few routers on the Internet, which can have far-reaching effects. Similarly, infection of an IT network with a computer virus is not problematic until essential hub nodes, i.e. servers, are infected, at which point the virus spreads extremely rapidly. Even in COVID-19 times, we have experienced that there are so-called *super spreaders*, i.e. people in the health sector (with many contacts to people at risk due to their job), or *super spreader events* such as carnivals (where many people at risk come in contact with the virus).

Barabási now applied this concept to diseases and disease-relevant genes and proteins. If a *hub* protein is too essential, a defect may be incompatible with life; if the protein is important but will not cause symptoms, additional neighbouring proteins within the same cluster need to be affected until symptoms arise, either directly or when the cell is put under stress. Of our approximately 25,000 genes, only about 1 in 20 genes is so essential that a defect will result in an abortion or stillbirth;[9] only about 1 in ten has been associated with a disease. Since at least a quarter of all our genes are active in all our cells, it can be assumed that disease genes or a group of disease genes will cause symptoms in more than one organ. Thus, the probability is high that two or more of the currently organ-based diseases have the same genetic origin and are thus genetically the same disease needing the same treatment. Consequently, naming a disease according to a gene or set of genes will lead to completely different disease definitions.

What Barabási did was to combine all diseases, and all disease-associated genes known at that time, and construct a network of all human diseases, the so-called *diseasome*. This was an epoch-making work. When I saw it, my entire coordinate system of how and what to research turned 180°. Nothing was the same after that, because the conclusion to be drawn from it was as clear as day to me. The whole concept of biomedical science had to change. It was a eureka moment, the likes of which one rarely has. What had Barabási observed? When diseases were made nodes and risk genes connected these nodes, some diseases had a lot of common risk genes formed a cluster of diseases (Fig. 11.2). On my homepage I have a 3D visualization of this network from a TEDMED

[9] Goh K-I et al. (2007) The human disease network. Proceedings of the National Academy of Sciences of the United States of America 104:8685–8690, https://doi.org/10.1073/pnas.0701361104; Barabási AL (2011) Network medicine: a network-based approach to human disease. Nat Rev. Genet 12:56–68, https://doi.org/10.1038/nrg2918; Ramsköld D et al. (2009) An Abundance of Ubiquitously Expressed Genes Revealed by Tissue Transcriptome Sequence Data. PLoS Comput Biol 5:e1000598, https://doi.org/10.1371/journal.pcbi.1000598

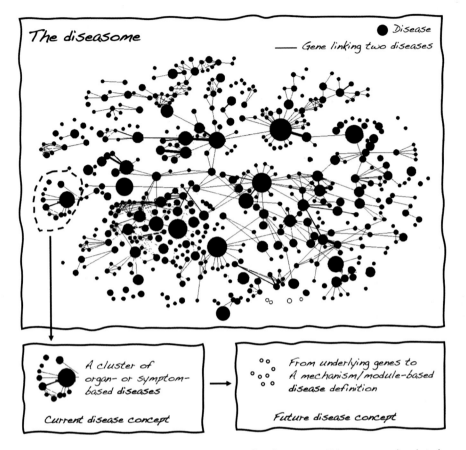

Fig. 11.2 The network of all human diseases, the diseasome. Diseases are the dots (so-called nodes). They are linked through shared risk genes (lines = so-called edges). Diseases with a lot of common risk genes cluster together (dashed cluster and lower left). This group of shared risk genes then becomes the new disease definition, while the current diseases become just symptoms (lower right)

talk by Barabási, which I highly recommend listening to.[10] In Fig. 11.2, I use only black and white line graphics to visualize the essentials of this network as simply as possible. You can easily see that the diseasome is not regular but rather several clusters of diseases loosely linked. One exciting conclusion that follows from this is that the genes specific to each disease cluster are keys to the underlying causes of these diseases. Thus, the group of genes becomes the

---

[10] Bonus 3-D visualization of diseasome, https://3hwschmidt.wordpress.com/geheiltstattbehandelt/, from Barabási's TEDMED talk, https://youtu.be/10oQMHadGos

new precise disease definition, and what we called diseases so far will be "degraded" to become just the symptoms of this genetic cause.

This meant that diseases (or, from now on, symptoms) that have been treated by completely different specialists and dealt with by completely different scientific disciplines belong together. Thus, the whole concept of medicine must change from organ to the whole human but not in an esoteric but evidence-based manner. This marked *the end of medicine as we know it*.

A cluster in this consideration are, for example, all tumour diseases, completely independent of the organ in which the tumour occurs. Designations such as breast cancer, colon cancer, lung cancer, or brain tumour are—as understandable as this may be since it designates the localization—virtually meaningless from a diagnostic-therapeutic point of view. Two tumours that look microscopically identical and affect the same cell type in the same organ can be completely different genetically—and thus in terms of the treatable cause. They look identical but are diagnosed and treated completely differently. I already mentioned that in oncology, in every better clinic, all tumours are now discussed within a tumour board, completely independent of where the tumour is located. The same happens with autoimmune diseases and some eye diseases.

My group is leading *repo-trial*, a large European Union project that is working on a cluster of diseases that you really wouldn't lump together: diabetes, obesity, Parkinson's disease, asthma, heart failure, stroke, atherosclerosis, dementia, myocardial infarction and coronary heart disease, hypertension, and Alzheimer's disease, and there could be a few more. Now not all these diseases have the same cause, but in a large enough proportion of patients with these symptoms, a group of genes is obviously causative. We've recently been able to show for hypertension that you can filter these out. Here we are confident that we have found the cause of hypertension for one fifth of all hypertensive patients—and a way to diagnose it.[11] The genes associated here

---

[11] Elbatreek MH et al. (2020) NOX5-induced uncoupling of endothelial NO synthase is a causal mechanism and theragnostic target of an age-related hypertension endotype. PLOS Biology 8:e3000885, https://doi.org/10.1371/journal.pbio.3000885; Casas AI et al. (2019) From single drug targets to synergistic network pharmacology in ischemic stroke. Proceedings of the National Academy of Sciences 116:7129–7136, https://doi.org/10.1073/pnas.1820799116; Casas AI et al. (2019) Calcium-dependent blood-brain barrier breakdown by NOX5 limits postreperfusion benefit in stroke. Journal of Clinical Investigation 129:1772–1778, https://doi.org/10.1172/JCI124283; Langhauser F et al. (2018) A diseasome cluster-based drug repurposing of soluble guanylate cyclase activators from smooth muscle relaxation to direct neuroprotection. NPJ Systems Biology and Applications 4:8, https://doi.org/10.1038/s41540-017-0039-7; Casas AI (2017) NOX4-dependent neuronal autotoxicity and BBB breakdown explain the superior sensitivity of the brain to ischemic damage. Proceedings of the National Academy of Sciences of the United States of America 114:12315–12320, https://doi.org/10.1073/pnas.1705034114;

are also risk genes for stroke, coronary heart disease, and heart failure, both possible late effects of hypertension. This now offers the first opportunity to develop a curative therapy for this subgroup of hypertensive patients that not only lowers blood pressure, but above all prevents the late effects of stroke, heart attack, and heart failure, because that is the real reason why we want to treat hypertension.

Of course, the first gene-based *diseasome* still had some weaknesses. Some diseases were missing. This is because a disease for which no genetic association study had been performed at the time could not possibly appear in a gene-based network. Moreover, two different genetic mechanisms could result in similar symptoms. In the diseasome, a disease/symptom can however only appear in one cluster. Thus, eventually symptom-based diseases need to be subtyped and split up into different clusters (see the hypertension example above). But these are details that are currently worked out. What counted was the concept.

Another attractive outcome of this concept was that if all diseases/symptoms in one cluster all share the same mechanism, then any drug targeting that mechanism should be applicable to any other disease/symptom within the same cluster. This is indeed what my research group observed and is now pursuing in so-called drug repurposing clinical trials. This rapid move from some bioinformatics findings to a clinical trial has additional consequences. Our previous dogma of research and innovation, which is broken anyway as you know by now, from basic to pre-clinical to clinic is redundant. Most animal models of disease maximally mimic a symptom of a human disease, but how could one be sure about their translational relevance when the mechanism of the human disease is not known. This may have contributed to the low success rate of translating basic research into patient benefit. With our new concept animal work is hardly necessary nor justifiable anymore, at least not to pre-test new therapies.

For repositioned already approved drugs the retail prices to be achieved by the pharmaceutical industry will be much lower than for a new drug. As a pro the development is shorter and cheaper and—if a patent can be claimed—the time for economic exploitation for the new indication is longer. Due to the limited number of possible disease genes and approximately 7000 approved drugs worldwide, it can be assumed that a drug is already there for every disease. We just need to find the right application for the right disease. Still, repositioning is not very popular with Big Pharma, which still dreams the

Kleinschnitz C et al. (2010) Post-stroke inhibition of induced NADPH oxidase type 4 prevents oxidative stress and neurodegeneration. PLoS Biology 8;e1000479, https://doi.org/10.1371/journal.pbio.1000479

billion-dollar-drug dream. Nevertheless, only a few completely new drugs may still be needed, so that the downward trend of classical drug research will accelerate again and only those companies that specialize in drug repositioning and generic out-of-patent drugs. After that, of course, there must still be companies that produce drugs, but more as generic producers and no longer as research companies with large profit margins for patent-protected, new drugs. It may also still be the case that a drug substance is optimized here and there in terms of potency, duration of action and side effects, but big pharma as we know it today will no longer exist. Pharmaceuticals will then become relatively insignificant as a cost factor in the healthcare system. And this, of course, not only for industrialized countries, but worldwide. This will be a first big step in what I would call the democratization and de-commercialization of medicine.

What will further accelerate and facilitate this process is the fact that the classical concept that one drug binds to only one protein is outdated. Drug repositioning studies have shown already that one drug can be used for multiple targets and diseases. With a digital 3D modelling of 400 approved drug molecules onto 7895 different known protein structures, it could also be shown and experimentally verified that practically all known drugs bind not only to one protein, but on average to 30 and more, i.e. even to those for which the drug was not originally developed.[12] This could explain the long-known observation that drugs that belong to the same class, i.e. have the same target structure and the same mechanism, can sometimes differ significantly in terms of their efficacy or undesirable side effects, precisely because they bind to different additional proteins. This again increases the repositioning potential for approved drugs, namely, not only for the original target protein but also to additional target proteins and thus for further diseases.

From Symptom to Cause

How exactly do we get to the causes of the diseases—we no longer want to treat symptoms; how are they then named, we will no longer call asthma asthma and high blood pressure high blood pressure; and how are they to be treated? How do we find the right drugs, be they new or repositioned? In the case of rare, monogenetic diseases, the first two questions had clear answers:

---

[12] Chartier M (2017) Large-scale detection of drug off-targets: hypotheses for drug repurposing and understanding side-effects. BMC Pharmacology and Toxicology 18:18, https://doi.org/10.1186/s40360-017-0128-7

the cause is a single gene or protein, and the disease is named after the gene or protein, and the drug must correct the genetic defect or its consequence. Often the defective protein molecule is replaced, for example, velmanase alfa in alpha-mannosidosis, factor X in factor X deficiency, factor VIII or IX in haemophilia A or B, migalastat in Fabry disease, or eliglustat or velaglucerase alfa in Gaucher disease, to name but a few. Insulin in type 1 diabetes is also one of them.

In more complex diseases where multiple genes are affected forming a small signalling network, such a network of drug targets is best treated with several drugs. In the future, the diagnostics leading to this may be whole genome sequencing. Only few people have done this yet. Alternatively, other tests are developed to filter out those patients who exhibit both the disease symptom and the causal genetically defined disease mechanism, e.g. from a simple blood sample. My group's hypertension subtype is such an example. Similar approaches have been described for 33 different types of cancer, which can be defined by a combination of ten different signalling pathways that are affected. The more signalling pathways that are affected, i.e. the more complex a tumour becomes, the more difficult a potential therapy becomes and could easily end up consisting of six, nine, or more drugs; but there is no other way to get such a tumour under control. An example of this is the *coordinated undermining of survival pathways by 9 repurposed* drugs (CUSP9) study in which a total of nine repurposed drugs are used with another new drug to treat a brain tumour.[13] On the other hand, there is hope that this will include drugs with fewer side effects than those used in current tumour therapy. The aim does not have to be to "kill" the tumour anymore with side effect-prone drugs, but merely to give the immune system the upper hand again, similar to a bacterial infection. There, an antibiotic is also usually sufficient, as it only slows down bacterial growth. We make cancer cells every day, and our immune system eliminates them all.[14] Similar approaches have been found for autoimmune diseases such as ankylosing spondylitis, Crohn's disease, psoriasis, primary sclerosing cholangitis, and ulcerative colitis and various retinal diseases,

---

[13] A proof-of-concept clinical trial assessing the safety of the coordinated undermining of survival paths by 9 repurposed drugs combined with metronomic temozolomide for recurrent glioblastoma (CUSP9v3), https://www.anticancerfund.org/en/projects/combination-9-repurposed-drugs-low-dose-chemotherapy-brain-cancer, https://www.anticancerfund.org/sites/default/files/attachments/poster_sno.pdf

[14] Sanchez-Vega F et al. (2018) Oncogenic Signaling Pathways in The Cancer Genome Atlas. Cell 173:321–337, e10, https://doi.org/10.1016/j.cell.2018.03.035; Ellinghaus D et al. (2016) Analysis of five chronic inflammatory diseases identifies 27 new associations and highlights disease-specific patterns at shared loci. Nature Genetics 48:510–518, https://doi.org/10.1038/ng.3528; Kiel C et al. (2017) Simple and complex retinal dystrophies are associated with profoundly different disease networks. Scientific Reports 7:41835, https://doi.org/10.1038/srep41835

respectively. Although the final clinical evidence is still pending, it is foreseeable that this concept of dividing common, chronic diseases according to the associated genes, comorbidities, and signalling pathways and defining them mechanistically-molecularly, in principle very similar to the rare diseases, will be the solution to the problem of diseases now defined only by symptom and organ. In this way, these diseases will be treated so effectively that they will disappear. Chronic treatment may still be necessary if, for example, the genetic mutation is not corrected, and the causative mechanism remains. But the patient will remain symptom-free and will not have to fear the late effects, so is in effect no longer sick, but chronically symptom-free. To use a car analogy: Let's assume that the brake pads on your model wear out somewhat quickly; this would have led to damage to the brakes earlier (symptom) and at worst to a serious accident (late effects). That's why they would have kept installing new brakes (a symptomatic drug), and if they hadn't done it in time, there would have been serious accidents all the time. Now the brake pads are regularly renewed (a causally acting medicine), the brakes no longer break down, and serious accidents do not happen either.

So, the scientific concept for this fundamental innovation in medicine is in place, but to work through all this we need a completely new kind of biomedical research: maximally patient-oriented and not primarily aimed at publications, and if so, the publication process must also be different. Above all, the data must be transparent and reproducible, and if the research has been publicly funded, then the results should also be publicly available. And of course, organ-based research will no longer play a role in the elucidation of most diseases. The new medicine is called systems medicine and it must heal, not treat.

12

Research for Patients

The insight into the far-reaching unsuccessfulness of our current biomedical research approach—at least as far as its relevance for you as a (potential) patient is concerned—must lead to a radical rethinking if we do not want to continue to waste a large part of the resources and lead bright minds on wrong tracks with false incentives (publications instead of medical progress). None of this is a criticism of my scientific colleagues, by the way. I am sure that the same brilliant minds who now invest all their energy and strategy into producing Nature, Cell, and Science publications, and are thus among the biomedical elite, will also be the ones who make great patient-relevant discoveries with different incentives in place. In terms of content, I am convinced that abolishing disciplines organized by organ will be essential for clinics, doctors, and biomedical scientists alike (e.g. neurology, neurologist, neuroscientist). This should be easier for scientists than for clinicians and specialists whose entire career strategy has been focused on one organ. But more on that later. First, how to reform biomedical research on which medical practice is based.

A New Way to Research

Biomedical scientists must leave their *organ silos* and ivory towers if they want to do research that is relevant to patients. Medical faculties, university hospitals, biomedical research institutes, and other research institutions that claim to do medically relevant research related to diseases and for patients must in future be measured solely based on their relevance to patients. Universities

© The Author(s), under exclusive license to Springer Nature Switzerland AG 2022
H. H. H. W. Schmidt, *The end of medicine as we know it - and why your health has a future*,
https://doi.org/10.1007/978-3-030-95293-8_12

and university hospitals must no longer be allowed to steer career paths based on publication parameters. Some examples of reforming biomedical research incentives are the Dutch Recognition and Rewards System,[1] which differentiates career paths, and the San Francisco Declaration on Research Assessment (DORA).

Another structural dilemma is that schools of medicine and schools of public health often work separately or that public health as an academic subject is underdeveloped. In contrast, health scientists often have a much closer approach to patients and can offer a more patient-centred perspective through collaboration with clinicians and theorists. The inclusion of social determinants of health in medical research in a single united approach is the strategy of university hospitals in the United States, where the term Academic *Health Centers* is an adequate and better description of what medical research organizations—mainly university-associated—should develop into.[2] Consequently, research in Academic Health Centers is therefore increasingly directed at the system level.

One of the key work and career incentives is how to obtain research funding. Currently most funding institutions are too lazy to dig deep into the outcomes of their research when allocating funds. It's easier to delegate the evaluation to peers, who look mainly at the publication track record, i.e. number of high impact papers in high impact journals. Research income and again papers also determine the intra-institution careers, where the number of papers and impact points are literally counted and added up to rank people. I am sure that in a couple of years this practice will be viewed as grotesque. Research funders who in the end distribute tax or donors' funds must support biomedical research exclusively according to the patient benefit achieved by a researcher or a group to date (ideal) and planned (suboptimal, as this must be assessed for feasibility). A group that has for the past 5–10 years achieved important patient benefit is very likely to do so in the future. So why not just fund this group for another 5 years? Where is the risk when the current

[1] VSNU, NFU, KNAW, NWO & ZonMw (2019) Room for everyone's talent: Towards a new balance in recognising and rewarding academics. The Hague, https://www.vsnu.nl/files/documenten/Domeinen/Onderzoek/Position%20paper%20Room%20for%20everyone's%20talent.pdf; Hatch A (2020) San Francisco Declaration on Research Assessment, The American Society for Cell Biology, https://sfdora.org/read/

[2] Association of Academic Health Centers. Academic health centers and the social determinants of health: challenges & barriers, responses & solutions, http://wherehealthbegins.org/pdf/AAHC-SDOH-Report-ExecSum-Final.pdf; Dzau VJ et al. (2010) The role of academic health science systems in the transformation of medicine. Lancet 375:949–953, https://doi.org/10.1016/S0140-6736(09)61082-5; Channing Division of Network Medicine, Harvard University, https://www.brighamandwomens.org/research/departments/channing-division-of-network-medicine/overview

funding allocation has a success rate of 1:24,000?[3] Less time is wasted on writing grants, and the review process is much easier. Publications must no longer play any role, neither by impact nor by mass.

Content-wise, biomedical research must be medical, not biology in only one species, homo sapiens, but exclusively revolve around the patient (see Fig. 12.1). Biological research has its home in biology, which I do not feel entitled to judge at all; medical research, in medicine. And within medical research there must be many more academic, i.e. investigator-initiated, clinical trials that address important therapeutic or diagnostic questions, beyond regulatory studies by the pharmaceutical or medical device industry. We do not want to cure mice; thus the ethical bar to justify an animal experiment must be much higher than it is currently. It must be much more questioned whether an animal "model" of a human disease is really a 1:1 model for this disease and allows direct conclusions. I am not at all against animal experiments and have conducted those myself for many years with good intentions, but with new insights I and others view this differently now. Instead of

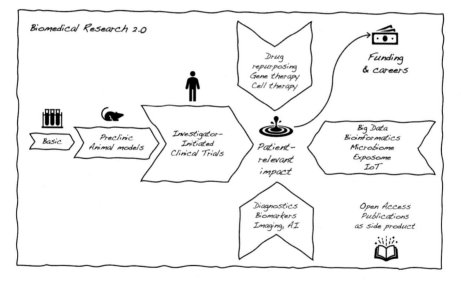

Fig. 12.1 To ensure patient-relevant outcomes become key performance indicators for research funding and career promotion (upper right), biomedical research needs to be redesigned. Basic and preclinical research need to focus on supporting clinical trials (left arrows) by therapeutics (top arrow), diagnostics (bottom arrow), and data (right arrow). Publications (lower right) are side products for dissemination and strictly full open access

[3] Contopoulos-Ioannidis DG et al. (2003) Translation of highly promising basic science research into clinical applications. The American Journal of Medicine, 114:477–484, https://doi.org/10.1016/S0002-9343(03)00013-5

permanently generating new data, we need to make much more use of the existing mass of patient data, and biomedical scientists should be stimulated to collaborate intensively with bioinformaticians to use electronic health records, biobanks, registries, genetic, microbiome, and exposome data (I'll get to all those terms) and the *Internet of Things*. As an end result, it will be key to develop a molecular, mechanistic disease theory instead of the current descriptive pathology or disease theory and to provide the necessary diagnostics, biomarkers, and new imaging techniques and their analysis by artificial intelligence (or better machine learning).

The focus of basic and preclinical research, which currently accounts for most of the unsuccessful biomedical research (in terms of added value for patients), will need to change dramatically. Animal models will become the exception and only justified if the "model" really mirrors the human disease and conclusions can be almost 1:1 translated or is required by regulators before a clinical trial. One supposed alternative, cell culture models and the increasingly hyped organoids, i.e. miniaturized and simplified versions of an "organ" produced in vitro in three dimensions from one or a few cells from a tissue, embryonic stem cells, or induced pluripotent stem cells, I view very critically. First, cells are typically kept in highly artificial conditions, e.g. ambient oxygen levels that nowhere exist in the body[4]; second, they are portrayed as an alternative to animal experiment, whereas their translational relevance is even less than for animal studies and they are by no means an alternative. The medium in which most cells are cultured requires large amount of serum from animal blood, quite often foetal calf serum. And a foetal calf's heart must be beating to obtain an adequate harvest for foetal calf serum production.

The monomaniac culture of science, i.e. the Nobel Prize, etc., also needs to reform itself. Nowadays, no single researcher can achieve anything in biomedicine without a team of essential, dedicated staff members or external collaborators. There are certainly scientists who are more innovative than others and can better entice and lead teams than others, but the other members are equally needed. Content-wise, the success of a biomedical scientist or, much better, of an interdisciplinary team of scientists should be assessed solely based on their success in patient care, prevention, or cure of diseases. The role of scientific publications as an essential determinant of biomedical research and career progression must drastically lose importance. While data on studies, methods, and so on must be published, it must be quite sufficient that

---

[4] Keeley TP & Mann GE (2019) Defining Physiological Normoxia for Improved Translation of Cell Physiology to Animal Models and Humans. Physiol Rev. 99:161–234. https://doi.org/10.1152/physrev.00041.2017

these are competently peer-reviewed (for which a fee needs to be paid or one pays back in being a peer reviewer yourself) and subsequently made publicly available. The journal in which this is done must become completely irrelevant. In fact, journals and their profit margins, which impose huge costs on researchers and their institutions, should become obsolete.

I am sure that this will drastically increase the translational success of biomedical research worldwide—without investing more funds—and I am even sure that all the scientists in biomedicine who are now struggling to get published in top journals will love to finally do research for what they studied medicine for, namely, to help patients, and not to fill printed pages in journals.

Funding must remain to some degree free or blue sky, but also be based on *top-down*, clearly formulated deliverables addressing unmet medical needs, and be formulated by those who hand out the grants, which in the end are money from us taxpayers or donors. But also, the process of how the allocation of these funds is organized needs to be revised. Scientists are already well involved as peer reviewers for publications to ensure quality. In addition, there are the reviews of doctoral theses, appointments of professors—and research proposals. The latter are becoming increasingly complex and extensive, as biomedical research is also becoming more interdisciplinary and extensive. Consequently, for example, European funders require to submit proposals of 45 pages and more plus hundreds of pages of attachments. Colleagues who would be very competent to assess these applications because they are close to the topic either do not have the time or—if honest—must declare a conflict of interest, because a potential scientific competitor is supposed to declare all future plans to research over the next 5 years. This usually leaves reviewers to be chosen, who are not really close enough to a complex topic, which in turn impacts on the quality of the review. Let's assume that for a specific European call over a hundred teams from all over the continent apply and only four are funded. On the one hand, it can be assumed that for 100 teams that apply each will have at least ten members each; thus approximately 1000 researchers from all over Europe apply in different teams. Being part of a team excludes a researcher from being a peer reviewer because of a potential conflict of interest. Thus, scientists review these research programmes whom none of the 100 team leaders has approached to take part in their team. There may be good reasons why this did not happen. Consequently, the most obviously competent scientists are excluded from the review process, although there are simple ways of avoiding conflicts of interest, for example, in the case of thematic overlap or if scientists from the same university have applied, a procedure that has been well established by the *Australian National Health and Medical Research Council*. But even then, many perceive that the allocation of funds, in particular those that are not mainstream or even challenge dogmas,[5] become a kind of lottery. And because peer review is so dramatically poor,[6] the *Health Research Council of New Zealand* has introduced just that—a lottery—and other research funders are thinking about it too.[7] This is, of course, a capitulation and a departure from performance and quality-based funding of science.

But what could an ideal, simple, and effective funding allocation in medicine look like? It's quite simple: over the next 5 years, funders support those teams that have demonstrably researched or achieved patient-relevant innovations over the last 5 or 10 years. Researchers and their teams, who have been successful achieving this in the past, are very likely to do so in the future. This so-called Matthew effect was observed as early as 1968 and has been confirmed several times.[8] Of 13,303 applications for research funding, 3455 were funded (26 per cent). For these, the easy-to-measure past performance allowed a better prediction of future scientific output than the 42,905 reviewer ratings. That is, by simply measuring past performance, research funds would be more targeted and effectively allocated, saving many reviewers a lot of time and good applicants a lot of frustration. It is grotesque that this 50-year-old insight is still not applied, but instead qualitatively obviously less suitable, labour-intensive reviews are used. Ideal criteria for such an award policy should not be something published, but which previously unmet medical need has been successfully researched in the past.

This will require a transition period, in particular for young investigators, who are told to become "independent" and are primarily evaluated by the number of papers. This disagrees with the fact that only teams can make substantial and relevant achievements in biomedicine. Thus, it will be essential to identify if a young team member has leadership qualities and orchestrate the ideal timepoint for him or her to form a new team and it must be OK not to be a team leader and just a productive team member. Not everyone who is passionate about opera is cut out to be an opera singer, and just because one finds research interesting doesn't mean they must be personally cut out for

[5] Chu JSG & Evans JA (2021) Slowed canonical progress in large fields of science. Proc Natl Acad Sci U S A. 118:e2021636118, https://doi.org/10.1073/pnas.2021636118

[6] Piper K (2019) Science funding is a mess. Could grant lotteries make it better? Vox, https://www.vox.com/future-perfect/2019/1/18/18183939/science-funding-grant-lotteries-research

[7] Adam D (2019) Science funders gamble on grant lotteries. A growing number of research agencies are assigning money randomly. Nature 575:574–575, https://doi.org/10.1038/d41586-019-03572-7

[8] Merton RK (1968) The Matthew Effect in Science. The reward and communication systems of science are considered. Science 159:56–63; Bornmann L et al. (2017) Does the hα-index reinforce the Matthew effect in science? The introduction of agent-based simulations into scientometrics. Quantitative Science Studies 1:331–346, https://doi.org/10.1162/qss_a_00008; Bol T et al. (2018) The Matthew effect in science funding. Proceedings of the National Academy of Sciences of the United States of America 115:4887–4890.

designing and leading meaningful projects. Moreover, permanent budgets and jobs at universities are fairly constant. Thus, in their entire professional life, one professor can have, in purely mathematical terms, only one successor. If two of a professor's doctoral students or postdocs later become professors themselves, this means that another professor somewhere else will have no successor—neither locally nor anywhere else. All their PhDs and postdocs will not have been able to find a permanent position in university research. That's just the way it is; professorial positions are constant.

Of course, it's good if many students do a Masters or a PhD and thereby have had some contact with research, but one shouldn't infer from that that there's even a remotely secure career path to a permanent position at a university. The universities' fixed budgets don't allow for that; these positions don't even exist. Teams also offer much better opportunities to discover, integrate, and develop young talent until the best of them can lead successful teams themselves. The days when individuals could make a difference in medicine are long gone. Today, even the best team leader is nothing without excellent scientists, technicians, and an administration around them.

A New Way to Publish

The previous shortcomings of biomedical publications, in terms of quality, reproducibility, and medical relevance, were exacerbated by the flood of COVID-19 publications in 2020, but also made their problems public for the first time. Many authors bypassed the traditional review process of biomedical science journals. In some cases, important data thus became known at a maximum early stage. On the other hand, a lot of irrelevant nonsense was published and partly retracted.

Journals with a peer-review system, in which one scientist reviews another's work to see if it should be accepted for publication, were originally created to free themselves from government regulators and their non-scientific agency staff. But that journals with a peer-review system only publish good science is something I have since refuted. I showed—at least for the crystal structures of proteins—that it is precisely the supposedly best journals that publish the studies of poorest quality.

In fact, the review process at journals leaves much to be desired. When a paper is submitted, only the two to five reviewers invited by the editor, usually anonymously, can influence its quality. Either the manuscript is rejected, or the authors are given the opportunity to revise their manuscript or to submit subsequent experiments. In contrast, a paper published as a preprint is peer-reviewed by any scientist, and anyone can publish their comments using annotation software such as hypothes.is or share them on social media for all readers to see. That's when a scientist will think twice about publishing prematurely if they're threatened with an avalanche of proofs of error afterwards. Conversely, any critic will also try to formulate their publicly viewable comments appropriately and to make a genuine contribution to the discussion. All in all, both the possibility for every scientist to write a publicly visible comment or an evaluation of a publication and the fact that this commenting can take place with a clear name and not anonymously would contribute to better science that is rigorously oriented towards the correctness of methods and data. And on top of that, neither publishing nor reading them costs money. This almost "revolutionary" system is commonplace in other disciplines such as physics.

In common practice at many journals, however, a scientist submits a paper, and it is reviewed anonymously. The accepted paper can either be published free of charge, but then lies behind a so-called paywall. Only by subscribing to the journal or paying a fee to read the specific article can it be read by other scientists. For example, reading a single, three-page article in the journal *Nature* can cost 200US\$ or more. Or the scientist pays an open access fee for the article to be published freely accessible (so-called golden open access).

Meanwhile, many research funders require that the results are published without a so-called paywall between the work and potential readers. Preprints, but also rather cryptic university-owned self-archiving systems, serve this purpose. Now, however, neither these nor preprints are read. COVID-19 preprints have been an atypical exception to this. But preprints also have problems because of the lack of coordinated, comprehensive formal peer review. Right now, most preprints receive very few, if any, reviews. And how to guarantee that unknown authors get attention, or how to prevent friends from writing glowing reviews of each other's articles?

The main argument for preprints and self-archiving, however, is to break the paywall of commercial scholarly publishers. It simply doesn't make sense for scientists to get their work funded by millions of dollars of research taxpayer money, then review and partially edit it for free for commercial journals, then in turn pay to make it freely available, or pay to read a paper that is not freely available. Although there is a countermovement with the shadow library Sci-Hub, which has over 60 million articles stored, and others like BookFi and LibGen, to get around this and make articles that are behind a paywall accessible, however, these services are increasingly facing legal disputes and therefore must constantly change their web address, for example. The best known and most extensive project Sci-Hub was founded by Alexandra

Elbakyan from Kazakhstan as Guerilla Open Access.[9]On the other hand, online databases like Sci-Hub are an open secret among scientists in countries that cannot afford the high subscription prices of publishing houses and are quasi-essential for staying scientifically up to date. Even Nature named them among the top 10 most influential people in science in 2016.[10]

In contrast, open access articles have the advantage of being just as freely accessible, but at the same time having been peer-reviewed. Thanks to free access, these publications are downloaded four times more often on average than non-open-access articles and cited 1.6 times more often. However, there is still a need to pay if one wants to make one's own article freely accessible. In 2021, the European Commission (EC) therefore introduced *Open Research Europe*,[11] a free peer-reviewed Open Access publishing platform. Here, a submitted paper is immediately publicly accessible and is additionally peer-reviewed. Parallel comments can also be made publicly. This corresponds to the self-archiving that already exists in principle, as in bioRxiv or medRxiv (so-called Green Open Access), but which is currently hardly used at all. After a positive review, the work is published. There are no fees, neither for the publication nor for the reader.

It is true that there were open access journals or journals that offered an open access option, and this with peer review, even before Open *Research Europe*. But these were not free of charge. For example, Nature, one of the *high impact journals* but with quality problems (remember?), has been offering *OA to* articles since 2020—for the hefty sum of US$9800 per article.[12] In addition, there were already free OA publishing platforms. But these did not include peer review.

So far, *Open Research Europe* is only intended for projects funded under the European Community's research programmes (Horizon 2020 and Horizon Europe). The European Community finances the editorial superstructure. After all, manuscripts must be checked and sent to reviewers and finally professionally typeset. Submitted articles cannot be published elsewhere but

---

[9] Herb U (2016) Guerilla Open Access and Robin Hood PR against market failure. Telepolis, https://www.heise.de/tp/features/Guerilla-Open-Access-und-Robin-Hood-PR-gegen-Marktversagen-3378648.html; Kühl E (2016) Who wants the knowledge? Die Zeit, https://www.zeit.de/digital/internet/2016-02/sci-hub-open-access-wissenschaft-paper-gratis; Hummel P (2016) Millions of scientific articles illegally available online, Spektrum der Wissenschaft, https://www.spektrum.de/news/sci-hub-millionen-fachartikel-illegal-im-netz-verfuegbar/1399718

[10] Van Noorden R (2016) Nature's 10: Paper pirate. The founder of an illegal hub for paywalled papers has attracted litigation and acclaim. Nature 540:512, https://www.nature.com/news/polopoly_fs/1.21157!/menu/main/topColumns/topLeftColumn/pdf/540507a.pdf

[11] https://open-research-europe.ec.europa.eu

[12] https://www.nature.com/nature-research/open-access

benefit from immediate publication after submission. Quick turnaround and review times are also planned. The entire publication service will be free to all scientists. The review process will be unusually open and transparent, with the extremely unusual opportunity to interact directly with reviewers. Researchers and citizens will have access to all published research and underlying data. All research papers are welcome. Highly subjective factors such as "general interest" or "novelty" are irrelevant. Replication studies that confirm or refute previous publications are also eligible. This counteracts one of the causes of the reproducibility problem, publication bias for false positives. Another initiative is Science Open (scienceopen.com), which offers content hosting, context building, and journal hosting to develop new open access paradigms for scholars.

However, we are in a time of transition and I'm having trouble making it palatable to my younger co-workers, who were all still socialized in a scientific world where the goal is to publish in *high-impact* journals if possible. Almost like an addiction. And now I must take away their *impact factor* drug. But I can't be the only one who must—and will—solve this and still promote their careers. It must be possible. Better research and innovations will be unstoppable, no matter how poorly organized they are. Let's take a detailed look at what the innovations will consist of in detail and which of your personal Big Data can already be collected for your very personal health or risk analysis.

13

Know your Genes

Sooner or later—depending on whether and how well and quickly biomedical research reforms—all genes and their importance in maintaining health and curing disease will be elucidated. However, you, dear reader, will personally only be able to benefit from this if you also know your own genes and variants. But what exactly does that look like and how does that work, "knowing your genes?"

Genes are encoded by four different "letters", A, C, T, and G (nucleic acids). Each letter is connected to the next by a sugar molecule (deoxyribose). The resulting chain of deoxyribose and nucleic acids, which can be up to two meters long, is called deoxyribonucleic acid (DNA). The totality of all genes encoded on the DNA is called the genome. Within our cells, the DNA is in the nucleus, densely packed into chromosomes. The DNA of all human beings is 99.9% identical. In the seemingly negligible few 0.1 per cent, however, sits all that distinguishes us humans from each other, makes us individuals, millions of letters at which variations can occur.

Why Is your DNA So Unique?

We have 46 chromosomes, 23 from our mother, 23 from our father. Thus, of each gene, we have two variants, one from our mother, one from our father. Only our cells for reproduction, i.e. egg cells in women and sperm cells in males, have only one set of each gene, i.e. 23 chromosomes, but not just the 23 from our mother or the 23 from our father, but a total mix.

During the formation of the germ cells, all genes are exchanged between maternal and paternal chromosomes, so that each sibling receives a completely different set of maternal and paternal genes from their parents and each chromosome contains a unique mixture of the genes of both parents. Rare exceptions are of course identical twins, who have still a unique mixture of genes but they are identical between the two—except for changes that can happen during the embryonic period or during development. This constant mixing of genes from generation to generation creates new characteristics, better, neutral, but also worse and even diseases. This is how evolution works.

Due to the uniqueness of our DNA, it is possible by examining several DNA markers to assign a DNA trace in forensic medicine to an individual without any doubt or to trace our genes in genealogy over many generations and continents. And for medical purposes, more and more information is becoming available about each of our genes as to whether certain variants can cause or impose a risk for a disease. The medical application of our genetic information has both a legal and practical aspects. Let's start with the former, because everything that will be possible has to first comply with national or European genetic diagnostics law.

The Genetic Diagnostics Act

In the USA, several federal agencies regulate genetic tests, the Food and Drug Administration, the Centers for Medicare and Medicaid Services, and the Federal Trade Commission. The UK is embedding genetic testing into the National Health Service with its Genomic Medicine Service. Similarly, the Danes are working toward a vision of personalized medicine for the masses through their National Genome Center. And in France, Genomic Medicine 2025 aims to link the health system with the research sector and industry. Between individual European countries, there are legislative similarities but still many differences. Fragmented regulation is difficult to enforce. Genetic Diagnostics Acts are to preserve the opportunities of the use of genetic testing for the individual, while at the same time preventing possible dangers and discrimination. Key quality parameters are:

- Analytical validity, i.e. how well the test predicts the presence or absence of a gene variant.
- Clinical validity, i.e. the evidence that the genetic variant is related to the presence, absence, or risk of a specific disease.

- Clinical utility, i.e. whether the test informs about diagnosis, treatment, management, or prevention of a disease that will be helpful to patients and lead to improved health outcomes.

For you as an individual, the right to informational self-determination is contained therein. This includes both the right to know your own genetic findings (right to know) and, conversely, not to know them (right not to know). Genetic testing may therefore only be carried out if you have consented to the testing. Genetic analyses are therefore to be accompanied by a doctor and detailed statement of the nature, significance, and scope of the test, as well as written patient consent. Regarding children, restrictions apply. Examinations concerning health impairments before or shortly after birth are permitted. However, prenatal genetic testing for diseases that may not manifest themselves until adulthood is prohibited. I will come back to this issue in my second interjection. The initial area of consumer application was, however, DNA genealogy, i.e. family history research based on DNA.

DNA Genealogy

For DNA genealogy, all that is usually needed is a saliva sample in a tube or, as in mass criminology tests, a few cells taken from the oral mucosa with a cotton swab. Saliva or cells are then sent to a laboratory that isolates the DNA. DNA genealogy usually involves decoding less than 1% of the DNA by examining individual differences in certain traits or markers. This means that not your entire genome, letter by letter, is analysed. The DNA marker technology usually comes from the company Illumina.[1] Their microarray chips can contain more than one million markers and are updated annually for optimal coverage or specific applications. The differences or similarities found between two or more people allow conclusions to be drawn about a closer or more distant relationship, and this over several generations. Moreover, people from certain regions show characteristic "patterns" of these markers, since in past centuries Spaniard men married mainly Spanish women, Swedish men mainly Swedish women, and Russian men mainly Russian women. But of course, there were migrations and intermixtures, so that your personal origin can be read from your individual "pattern" and how your ancestors are

---

[1] Wojcik GL et al. (2019) Genetic analyses of diverse populations improves discovery for complex traits. Nature 570:514–518, https://doi.org/10.1038/s41586-019-1310-4

composed regarding origin. So, I personally am genetically 53% Northwest European and 39% Eastern European. The small remainder is distributed over Southern Europe and Europe in general. I would recommend a DNA examination like this to any racist and nationalist wherever they are. Every single one would be amazed that they have genes from all over Europe or the World. This could be embarrassing among his fellow thinkers. On this occasion:

There are no races in humans.

nor even in wild animals. Animal breeds only exist in pets that have been purposefully bred for certain traits, which has nothing to do with natural evolution. Species already exist in animals, for example, the Indian or African elephant. But animal species are not defined by skin or fur colour, but by the fact that animals of two different species cannot have procreative offspring. Since all humans can have procreative offspring with all humans (of the opposite sex, of course):

There is only one species of human: Homo sapiens.

This had to be said at this point! The pioneer of DNA genealogy is the US company 23andMe, which for the first time published a database for comparison with other persons. Without such a database, the possibility of matching is missing. The number 23 in the name of 23andMe comes from the fact that each person has 23 maternal and 23 paternal chromosomes. Of these 46, two are sex chromosomes. Females have two X chromosomes; males have one X and one Y chromosome. What I have failed to mention so far is that there is still a small amount of DNA in the so-called mitochondria of the cell, which are "power plants" of the cell that burn oxygen and energy carriers like sugar to energy and carbon dioxide. Their DNA is also used for genealogy. Mitochondria are only ever passed from the mother's egg to her children, and analysis of their DNA therefore allows conclusions to be drawn about kinship in the direct all-female line and its geography over the last millennia. For example, according to 23andMed and my maternal gene share, I have type J1c, just like the fifteenth-century English King Richard III, which traces my family back to a woman who lived in Europe 13,000 years ago. Her ancestors lived in the Arabian Peninsula 57,000 years ago. And all our ancestors ultimately descend from a woman who lived in East Africa 150,000 to 200,000 years ago. Although there may have been thousands of women living there, only the descendants of that one woman have survived to this day. So, there may indeed be an Eva. Fascinating, isn't it? However, as always there is also discussion among paleoanthropologists whether there was The Cradle of Humankind and where.

In a legal grey area is the fact that a kind of paternity test is possible via a genealogical examination of parents and children. After all, parents and children should have about 50% of the same genome. However, it is an administrative offence, punishable by a severe fine, to carry out a genealogical DNA test to verify or disprove doubtful paternity on minors without the knowledge of all those who may be involved.

Meanwhile, there are numerous other providers besides 23andMe, for example, FTDNA, Ancestry, MyHeritage, Living DNA, and others. In Germany, however, DNA genealogy is not yet very well-known and used, because it is not necessary for family history research over a few generations due to the very good availability of written sources. However, to find out how your ancestors came to Europe from Africa and Asia over thousands of years, DNA genealogy is of course essential. Incidentally, to build up a reference database for finer DNA origin analyses in Central Europe, Living DNA has carried out different national sub-projects.

Besides DNA genealogy, 23andMe offers even more, for example, quite curious, but medically uncritical predictions; otherwise this would not be allowed even in Germany. These include, for example, that my skin is fair (true) and that I have no freckles on my face (true), no eyebrows that have grown together (true), no dimples (true), but blue eyes (almost true) and a problem with earwax (true). That I had hardly any hair at birth (true), then later slightly wavy (true), dark blonde (true) hair that fades quickly in the sun (true) and am unfortunately prone to baldness (true) and dandruff (true), but thankfully have no back hair for it (true). My ring finger is longer than my index finger (true) and I have a long, big toe (true). Also, I'm supposed to prefer salty over sweet (not true), not be afraid of heights (not true). These associations show that one can predict a relatively large amount of a person's individual features from his or her DNA, at least about appearance down to individual details of the human face.[2] At my age, I know all these features of course, but it might be interesting for a 40-year-old to know of his risk of baldness and consider hair transplants while the hair loss is not obvious yet. Smiley.

---

[2] White JD et al. (2021) Insights into the genetic architecture of the human face. Nat Genet 53:45–53, https://doi.org/10.1038/s41588-020-00741-7

Your Personal Genome

Medically, of course, it becomes more exciting and relevant when you can predict disease risks. With my first report of 23andMe, this was still displayed to me. In the meantime, this lack of supervision is prohibited in several countries due to Gene Diagnostics Acts, and the permitted information is limited exclusively to origin and harmless characteristics. The legal situation varies from country to country. France, for example, is extremely restrictive about genetic testing.[3]

If the evaluation involves medically relevant advice, this must be done by a physician and human geneticist. Such a service can also be done after the fact for medical or non-medical (not for diagnosis) raw data from 23andme, MyHeritage, AncestryDNA, and other formats. Examples include companies like DNAVisit (for medical and non-medical purposes) and HeartGentics' AddingKnowledge service (for non-medical purposes only).[4] For medical genetic diagnoses, both companies offer consultation with a certified human geneticist. HeartGenetics also markets a genetic test that evaluates 32 genes associated with the efficacy or risk of adverse side effects of more than 100 drugs in psychiatry, pain management, oncology, diabetes, and cardiovascular therapy. This type of one-time testing is called pharmacogenomics and is suitable for avoiding dangerous individual under- or overdoses of drugs. And in 2021, the FDA approved 23AndMe to report pharmacogenomic variants of the CYP2C19 gene relevant for drugs such as the antithrombotic, clopidogrel, and the antidepressant, citalopram.[5]

DNA genealogy does not sequence your entire genome (i.e. all genes), but only uses characteristic variants of individual DNA letters (nucleotides), so-called *single nucleotide polymorphisms* (SNPs, pronounced like snips), as markers and correlates these, for example, with origin, but also with disease risks. Nevertheless, these chips cover most of the rare gene variants and from only one million SNPs up to 85% of the genomic differences between individuals can be analysed by a statistical procedure (imputation).

One step further is the sequencing of expressed genes, i.e. individual letters. This is established for test that only analyse a single gene or parts of it in detail of to all (*Whole Exome Sequencing*). Of course, this only makes sense if the

---

[3] International Society of Genetic Genealogy (2016) Regulation of genetic tests, https://isogg.org/wiki/Regulation_of_genetic_tests

[4] https://www.heartgenetics.com/product/addingknowledge/

[5] AACC (2021) FDA OKs 23andMe to Report Pharmacogenomic Variants Without Confirmatory Testing, https://www.aacc.org/cln/articles/2021/july/fda-oks-23andme-to-report-pharmacogenomic-variants-without-confirmatory-testing

connection between gene variant and disease is clear. These include, for example, variants in the BRCA1 and BRCA2 genes (BRCA stands for *breast cancer*), in which the lifelong risk of breast cancer is between 70% and 80%, the HTT (Huntingtin) gene in Huntington's disease, or the CFTR (Cystic Fibrosis Transmembrane Conductance Regulator) gene in cystic fibrosis, or pharmacogenomics, which analyses genes that can affect drug metabolism, thereby raise or lower blood levels of the drug affecting both drug efficacy and side effects.

The final and ultimate step in genetic analysis is, of course, to have access to the complete DNA sequence of your entire personal genome (*Whole Genome Sequencing*). This will also cover the DNA left and right from our genes. Originally this was thought to be "junk" DNA, but now we know that also here regulatory elements are encoded which affect gene function and cause disease. What was considered a technical revolution just a few years ago is now a human genome project just for you. Since mistakes can sometimes occur when reading 3 billion nucleotides (i.e. DNA letters), the process is repeated 30–300 times or even more for the sake of thoroughness. As more and more people are sequenced over the next few years, the dataset available will become larger and larger, allowing us to make ever more precise statements. You can now practically track this increase in knowledge using your own DNA. Data generation and data analysis services are booming. The blog NebulaGenomics provides an up-to-date overview of many of the providers.[6] This blurs the lines between your personal genome, biomedical research, and medical practice.

The technology that made the human genome project possible saw an unprecedented drop in costs, exceeding even the drop in the price of memory and processor chips in the IT industry. To this end, Gordon Earle Moore, chemist, physicist, and co-founder of Intel, had formulated Moore's Law, named after him, back in 1965. It states that the number of transistors that can fit into an integrated circuit of a fixed size doubles approximately every 2 years (Fig. 13.1). This cost collapse has made genetic analysis available to a wider population. The first sequence of the human genome from Craig Venter's Celera, or *Human Genome Project*, was finally achieved in February 2001 with hundreds of sequencing machines in operation for years.[7] Now, a single machine can sequence a complete human genome in a matter of days, the price of pure analysis has dropped to around 500 euros, e.g. with the

---

[6] https://blog.nebula.org/de/dna-sites/

[7] Venter JC et al. (2001) The Sequence of the Human Genome, Science 291:1304–1351, https://doi.org/10.1126/science.1058040; Lander ES et al. (2001) Initial sequencing and analysis of the human genome. Nature 409:860–921, https://doi.org/10.1038/35057062

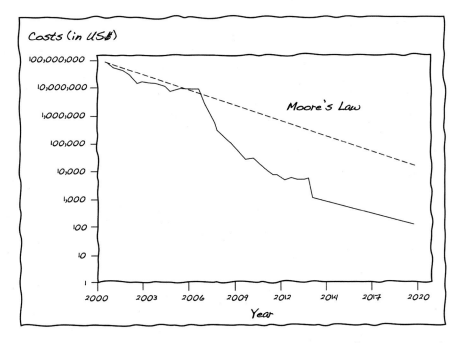

Fig. 13.1 Evolution of the costs of sequencing a human genome from 2000 to today compared to Moore's law, according to which the cost of equal computational or storage power is halved. The price drop for genome sequencing exceeds Moore's law (National Human Genome Research Institute (NHGRI), ARK Investment Management LLC)

DanteLabs company stripes2be, and there is no end in sight. Of course, this does not include any data analysis. A report on your data usually doubles the total cost.

You don't have to be a prophet to predict that the multiple total sequencing of a genome will become a standard part of medical diagnostics and prevention. Sequencing machines are becoming smaller and more affordable. For example, the MinION partial sequencing machine is now only as big as a bar of soap.[8] If a great deal of consideration and consultation is still required when interpreting the still imperfect knowledge about the significance of all gene variants, a doctor or geneticist will inevitably have to stand between technology and humans. But it is also not necessary to be a prophet that with the advance of artificial intelligence (see Chap. 15), the interpretation of the genome and the optimal recommendation from it will also become machine-learnable and thus more automated. The crucial question you will need to ask yourself before a doctor's email arrives with your personal human genetics report—or preferably before you even order the test—is, "Do I want to know

---

[8] https://nanoporetech.com/products/minion

all this?" One of the worst cases could be being accurately diagnosed with a serious but incurable or untreatable disease. But such cases will become fewer and fewer in the next 10–20 years because of more and more new and precise therapies, up to and including curative gene therapies, so that such decisions of conscience will then no longer be necessary. If all diseases are treatable or even preventable, then there must be no more hesitation in knowing about each of one's genes.

One example of what this could or will look like is the tumour gene HER-2, which is overactive in about 30% of breast cancer patients, resulting in poorer prognosis, increased tumorigenesis, metastasis, and resistance to classical chemotherapy.[9] However, in this group of patients, treatment with trastuzumab (Herceptin®), an antibody that binds to HER-2, is highly effective. This is one of the first and most impressive examples of pharmacogenetics—precise and effective drug therapy driven by genetics. This case also marked a turning point in tumour therapy. Whereas up to that point the focus had been almost exclusively on substances that were ultimately highly toxic, with the hope that the cancer cells would die sooner than the person, the time has now come for the concept of being able to treat the alteration of the tumour cell with highly specific drugs that have few side effects. In 2020, 2.7 million people in the European Union were diagnosed with cancer, and another 1.3 million people lost their lives to it, including over 2000 young people. Unless we take decisive action now, cancer cases are set to increase making it the leading cause of death in the EU. Europe's Beating Cancer Plan together with national cancer institutes around the globe will make cancer a controllable disease.

Personal "Omes"

Once we have elucidated the function of each DNA letter and its variants, we will know our genetic starting point from birth. But our cells are not only made up of genes. Genes basically do next to nothing themselves. They are

---

[9] Slamon DJ et al. (1989) Studies of the HER-2/neu proto-oncogene in human breast and ovarian cancer, Science, 244:707–712; Slamon DJ et al. (1987) Human breast cancer: Correlation of relapse and survival with amplification of the HER-2/neu oncogene. Science 235:177–182; Baselga J et al. (1999) Phase II study of weekly intravenous trastuzumab (Herceptin) in patients with HER2/neu-overexpressing metastatic breast cancer, Semin Oncol 26:78–83; Shak S et al. (1999) Overview of the trastuzumab (Herceptin) anti-HER2 monoclonal antibody clinical program in HER2-overexpressing metastatic breast cancer. Herceptin Multinational Investigator Study Group, Semin Oncol 26:71–77; Editor (1998) Pharmacogenomics at work. Nat Biotechnol 16:885; Mass R (2000) The role of HER-2 expression in predicting response to therapy in breast cancer. Semin Oncol 27:46–52; Haseltine WA (2000) Not quite pharmacogenomics. Nat Biotechnol 16:1295

merely blueprints for the actual machines in our cells, the protein molecules, or proteins. Understanding this is also important for later understanding how gene therapies work.

The DNA or our chromosomes with our genetic information are in the cell nucleus and thus somewhat better protected from environmental influences on a cell. However, everything that happens in the cell is mediated by proteins, and this mostly happens outside the cell nucleus. Even the proteins themselves are made outside the nucleus. For all of this to happen, the blueprints on the DNA from the nucleus must enter the cell in the form of a copy. For this purpose, not the entire DNA of a chromosome is copied, but only the part that contains the blueprint for a single protein. This copy is again written with nucleic acids as letters, of which, however, one letter (U instead of T) is different from DNA and is also linked to a slightly different sugar molecule, ribose. Consequently, this copy of DNA is chemically called ribonucleic acid (RNA). Inside the cell, a construction machinery is waiting to build proteins based on these RNA copies. The building blocks for protein are amino acids. The resulting various proteins are the workhorses in our cell and can specialize in any cellular function. In total, our cells can build over 20,000 different proteins that, for example, form a cell scaffold, connect cells together, metabolize small molecules but also other proteins to form new molecules, recognize molecules to send signals into or out of the cell, and much more. In the process, they are packed tightly together in the cell and the totality of their interactions form the interactome, which we have met before, in the definition of disease modules.

At some point, we may have understood the effect of each letter of DNA on its way to RNA, protein, and metabolites. However, this could take quite a long time, longer than my usual "in 10–20 years" estimate. One reason is that, at least from a medical point of view, the goal of research is not to clarify the function of all DNA letters, but the causes of all diseases. These causes of diseases can originate in single or multiple altered genes. However, these alterations are subsequently also reflected in RNA, altered proteins, and altered metabolites. This means that the diagnosis of the disease and elucidation of the mechanism can take place at all these levels. Thus, altered RNA amounts, altered protein amounts or changes in a protein, or altered metabolites can all equally provide the decisive clue.

In the COVID-19 pandemic, you could follow this diagnostic to some extent. Since the SARS-Cov2 virus is an RNA virus, it was identified by its RNA. That was the PCR test, which technically "translates" the RNA into DNA first, but that is purely methodological. What was detected was the RNA. The rapid tests that came later, on the other hand, detected the spike protein of the virus in the pharyngeal mucosa. Proteins can also sometimes be detected in the blood, especially when cells are dying, for example, protein from the liver in cases of liver damage or the prostate-specific antigen (PSA test) for prostate cancer screening. Metabolites such as cholesterol and uric acid are also part of routine diagnostics at the family doctor. In these cases, however, one already knows what one is looking for, and the statements are therefore very limited to a single disease. The detection of cell-free DNA, which is leached into the blood by many tumours, could facilitate the early detection of cancers in the future. The multi-cancer early detection (MCED) test of a US manufacturer GRAIL (grail.com) detected about half of the diseases in 50 different types of cancer in a case-control study. False-positive tests could be largely avoided in the process.[10]

But if you want to capture all diseases, and not just via the genome, then you would have to measure all RNAs (the transcriptome), all proteins (the proteome), and all metabolites (the metabolome). Crazy? No. The feasibility was proven already back in 2012.[11] The rest, that is, the gradual introduction into normal diagnostics, is solely a matter of mass, as with the *Human Genome Project*, and costs. If more and more such analyses are performed, more equipment will be built, improved, and costs will come down. Where would that leave us? For example, one such integrative Personal Ome profile—"Ome" because of the word ending of genome, transcriptome, proteome, and metabolome—was performed on a single individual over a 14-month period. Various medical risks were identified, including a sudden onset of type 2 diabetes shortly after a viral infection. The course could be followed quasi-live based on the measured values. After a radical change in diet and physical training program, which were initiated immediately, the diabetic metabolism returned to normal. Type 2 diabetes was averted (for the time being). This means that "know your genes" will in all probability also extend to all gene copies (RNAs or transcriptome), all gene products (proteins or proteome), and the products of the gene products (metabolites or metabolome) in the future.

Then we will know incredibly much more about ourselves—if we want to. But will this mass of data be enough? Unfortunately, not yet. Because we are more than our own genes and our own gene products. We also live in symbiosis with billions of bacteria: on our skin, in our lungs, in our intestines. A few

---

[10] Klein EA et al. (2021) Clinical validation of a targeted methylation-based multi-cancer early detection test using an independent validation set. Annals of Oncology 32:1167–1177, https://doi.org/10.1016/j.annonc.2021.05.806

[11] Chen R et al. (2012) Personal Omics Profiling Reveals Dynamic Molecular and Medical Phenotypes. Cell 148:1293–1307, https://doi.org/10.1016/j.cell.2012.02.009

bacteria, you might think. Let me surprise you. And even that will not be enough. In addition to your genes and bacteria, there is also your lifestyle and your environment. I mentioned earlier that some genetic risks can be kept in check with an optimal lifestyle. Similarly, a risk of lung cancer or heart attack will depend on whether we smoke, a risk of severe lung disease will depend on whether we live on a major traffic road with high levels of particulate matter or nitrogen dioxide in the air, a risk of colon cancer will depend on whether we eat a lot of red meat and little fibre. All this is what the next two Chaps. 13 and 14 are about.

14

Outnumbered

So far, it's always been about genes. And most likely you have been considering only the cells of your body and their genes. However, you may have heard
that there are microbes in and on us. This refers primarily to bacteria, viruses,
and fungi, which in their entirety are referred to as our microbiome. "But it
can't be that important", you might think to yourself, right? The amazing
thing is that you as an adult consist of about 30 trillion cells, the number of
all your bacteria in you (lungs, intestine) and on you (skin) is about 38 trillion, which is about 1.3 times as many as your own body has cells.[1] These
bacteria are not just one strain but different ones and thus all genetically different. This multiplies to a total of 3.3 million bacterial genes, which is 150
times the amount of our own human genes.[2] Moreover 142,809 different
viruses (so-called bacteriophages) that infect our gut bacteria have been identified which further increase our microbial complexity.[3] So genetically you are
clearly outnumbered by your microbiome. You could view this as if we live in
a symbiosis with our microbiome. Our microbiome influences us and we our
microbiome, positively or negatively, respectively. So, whenever you think
about yourself, you should also consider that half of you are your bacteria,
viruses, and fungi. These are not unhygienic contamination, as some people
think and exaggerate especially in skin hygiene or carelessly take antibiotics,

---

[1] Sender R (2016) Revised Estimates for the Number of Human and Bacteria Cells in the Body. PLOS
Biology 14:e1002533, https://doi.org/10.1371/journal.pbio.1002533

[2] Qin J et al. (2010) A human gut microbial gene catalogue established by metagenomic sequencing.
Nature 464:59–65, https://doi.org/10.1038/nature08821

[3] Camarillo-Guerrero LF et al. (2021) Massive expansion of human gut bacteriophage diversity. Cell
184:1098–1109.e9, https://doi.org/10.1016/j.cell.2021.01.029

© The Author(s), under exclusive license to Springer Nature Switzerland AG 2022   **177**
H. H. H. W. Schmidt, *The end of medicine as we know it - and why your health has a future*,
https://doi.org/10.1007/978-3-030-95293-8_14

but we live in a symbiosis. We need each other. Most of the microbiota is found in the intestine. This means that after a bowel movement we might be—for a short moment—in the majority with our cells, but otherwise it is probably more of a draw. But let's start with the skin.

Excessive Hygiene

On the one hand, the human skin microbiome consists of bacteria that are found on every human skin and make up the majority in percentage—the so-called core microbiome. Beyond that, however, the skin microbiome is highly individual, varying between different people, but also in different areas of the body. The biggest risk factor for our microbiome is ourselves. Our microbiome and its diversity are greatly influenced by our lifestyle. Our often-exaggerated hygiene behaviour and—in the case of our gut—uncritical intake of antibiotics can damage our skin and oral microbiome and make us more sensitive to diseases. This is due to antimicrobial agents such as triclosan, silver, aluminium salts, chlorine compounds, alcohols, phenols, hydrogen peroxide, and preservatives, as well as "natural" substances such as grape seed extracts in personal care products, cosmetics, toothpastes, and mouthwashes. This was accentuated during the COVID-19 pandemic by more intensive hand hygiene and the wearing of rubber gloves.[4] Our microbiome is necessary for the formation of a balanced immune system—not too weak, but also not overreactive. Children who grow up in excessively "hygienic" conditions tend to develop allergies and autoimmune diseases because their immune system has not been sufficiently trained with harmless bacteria and thus overreacts easily and chronically.[5] In one of the few intervention studies against excessive hygiene, ten Finnish day-care centres were investigated. Three of them were close to nature and served as positive controls. The urban day-care centres had yards with little or no green space. The intervention consisted of covering part of the gravel in some of the urban day-care centres with forest soil and sod for over a month, plants, and peat blocks for climbing and digging. The intervention diversified the skin microbiome and, in the blood, the proportion of

---

[4] Editor (2020) Physicians expect more skin damage due to frequent hand washing. Deutsches Ärzteblatt, https://www.aerzteblatt.de/nachrichten/112786/Aerzte-rechnen-mit-mehr-Hautschaeden-wegen-haeufigen-Haendewaschens; Larson EL et al. (1998) Changes in bacterial flora associated with skin damage on hands of health care personnel. Am J Infect Control 26:513–21, https://doi.org/10.1016/s0196-6553(98)70025-2

[5] Vandegrift R et al. (2017) Cleanliness in context: reconciling hygiene with a modern microbial perspective. Microbiome 5:76, https://doi.org/10.1186/s40168-017-0294-2

regulatory immune cells. Anti-inflammatory factors were increased, and inflammatory ones decreased. Such a so-called biodiversity intervention targeting the microbiome therefore improves immune regulation and reduces the risk of (auto)immune-mediated diseases.[6] A large variety or diversity of different bacteria correlates positively with our health. The composition varies between people and even in the same person over time. People who live together, as well as dog owners and dogs, incidentally, equalize their microbiomes, which in both increases diversity and is recommended.[7]

Your Gut Microbiome

Our intestine has not only the function of absorbing food components but also plays an important role for our immune system. With a length of six to nine meters and an internal surface area equivalent to two tennis courts, the intestine is our largest organ. This is good for absorbing food efficiently, but also provides an opportunity for germs that have passed through the stomach acid to infect us. To prevent this, our intestines have more defence cells than the skin and airways combined. On the other hand, intestinal bacteria produce for us, for example, biotin, folic acid, and vitamins B_2, B_{12}, and K. Obviously, nutrition plays an important role in regulating the composition of our intestinal microbiome, but also exercise, stress, lifestyle, age, gender, and medications.[8] By uncritically taking antibiotics for trivial infections, for example, one can destroy one's microbiome for months. Qualitative classification of individual bacteria into healthier and unhealthier has begun to make predictions about the overall health status of our gut microbiome.[9] How can you find out more about your personal microbiome?

In the past, it was necessary when diagnosing bacteria to isolate and cultivate them alive, multiply them, and then stain, detect, and count them under the microscope. However, most bacteria (approximately 90–95%) cannot be multiplied or only with great difficulties, and it is impossible to detect thousands of different bacterial strains from a stool sample in this way. Today,

---

[6] Roslund M et al. (2020) Biodiversity intervention enhances immune regulation and health-associated commensal microbiota among daycare children. Science Advances 6:eaba2578, https://advances.sciencemag.org/content/6/42/eaba2578

[7] Song SJ et al. (2013) Cohabiting family members share microbiota with one another and with their dogs. Elife 2:e00458, https://doi.org/10.7554/eLife.00458.001

[8] Rothschild D et al. (2018) Environment dominates over host genetics in shaping human gut microbiota. Nature 555:210–215, https://doi.org/10.1038/nature25973

[9] Gupta V et al. (2020) A predictive index for health status using species-level gut microbiome profiling. Nature Communication 11:4635, https://www.nature.com/articles/s41467-020-18476-8

bacteria are therefore not analysed by culture, but a specific DNA is sequenced, which provides sufficient information for a specific detection of each bacterial strain in the intestine. If you want to have your microbiome determined, this starts, for example, with a small kit consisting of a sterile sample container plus cotton swabs and a back envelope. You dab a sample from your stool with a swab and stir it into a sample jar, seal it, and off it goes in the mail. That's it. A few weeks later you will get the results. For this purpose, DNA is extracted from your stool sample, and a gene is sequenced that is specific for bacteria but different in each strain. The DNA-based bacterial composition then allows conclusions about diversity, inflammatory factors, and unwanted bacteria. Your data will be compared to the results of thousands of other microbiome analyses, matching your geographic region and lifestyle, i.e. a 70-year-old "omnivore" with other older "omnivores" and an 18-year-old vegan with other young vegans.

However, different companies take different approaches to this. Many distinguish three intestinal types depending on dominant bacterium types and eating habits: Type 1 in meat eaters with mainly *Bacteroides* bacteria and the lowest diversity, Type 2 in vegetarians and vegans with mainly *Prevotella* bacteria, and Type 3 with mainly *Ruminococcus* bacteria. Predispositions to certain diseases or obesity also correlate with dominant bacteria, as some, for example, can break down food more thoroughly than others. Thus, more energy can be obtained for the body, which can lead to obesity, while with other bacteria food components are excreted unutilized. For the sake of completeness, it must be said that a rather heated discussion has flared up about the usefulness of microbiome analyses.[10] The interpretation is also complicated by the fact that completely different bacteria are and should be at home in different parts of our digestive organs—i.e. the mucous membranes of the stomach, different sections of the intestine, or the mouth.[11] How these are represented in a stool sample is unclear. Moreover, the result of each stool sample represents only a snapshot. Food also quickly has a big impact: glutamate—often used in Chinese cooking—drastically changes the composition of the microbiome for 24 hours. Likewise, large amounts of milk, sugar substitutes, emulsifiers, or unfamiliar spices have an impact, as well as just a few

---

[10] DCCV e.V. (2018) Expensive and pointless: DGVS advises against stool tests to analyse the gut microbiome, https://www.dccv.de/aktuelles/nachricht/news/detail/News/teuer-und-sinnlos-dgvs-raet-von-stuhltests-zur-analyse-des-darm-mikrobioms-ab/

[11] Martinez-Guryn K (2019) Regional Diversity of the Gastrointestinal Microbiome. Cell Host & Microbe 26:314–324, https://doi.org/10.1016/j.chom.2019.08.011; Vasapolli R (2019) Analysis of Transcriptionally Active Bacteria Throughout the Gastrointestinal Tract of Healthy Individuals. Gastroenterology 157:1081–1092.E3, https://doi.org/10.1053/j.gastro.2019.05.068

days of vegan eating. So, one should eat a representative diet, the same as usual, in the days leading up to a stool test. In fact, no evidence of specific diseases can currently be derived from the analysis, and it is impossible to define a healthy or an unhealthy microbiome.

So, what about the possibilities of healing an intestinal microbiome that is out of balance, i.e. is no longer diverse? In principle, there are two possibilities: on the one hand, to have the entire microbiome of a healthy person "transplanted" in the form of fresh bowel movements, or to take a mixture of bacteria (probiotics) or bacteria-promoting food supplements (prebiotics), whereby the transition from prebiotics to drugs is fluid, since the latter—like antibiotics, for example—can also influence our microbiome.[12] Recently, also products of gut bacteria, postbiotics, for which beneficial effects have been identified have gained attention and may represent an alternative analysis and intervention.

Prebiotics ➜ Probiotics ➜ Postbiotics.

Prebiotics and Probiotics

Unfortunately, both prebiotics and probiotics are currently swamping the market and taken without criticism. Prebiotics are mostly so-called dietary fibres, which pass unchanged from the small intestine into the large intestine where they are broken down by bacteria. This means that for us dietary fibres are "indigestible ballast", but for our microbiome they are essential food. They stimulate the growth of certain bacteria in the intestine, for example, bifido. Probiotics are lactobacillus and other bacteria as well as yeasts. Although the name probiotics suggests that they could be used to compensate for or correct damage to the intestinal microbiome caused by antibiotics, for example, this is not yet possible. Probiotics usually contain different bacteria than those lost through antibiotics or lifestyle, and which are the important ones is not clear yet. Ingesting the wrong bacteria can even disrupt or worsen the normalization process of the individual gut microbiome after antibiotic therapy and cause irritable bowel symptoms.[13] Despite this knowledge gap, the Internet is

---

[12] Heuer H (2016) Drugs and the microbiome. Deutsche Apotheker Zeitung 45:52, https://www.deutsche-apotheker-zeitung.de/daz-az/2016/daz-45-2016/arzneistoffe-und-das-mikrobiom

[13] Palleja A et al. (2018) Recovery of gut microbiota of healthy adults following antibiotic exposure. Nature Microbiology 3:1255, https://www.nature.com/articles/s41564-018-0257-9; Suez J et al. (2018) Post-Antibiotic Gut Mucosal Microbiome Reconstitution Is Impaired by Probiotics and Improved by Autologous FMT. Cell 174:1406–1423.E16, https://doi.org/10.1016/j.cell.2018.08.047

full of probiotics, live bacteria that are intended to have health benefits when consumed. At present, only a few bacteria can be cultivated in therapeutically relevant quantities. There is at present no evidence that the administration of such probiotics, e.g. to re-diversify the composition of the intestinal flora, would be beneficial. In addition, for most of the possible applications there are only correlations between microbiome and disease, but no placebo-controlled studies on the treatment, cure, or prevention of diseases with probiotics.

An exception is hospitalized patients who suffer from a rare but severely pathological colon colonization with *Clostridium difficile* bacteria, e.g. through use of antibiotics. This is associated with fever, abdominal pain, and diarrhoea, but can also result in life-threatening bowel obstruction and sepsis. Here, probiotic intervention can indeed prevent this antibiotic-associated colitis if they are taken shortly before or after the first antibiotic.[14] Therefore, at this time, except for this one exception—and may be some very few intestinal conditions that I may have missed—the administration of probiotics cannot be widely recommended. The still justified criticism or limitation of probiotic therapies can be contrasted at the other end with the extreme, namely, the rather drastic-seeming but effective stool transplants from which the search for more acceptable probiotics derived.

Stool Transplant

"Stool?!", you might ask. Yes, it sounds extreme, but this is the only way to ensure that the entire health-promoting microbiome is transferred or "transplanted". No need to identify, select, culture, and apply hundreds of specific bacteria. In this case, freshly produced stool is transferred by means of a nasal probe that leads directly into the duodenum, so that reflux of stool into the stomach or even the oesophagus is virtually impossible. And with this, therapeutic successes can be achieved, which thus prove a causal or at least effective symptomatic therapy option by means of correction of the total gut microbiome. Here, too, we are still at the beginning, with the two main knowledge gaps and risk as follows: One can define a healthy donor, but not yet a healthy microbiome, and one does not know whether stool transplants can also transfer (unrecognised) diseases.

---

[14] Shen NT et al. (2017) Gastroenterology 152:1889–1900.e9, https://doi.org/10.1053/j.gastro.2017.02.003

Here again, *Clostridium difficile* infections can be treated,[15] but also type 1 diabetes mellitus, which unlike type II diabetes is not a lifestyle problem, but an autoimmune disease. In type I diabetes, the insulin-producing cells in the pancreas are progressively destroyed until the patient, who is usually still young, must substitute, i.e. inject, insulin several times a day with a syringe or a mini-pump. The cause of type 1 diabetes mellitus, i.e. why this autoimmune reaction occurs, was unclear until now. Some drugs that inhibit our immune defences can stop this process, but they do so only temporarily (at best), have no effect on the long-term progression of the disease, and are sometimes associated with serious side effects.[16] More and more data suggest that type 1 diabetes mellitus is at least correlated with an altered gut microbiome.[17] For example, there are clear differences between type 1 diabetics and healthy control subjects with regard to the small intestinal microbiome and their genes.[18] Harmful bacteria appear to have surface proteins or structures that are tragically identical to surface proteins or structures of insulin-producing cells in the pancreas. Thus, the intestinal immune system reacts first against these bacterial structures, but then also against the body's own insulin-producing cells in the pancreas, causing them to gradually decrease in number and function until the body's own insulin production ceases. A generally impaired barrier function of the intestinal mucosa could accelerate this process or make it possible in the first place.[19] If fresh faeces from slim, healthy, and same-sex

---

[15] McDonald LC et al. (2018) Clinical Practice Guidelines for Clostridium difficile Infection in Adults and Children: 2017 Update by the Infectious Diseases Society of America (IDSA) and Society for Healthcare Epidemiology of America (SHEA). Clin Infect Dis 66:e1

[16] Roep BO et al. (2019) Antigen-Based immune modulation therapy for type 1 diabetes: the era of precision medicine. Lancet Diabetes Endocrinol 7:65–74, http://www.ncbi.nlm.nih.gov/pubmed/30528100; Atkinson MA et al. (2020) The challenge of modulating β-cell autoimmunity in type 1 diabetes. Lancet Diabetes Endocrinol 7:52–64, http://www.ncbi.nlm.nih.gov/pubmed/30528099

[17] Brown CT et al. (2011) Gut microbiome metagenomics analysis suggests a functional model for the development of autoimmunity for type 1 diabetes. PLoS One 6:e25792, http://www.ncbi.nlm.nih.gov/pubmed/22043294; de Goffau MC et al. (2014) Aberrant gut microbiota composition at the onset of type 1 diabetes in young children. Diabetologia 57:1569–77, http://www.ncbi.nlm.nih.gov/pubmed/24930037; de Goffau MC et al. (2013) Fecal microbiota composition differs between children with β-cell autoimmunity and those without. Diabetes 62:1238–44, http://www.ncbi.nlm.nih.gov/pubmed/23274889; Davis-Richardson AG & Triplett EW (2015) A model for the role of gut bacteria in the development of autoimmunity for type 1 diabetes. Diabetologia 58:1386–93, http://www.ncbi.nlm.nih.gov/pubmed/25957231; de Groot PF et al. (2017) Distinct fecal and oral microbiota composition in human type 1 diabetes, an observational study. PLoS One 12:e0188475, http://www.ncbi.nlm.nih.gov/pubmed/29211757

[18] Pellegrini S et al. (2017) Duodenal mucosa of patients with type 1 diabetes shows distinctive inflammatory profile and microbiota. J Clin Endocrinol Metab 102:1468–77, http://www.ncbi.nlm.nih.gov/pubmed/28324102; Vatanen T et al. (2018) The human gut microbiome in early-onset type 1 diabetes from the TEDDY study. Nature 562:589–594, https://doi.org/10.1038/s41586-018-0620-2

[19] Culina S et al. (2018) Islet-reactive CD8+ T cell frequencies in the pancreas, but not in blood, distinguish type 1 diabetic patients from healthy donors. Sci Immunol 3:eaao4013, http://www.ncbi.nlm.nih.

faecal donors are now transferred to a type 1 diabetic, in whom, however, the onset of symptoms must not have occurred more than 12 months previously, the decline in the body's own insulin production and thus the demise of the insulin-producing cells stops.[20] But the intestinal microbiome also plays a role in type II diabetes.

Another successful example of a stool transplant is in cancer therapy. Cancer patients with malignant melanoma who did not respond to treatment with the checkpoint inhibitor drug, pembrolizumab, responded after they received a stool transplant from other patients who had responded well to this therapy.[21] It is not entirely clear which bacteria in the gut were responsible for the change, but *F. prausnitzii* and *Akkermansia muciniphila* might increase the response, while *Bacteroides* might decrease it. The effects of stool transplantation in other forms of cancer are under investigation. *Akkermansia muciniphila* also popped up in obesity.

Does the Wrong Gut Flora Make you Fat?

The intestinal microbiome of overweight people differs significantly from that of normal-weight people, is less diverse, and individual bacterial species are increased, while others such as *Akkermansia muciniphila* are decreased.[22] Frequent use of antibiotics in childhood can also permanently alter the gut flora, with a higher risk of obesity.[23] However, for most cases there is still a "chicken-or-egg" problem. Which came first, the altered microbiome or the obesity? What is certain is that people with a microbiome typical of obesity gain weight more easily and are likely to have greater difficulty losing

---

gov/pubmed/29429978; Hand TW et al. (2020) Acute gastrointestinal infection induces long-lived microbiota-specific T cell responses. Science 337:1553–6, http://www.ncbi.nlm.nih.gov/pubmed/22923434

[20] de Groot P et al. (2021) Faecal microbiota transplantation halts progression of human new-onset type 1 diabetes in a randomised controlled trial. Gut 70:92–105, https://doi.org/10.1136/gutjnl-2020-322630

[21] Davar D et al. (2021) Fecal microbiota transplant overcomes resistance to anti-PD-1 therapy in melanoma patients. Science 371:595–602, https://doi.org/10.1126/science.abf3363

[22] Crovesy L et al. (2020) Profile of the gut microbiota of adults with obesity: a systematic review. Eur J Clin Nutr 74:1251–1262, https://doi.org/10.1038/s41430-020-0607-6; Forslund K et al. (2015) Disentangling type 2 diabetes and metformin treatment signatures in the human gut microbiota. Nature 528, 262; Zhernakova A et al. (2016) Population-based metagenomics analysis reveals markers for gut microbiome composition and diversity. Science 352:565–569; Fan Y & Pedersen O (2020) Gut microbiota in human metabolic health and disease. Nat Rev. Microbiol, https://doi.org/10.1038/s41579-020-0433-9

[23] Cox L & Blaser M (2015) Antibiotics in early life and obesity. Nat Rev. Endocrinol 11:182–190, https://doi.org/10.1038/nrendo.2014.210

weight.[24] Also, transferring the gut microbiome from an obese person to a lean animal induces obesity and diabetes in this animal. Conversely, transferring the gut microbiome from slim donors improves the metabolic situation in diabetics.[25] A first step towards a tailored and less drastic treatment of the microbiome in type 2 diabetes was the observation that compensating for the deficiency of *Akkermansia muciniphila* leads to a slight weight reduction, decreased body fat per centage and hip circumference, improved liver values, and decreased inflammation levels in the blood.[26] But the role of the gut microbiome seems to go beyond local effects, i.e. in the gut or on the skin.

The Gut-Heart and Gut-Brain Axis, Respectively

The same microbiome constellations that correlate with obesity also correlate with inflammation, hypertension, atherosclerosis, cardiovascular disease, and depression, so that gut-heart and gut-brain axes have been postulated. But again, correlations don't prove causality, after all. Other risk factors for these diseases, such as smoking, obesity, and diet, also influence the microbiome, so that disease and microbiome change may also be parallel symptoms of a common cause, so that the disturbed microbiome is not necessarily the cause of the disease. However, what does speak—at least in part—for a causal relationship and a gut-heart axis are numerous metabolites, such as trimethylamine(-N-oxide) and certain fatty and bile acids, that gut microorganisms produce from our food, e.g. red meat, and which can be directly

---

[24] Haslam DW & James WP (2005) Obesity. Lancet, 366:1197–209; Turnbaugh PJ et al. (2009) A core gut microbiome in obese and lean twins. Nature. 457:480–4; Mayengbam S et al. (2018) Impact of dietary fiber supplementation on modulating microbiota-host-metabolic axes in obesity. J Nutritional Biochem 64:228–236, https://doi.org/10.1016/j.jnutbio.2018.11.003; Tims S et al. (2013) Microbiota conservation and BMI signatures in adult monozygotic twins. Isme J 7:707; Million M et al. (2011) Obesity-associated gut microbiota is enriched in Lactobacillus reuteri and depleted in Bifidobacterium animalis and Methanobrevibacter smithii. Int J Obesity 36:817

[25] Fei N & Zhao L (2013) An opportunistic pathogen isolated from the gut of an obese human causes obesity in germfree mice. ISME J 7:880–884, https://doi.org/10.1038/ismej.2012.153; Turnbaugh P et al. (2006) An obesity-associated gut microbiome with increased capacity for energy harvest. Nature 444:1027–1031, https://doi.org/10.1038/nature05414; Pérez-Matute P et al. (2020) Autologous fecal transplantation from a lean state potentiates caloric restriction effects on body weight and adiposity in obese mice. Sci Rep 10, 9388, https://doi.org/10.1038/s41598-020-64961-x; Vrieze A et al. (2012) Transfer of intestinal microbiota from lean donors increases insulin sensitivity in individuals with metabolic syndrome. Gastroenterology 143:913–6.e7, https://doi.org/10.1053/j.gastro.2012.06.031, Erratum in: Gastroenterology 144:250

[26] Depommier C et al. (2019) Supplementation with Akkermansia muciniphila in overweight and obese human volunteers: a proof-of-concept exploratory study. Nat Med 25:1096–1103, https://doi.org/10.1038/s41591-019-0495-2

linked to cardiovascular diseases such as atherosclerosis, hypertension, heart failure, and chronic kidney disease.[27]

With respect to the gut-brain axis,[28] it is noteworthy that the intestine has the second largest nerve network in the body—after the brain of course—with 100 million nerve cells. These nerve cells both regulate intestinal movement of the bowel to slowly transport its contents towards the exit, but also send signals to the brain in the form of messenger compounds.[29] A key substance in this communication appears to be serotonin, the brain's so-called happiness hormone. However, most of our serotonin is not located in the brain; 95% of serotonin is produced in the intestines, where it influences intestinal motility, for example. To produce serotonin, our body needs tryptophan, an essential amino acid that we cannot produce ourselves. However, tryptophan is found in abundance in eggs, dairy products, oats, almonds, and chocolate, among other things. Dietary changes are indeed effective in depression.[30] These are always accompanied by changes in the gut microbiome, which both influences how much tryptophan is absorbed from the diet and directly regulates how much serotonin is produced in the gut cell.[31] And so increased (*Anaerostipes*, *Klebsiella*, and *Streptococcus*) as well as decreased (*Faecalibacterium* and the *Bifidobacterium*) levels of certain bacterial species correlate with depression,[32] possibly allowing in future the option to achieve faster or more effective therapy through combinations of drugs, dietary changes, and specific probiotics.

Studies in mice—and preliminary work in humans—suggest that bacteria are involved in Parkinson's disease, autism spectrum disorder, and motor neuron disease. Gut bacteria can produce clumping proteins, called curli, that have a similar structure to the misshapen α-synuclein proteins found in the

[27] Tang WHW et al. (2019) Dietary metabolism, the gut microbiome, and heart failure. Nat Rev. Cardiol 16:137–154, https://doi.org/10.1038/s41569-018-0108-7

[28] Willyard C (2021) How gut microbes could drive brain disorders. Nature 590:22–25, https://doi.org/10.1038/d41586-021-00260-3

[29] Khlevner J et al. (2018) Brain-Gut Axis: Clinical Implications. Gastroenterol Clin North Am 47:727–739; Martin CR (2018) The brain-gut-microbiome axis. Cell Mol Gastroenterol Hepatol 6:133–148.

[30] Francis HM et al. (2019) A brief diet intervention can reduce symptoms of depression in young adults—A randomised controlled trial. PLoS One 14:e0222768, https://doi.org/10.1371/journal.pone.0222768

[31] Yano JM et al. (2015) Indigenous bacteria from the gut microbiota regulate host serotonin biosynthesis. Cell 161:264–276, doi:10.1016/j.cell.2015.02.047; Sugisawa E et al. (2020) RNA Sensing by Gut Piezo1 Is Essential for Systemic Serotonin Synthesis. Cell 182:609–624.e21, https://doi.org/10.1016/j.cell.2020.06.022; Matute JD et al. (2020) Microbial RNAs Pressure Piezo1 to Respond. Cell 182:542–544, https://doi.org/10.1016/j.cell.2020.07.015

[32] Cheung SG et al. (2019) Systematic Review of Gut Microbiota and Major Depression. Front Psychiatry 10:34

brain of Parkinson patients. Curli might be a template for misfolding leading to more α-synuclein in the brain.[33] One likely gut-brain conduit is the vagus nerve, the longest of the 12 cranial nerves that carry signals from the brain to the rest of the body. Gut curli may transmit protein misfolding up the vagus until proteins in the brain misfold. Indeed, patients who have had stomach ulcers and whose vagus nerve was removed to reduce acid production are less susceptible to Parkinson's disease.[34] And because misfolded proteins are a hallmark of several other brain conditions, e.g. Alzheimer's and motor neuron disease (amyotrophic lateral sclerosis), bacterial proteins could be implicated in subtypes of these diseases as well.

The complete elucidation of the microbiome and association with gut, cardiovascular, psychiatric, and other diseases is a gigantic, ongoing endeavour.[35] Personally, I am sceptical whether this will be possible in the necessary detail. Moreover, any malnutrition will negate any future microbiome therapy—be it faecal transplantation, pre- or probiotics—no matter how targeted. Therefore, it will always be advisable to pay attention to a healthy diet at the same time, which in this context means above all a diet high in fibre, low in sugar, and low in red meat because of the risk of colon cancer.[36] However, a recent trend may be more feasible, namely, to focus on the gut products, i.e. the postbiotics. They are smaller in number, easier to measure, and to supplement.

Postbiotics, the Real Future?

At least half of all small molecules circulating in our bloodstream are either derived from bacteria or modulated by them. Nicotinamide—also known as vitamin B3—is such a molecule produced by beneficial bacteria and enters the brain. Patients with amyotrophic lateral sclerosis have lower nicotinamide levels than unaffected family members, and supplementing nicotinamide improves symptoms, whereas control patients decline in health.[37] Over 22,000

---

[33] Sampson TR et al. (2020) A gut bacterial amyloid promotes α-synuclein aggregation and motor impairment in mice. Elife. 9:e53111, https://doi.org/10.7554/eLife.53111

[34] Svensson E et al. (2015) Vagotomy and subsequent risk of Parkinson's disease. Ann Neurol 78:522–9, https://doi.org/10.1002/ana.24448

[35] Proctor LM et al. (2019) The Integrative Human Microbiome Project. Nature 569:641–648, https://doi.org/10.1038/s41586-019-1238-8

[36] Zmora N et al. (2018) You are what you eat: diet, health and the gut microbiota. Nat Rev. Gastroenterol Hepatol 16:35–56

[37] Blacher E et al. (2019) Potential roles of gut microbiome and metabolites in modulating ALS in mice. Nature 572:474–480, https://doi.org/10.1038/s41586-019-1443-5; de la Rubia JE et al. (2019) Efficacy

bioactive bacterial metabolites have been identified. Some of the better known postbiotics include:

- Vitamins: B-vitamins (biotin, cobalamin, folates, nicotinic acid, pantothenic acid, pyridoxine, riboflavin, and thiamine) and vitamin K.
- Acids: short-chain fatty acids (butyric acid), phenyl lactic acid, D-amino acids, and fulvic acids.
- Organic compounds: glutathione, phytoestrogens, volatile organic compounds, and urolithins.
- Inorganic compounds: hydrogen peroxide.
- Peptides and proteins: antimicrobial peptides.[38]

Medications based on postbiotic metabolites may have fewer side effects because they are naturally produced in the body.[39]

But your genome and your microbiome are not the end of complexity to understand your body. What is still missing is all the environmental influences and your own behaviour and lifestyle (you remember the seven factors that are responsible for 80% of the costs of all chronic diseases), i.e. all the exposures to which your body is exposed, summarized as another "Om", the exposome. Since ultimately everything is related to everything else, i.e. your genome, microbiome, and exposome, we also need to capture this as accurately as possible. Until recently, this seemed to be an unsurmountable technical challenge, but now is becoming a realistic part of comprehensive medical diagnostics.

---

and tolerability of EH301 for amyotrophic lateral sclerosis: a randomized, double-blind, placebo-controlled human pilot study. Amyotroph Lateral Scler Frontotemporal Degener. 20:115–122, https://doi.org/10.1080/21678421.2018.1536152

[38] Hill MJ (1997) Intestinal flora and endogenous vitamin synthesis. Eur J Cancer Prev 6:S43–S45; Hill MJ (1997) Intestinal flora and endogenous vitamin synthesis. Eur J Cancer Prevent 6:S43; Morrison DJ & Preeston T (2016) Formation of short chain fatty acids by the gut microbiota and their impact on human metabolism. Gut Microbes 7:189–200; Mikelsaar M & Zilmer M (2009) Lactobacillus fermentum ME-3: an anti-microbial and anti-oxidative probiotic. Micro Ecol Health Dis 21:1–27; Dobson A et al. (2012) Bacteriocin Production: a Probiotic Trait? Applied and Environmental Microbiology 78:1–6; Ohhira I et al. (2004) Identification of 3-phenyllactic acid as a possible antibacterial substance produced by Enterococcus faecalis TH10. Biocontrol Science 9:77–81; Cava F et al. (2011) Emerging knowledge of regulatory roles in D-amino acids in bacteria. Cell Mil Life Sci 68:817–831; Hertzberger R et al. (2014) H_2O_2 Production in Species of the Lactobacillus acidophilus Group: a Central Role for a Novel NADH-Dependent Flavin Reductase. Applied and Environmental Microbiology 80:2229–2239; Bos LD et al. (2013) Volatile Metabolites of Pathogens: A Systemic Review. PLoS Pathog 9:e1003311; Frandenfeld CL et al. (2014) Obesity prevalence in relation to gut microbial environments capable of producing equol or O-desmethylangolensin from the isoflavone daidzein. Eur J Clin Nutrition 68:526–530; Larrosa M et al. (2006) Urolithins, Ellagic Acid-Derived Metabolites Produced by Human Colonic Microflora, Exhibit Estrogenic and Antiestrogenic Activities. J Agric Food Chem 54:1611–1620.

[39] Brown JM & Hazen SL. Targeting of microbe-derived metabolites to improve human health: The next frontier for drug discovery. J Biol Chem 292:8560–8568

15

Your Exposome

Supposing you knew all your personal "omes", i.e. your genome, transcriptome, proteome, metabolome, and microbiome, would that be enough to predict your health risks, to carry out effective prevention or to intervene curatively? No, this self-referential approach is unfortunately not yet sufficient, because you are more than the sum of your "omes".[1]

Most of your possible disease gene variants are rather weak spots. If you don't overuse them, nothing happens. If a garden hose has become a bit brittle, I don't turn up the water to the maximum; if I have a risk of lung disease such as COPD, I try not to live on a main road with high particulate matter and nitrogen dioxide pollution (in this case, e.g. a vegan diet and lots of exercise would not help me as lifestyle measures). This causality became apparent during the COVID-19 lockdown in 2020, when hospitalization rates due to exacerbated cases of chronic obstructive lung disease were halved.[2] If I'm at risk for diabetes, then I'll just have to cut back on sugar, even if my neighbour eats triple that and just doesn't get diabetes.[3] If I'm at risk for atherosclerosis and stroke, then I just have to watch my weight, stress management, and

[1] Wild CP (2005) Complementing the Genome with an 'Exposome': The Outstanding Challenge of Environmental Exposure Measurement in Molecular Epidemiology. Cancer Epidemiology, Biomarkers & Prevention 14:1847–50.

[2] So JY et al. (2021) Population Decline in COPD Admissions During the COVID-19 Pandemic Associated with Lower Burden of Community Respiratory Viral Infections. Am J Med. 134:1252–1259. e3, https://doi.org/10.1016/j.amjmed.2021.05.008

[3] Tamayo T et al. (2016) The prevalence and incidence of diabetes in Germany-an analysis of statutory health insurance data on 65 million individuals from the years 2009 and 2010. Dtsch Arztebl Int 113:177–82, https://doi.org/10.3238/arztebl.2016.0177

© The Author(s), under exclusive license to Springer Nature Switzerland AG 2022
H. H. H. W. Schmidt, *The end of medicine as we know it - and why your health has a future*,
https://doi.org/10.1007/978-3-030-95293-8_15

healthy eating more than others.[4] You remember all these types of factors—air pollution, diet, stress, and in future increasing climate change—are part of the external risks (like environment) and personal behaviours (like overeating, malnutrition, lack of exercise, poor stress management, lack of sleep, smoking, alcohol) that account for 80 per cent of all chronic disease costs. That means, for all the "ome" technologies, the bulk of our health still depends on our behaviour and environment. The good thing is that we have it in our power to influence all these factors, if they are relevant to our genetic risk profile. So, there is no reason to surrender to high-tech medicine and abdicate responsibility for our own health altogether. We are still responsible for ourselves, only more precisely and effectively than ever before.

But one problem with the current "healthy living" recommendations is that we recommend everything to everyone. We don't know who has what genetic risk. And everyone knows the 95-year-old who smoked for the whole of his life and never exercised. Maybe I have healthy genes too. Maybe you do. Maybe not. At the latest after the first heart attack, the proportion of men who are suddenly interested in their weight and cycling increases. If they had known about their risk a little earlier—before the heart attack, when there was still time to take countermeasures—and with a 100 per cent reliability that they are really at risk, then they would certainly have been much more motivated to act.

But how could one possibly record lifestyle and environment, i.e. all the influences on which we expose our bodies (our exposome)? Our own health data so far has already become "relatively Big Data", but if you want to capture your exposome 24/7 and add to that, we are most certainly talking about "really Big Data". At the risk of repeating myself, without our exposome we won't be able to predict our health risks, effectively prevent, or be cured. So, no matter how big it is, we will need to know it. Its influence is just too important. But what exactly do we need to measure?

What Is your Exposome?

The exposome describes the sum of all environmental influences (including our behaviour) that affect our body, starting even before birth until our death (see Fig. 15.1). Simplified, one could say: everything that was not defined by the previous "ome".

---

[4] Wirth A (2004) Lifestyle modification for prevention and therapy of atherosclerotic diseases. Dtsch Arztebl 101:A 1745–1752

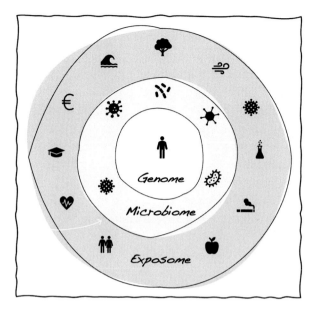

Fig. 15.1 Our exposome. The exposome describes the totality of all factors acting on our body—in addition to our genome and microbiome. Clockwise (from "one o'clock"): air pollution, infections, chemicals, addictive substances, nutrition, partnership/social contacts, stress, education, financial security, water quality, and green living environment

Many influences (e.g. UV radiation of our skin, smoking, fine dust and nitrogen oxides in the air, the consumption of red meat) accumulate over time. So, it is always a question of what affects us and for how long. These two factors not only sort of sit on top of our genome and microbiome but interact with them in both directions. Environment and our behaviour can alter our genome and microbiome but can also cause a genetic disease risk to convert into disease. Conversely, our behaviour also has genetic roots. Health-related aspects of our behaviour include nutrition, physical fitness (endurance, strength, and flexibility), ability to cope with stress, involvement in partnerships and social contacts, and financial security. Environment includes aspects such as air pollution, infections, chemicals,[5] addictive substances such as smoking and alcohol, water quality, and green living environments. But how could you capture your extremely complex exposome?

---

[5] Vermeulen R et al. (2020) The exposome and health: where chemistry meets biology. Science 367:392–396, https://doi.org/10.1126/science.aay3164

How to Measure your Exposome?

Research on the exposome was originally initiated to trace the relationships between exposures and their effects in occupational diseases[6], first in mines and factories by recording the dust and chemical compounds inhaled by workers, and since the 1950s also in relation to urban pollutants in the air and water supply. In the urban environment, technologies used include GPS tracking, and with it the ability to account for minute-to-minute variations in exposure levels and pollutants in the environment in real time.

In terms of coverage, the Health and Environment-wide Associations based on Large Population Surveys (HEALS) study was a milestone. It successfully refined the methodology for measuring and quantifying the many exposures and specific biomarkers to which people are exposed in their environment, including all internal, general, and[7] specific external factors. The main drawback was that the study was very expensive and extremely time-consuming, which precludes conducting this type of study on a larger scale or over a longer period for entire populations. Instead, the Internet of Things (IoT) and Internet of Medical Things (IoMT) have become more and more relevant for exposome research. Internet of (Medical) Things helps collecting data, for example, via the use of so-called wearables such as fitness watches, mobile phones, but also other devices connected to the Internet such as refrigerators, stoves, TVs, and so on. Just knowing where we are or even where we live, for example, whether we live next to a major city highway with heavy air pollution or stayed for 15 minutes at McDonald's, leads to medically relevant information. Thus, the Internet of (Medical) Things industry is helping to create greater awareness of lifestyle factors and to encourage or—one could almost say—playfully seduce people to adopt a healthy lifestyle, for example, through gamification (applying game-typical elements in a non-game context) or nudging (influencing people's decisions through positive reinforcement and indirect suggestions without classical ways of achieving compliance, i.e., commanding, criticizing, or punishing).

Already today, the benefits of gamification and nudging are considerable, for example, via a smartwatch in monitoring patients including informing and notifying caregivers in case of a fall or medical emergency. In addition,

---

[6] Olympio KPK et al. (2019) The Human Exposome Unraveling the Impact of Environment on Health. Revista de Saúde Pública 53:6

[7] Steckling N et al. (2018) Biomarkers of Exposure in Environment-Wide Association Studies - Opportunities to Decode the Exposome Using Human Biomonitoring Data. Environmental Research 164:597–624

health problems (such as cardiac arrhythmia) can be detected sooner before they become critical (heart attack), enabling preventive medical intervention.[8] With these or other components of the Internet of (Medical) Things, activity levels, dietary and lifestyle habits, and sleep patterns and abnormalities can be measured early and, most importantly, objectively, making more precise interventions possible. Once you have consented to data transfer to and analysis by your doctor, he or she doesn't even need to ask you if you're exercising regularly and sleeping well. They see objectively that you sit far too much and that your sleep is irregular and too short and that you are totally overestimating your physical activity. Before, you might have said, "No, doctor, I'm fine". Thus, the use of wearables can lead to a better awareness of your personal health and encourage you to pay attention to a healthy lifestyle— that is, enough physical activity, healthy eating, etc. In this way, wearables and the Internet of (Medical) Things can promote and maintain a healthy lifestyle and improve and ensure physical and mental health. Finally, the Internet of (Medical) Things can be used to collect health-related data anonymously over time. This will allow the impact of lifestyle and the need for medical interventions to be scientifically assessed. Regular check-ups at your general practitioner could thus be replaced by electronic examinations, combined with regular medical and non-medical telemedical coaching. Moreover, since lifestyle changes are in principle cost-effective and preventive, the efficiency of the health sector would be improved, and costs reduced. But how realistic is it that this is not one of these futuristic hypotheses but that you can really apply all of this for your own health and soon. Surprisingly, very realistic.

Exposome in Practice

For example, since 2020, the European Union has been funding several synergistic exposome projects (humanexposome.eu) to decipher the lifelong effects of external and internal exposures on human health. Some highlights from these give an idea of the realistic and rapid development of this field: The ATHLETE programme measures environmental exposures (urban, chemical, lifestyle, and social risk factors) during pregnancy, childhood, and adolescence and correlates them with incident disease. EPHOR investigates

---

[8] Marr B (2018) Forbes. Why the Internet of Medical Things (IoMT) Will Start to Transform Healthcare in 2018, https://www.forbes.com/sites/bernardmarr/2018/01/25/why-the-intern...ngs-iomt-will-start-to-transform-healthcare-in-2018

the burden of disease caused by occupational exposures. EXPANSE addresses how to maximize one's health in a modern urban environment by pooling and correlating chemical exposure and health data from more than 55 million Europeans. HEDIMED seeks to identify exposome factors that may explain the rapid rise in immune-related diseases such as type 1 diabetes, celiac disease, allergies, and asthma in recent years. Finally, LONGITOOLS investigates which is the latest time in life to intervene to reduce different environmental health risks.

The Exposome Economy

In addition to patient benefit, the Internet of Medical Things and exposome technology built on top of it are, of course, a huge market that is now worth $137 billion. A key to this has been the miniaturization of chips and sensors (i.e. the fifth Kondratieff wave) while delivering better performance and negligible cost. In keeping with the Exposome initiative, the European Commission has launched the *Alliance for Internet of Things Innovation* (aioti.eu), in part to develop a free flow of data across national borders in the EU. In parallel, of course, Google's holding company Alphabet will add to its portfolio, as demonstrated by its purchase of Fitbit, for example. With Apple's HealthKit, third-party developers can access data from the Health app to create sound health analytics and fitness solutions with little effort. Successful examples include apps focused on exercise, sleep, heart health, and nutrition, which are also currently used to provide scientific evidence and insight into principal feasibility. For example, the CareKit and ResearchKit apps have enabled the detection of heart arrhythmias, which is being refined with the Research app and the Apple Heart and Exercise Study.[9] Here, heart rate and exercise signals—for example, walking pace and stair climbing—are correlated with hospitalizations, falls, and heart health to promote minimum healthy levels of exercise and heart health. The Apple Hearing Study examines factors that impact hearing health and seeks to understand how daily sound exposure can affect hearing. Based on these pilot studies, future apps will be able to anonymously use smartwatch-derived sensor data for scientific studies, and in turn provide their results to you, the individual user, and your electronic health record as a personalized

---

[9] Falter M et al. (2019) Accuracy of Apple Watch Measurements for Heart Rate and Energy Expenditure in Patients With Cardiovascular Disease: Cross-Sectional Study. JMIR Mhealth Uhealth 7:e11889, https://doi.org/10.2196/11889

risk analysis or for coaching. Of course, Apple is not doing this for philanthropic reasons, but because the company knows that personalized health monitoring is one of the components of the "sixth wave." Apple also can't invent every solution to every problem on its own, so it needs to cooperate. Other developers can focus on the software; Apple provides the hardware and, most importantly, platform. It will be difficult to counter this with something equivalent on a national or European level. However, a national or European strength could be to have a maximal degree of data security and ownership of one's own data.

An economically relevant question is, of course, who pays? Now, exclusively you as the user. Everyone wants more prevention, but how analyses of the exposome and the resulting health-related services will be reimbursed is unclear. The US insurer Medicare has already approved reimbursements for remote monitoring and patient-generated health data and included them in care plans and for interventions.[10]

To analyse the individual effect of your exposome, you obviously need to wear one or more wearables. Would you do that, and who then bears the costs? Always you personally, or shouldn't the health insurance company participate since it's all about prevention and you ultimately save the health insurance company money? The number of users is still relatively small. However, the analysis of the exposome through data collection is only valuable for you when there is enough data from other people. That this technology is coming is not the issue, only the speed at which it happens and whether you can profit from it will depend critically on how quickly critical mass is reached and enough people have adopted this innovation until it becomes self-sustaining through word-of-mouth.[11]This kind of advertising and marketing used to be Apple's forte.[12] Alongside this health motive could come financial incentives, such as a reduction in your insurance premium or in-app rewards. For example, Azumio, a platform that uses food recognition to track eating habits, uses the cryptocurrency Lifecoin. Lifecoins are awarded to users of the app, who can then exchange them for gift cards and products.

---

[10]Comstock B (2018) Big changes are coming to Medicare reimbursement for connected health. Retrieved from: https://www.mobihealthnews.com/content/big-changes-are-coming-medicare-reimbursement-connected-health

[11]Rogers E (1983) Diffusion of Innovations. third Edition. New York: The Free Press; Sattler DN & Kerr NL (1991) Might versus morality explored: motivational and cognitive bases for social motives. Journal of Personality and Social Psychology, 60, 756–765.

[12]Krüger-Brand E (2020) Digital health: tech corporations as drivers. Dtsch Arztebl 117:A-375 / B-327 / C-315, https://www.aerzteblatt.de/archiv/212720/Digitale-Gesundheit-Tech-Konzerne-als-Treiber

From Exposome to Prevention

"Nothing is good. Unless you do it", said Erich Kästner. The first hurdle is, after all, that a critical mass of users and enough relevant data is created, which means that it may not help you much if a lot of users share their data in Asia or the USA, but not in your country, or in a different age group than yours. Then all predictions and tips will be less accurate. In this respect, Big Data for better health is an example of the "public goods dilemma". People want more efficient healthcare, but are reluctant to provide their own data, and so the public good is not realized. Another recent example is the COVID-19 pandemic, a now indisputable health threat, but one that some younger people and people without pre-existing conditions have found not so threatening to themselves and so have not used Corona apps and masks or kept social distancing. So, it's important to work with other users to develop the collective goal: "We need to improve the efficiency of medicine", for example, or "Systems medicine needs Big Data and can only work optimally if many provide their data".

But even after overcoming this critical mass, the data flow itself and the whole exposome and its analyses will mean little at first. The data only become valuable when you also use and implement them. They will often be lifestyle advice, not much dissimilar to now. The big difference, however, will be that it will be tailored to you. At present, everyone is suggested anything that is in any way suspected of being healthy: Everyone should exercise a lot, everyone should eat healthily, everyone should get enough sleep, and so on. This may make such general tips seem less binding to you personally, no more than an option you could stick to, but don't necessarily have to. In addition, you may also feel that the lifestyle changes to adhere to everything are too much work.

The difference in future Big Data-enabled lifestyle advice will be that it will be highly individualized based on all your personal "omes", including your exposome. You will then be given a ranking of tips, and some tips may not be given at all. For example, if you have no predisposition to severe lung disease, fewer tips would be given to avoid air pollution or respiratory infections; if you have an extremely high risk for colorectal cancer, on the other hand, you would be constantly reminded to eat lots of fibre, little red meat, and to make your colonoscopy appointment on time; and if you have a genetic risk for the most severe late effects of diabetes, you would be constantly reminded to get enough exercise; your nutrition app would watch your sugar intake and monitor your weight. This makes the tips more relevant to you and sets in what behavioural theory calls protective motivation. It assumes that your motivation to protect—in this case, to prevent health problems—stems from a perceived threat to you personally, rather than generally, and a desire to avoid negative consequences for you.[13] This is reinforced by an increase in the perceived severity of a threat, vulnerability to that threat, and perceived effectiveness of behaviour change. Specific to IT systems, the *Technology Acceptance Model*[14] exists on perceived usefulness and perceived ease of use.

The most important question about wearables and preparedness in general is: what are you trying to achieve? What exactly is your goal and how do wearables and provisioning help you achieve it? This is where most preventive care programmes currently fail, as they make blanket offers that may have nothing to do with your motivations. Doctors can use motivational *interviewing techniques* to do this, which is rarely done at present due to time constraints. Apps can achieve this via clever algorithms and game-like interactions (gamification). However, with the *Internet of Medical Things*, some of your goals may not be achieved immediately. For example, if the goal is rather general or long-term such as "Improve my health status" or "Live healthier and longer", the effects may not be observed for years or decades. An effective app would then either visualize the danger to you through clear genetic risk evidence or steer you to focus on goals that are closer in time, but demonstrably in line with your long-term goal, and that you are confident you can achieve. Something called self-efficacy in psychology.[15]

Your Data

But you may have other reservations that need to be taken very seriously. Even if you are willing to be a pioneer in sharing your data with others, and even if you are convinced that this is indeed for your own good and that you can derive some benefit from the analysis of your exposome and your other "omes", the nagging question remains, "How secure is my data, anyway?" Central to participating in the Internet of Medical Things will be privacy for you and everyone else. Without being able to guarantee the privacy of

[13] Floyd DL et al. (2000) A meta-analysis of research on protection motivation theory. Journal of Applied Social Psychology 30:407–429

[14] Davis FD et al. (1989) User acceptance of computer technology: a comparison of two theoretical models. Management Science 35:982–1003

[15] Martin J (2004) Self-regulated learning, social cognitive theory, and agency. Educational Psychologist 39:135–145

personalized patient data, the exposome and the self-tracking methods it requires would not stand a chance. The key technical solution here will be where the data is stored. Many current data strategies are based on cloud computing, i.e., the collection and centralization of all data in large data centres, which, moreover, are often not located in Europe and thus escape potentially stricter regulation.

By 2025, the trend towards data centralization will be massively reversed—at least within the EU: 80 per cent of all data in smart devices will then be able to remain with the user because it is already sufficiently processed there—i.e. not in the centre, but at the edge (edge computing). This means that your raw data will then never have to be transferred to the cloud. In such a functioning, secure Internet of Medical Things, aggregated data (features) from one or better multiple users will instead be passed on for analysis, ideally with blockchain protection. That is, any sharing of the data with a third-party unknown to you is precluded because they have not received blockchain clearance from you. Machine learning algorithms then must adapt to this. They no longer have the entire data set at their disposal, but only aggregated data from multiple users, within which the individual, however, is no longer identifiable. This makes one of the biggest potential weaknesses, data protection, much less relevant for the exposome.

Financial Incentives

The *Internet of Medical Things* can also help alleviate one of the main problems in the insurance industry, namely, information asymmetries, i.e. one party has information that the other party lacks. For example, an insurance company covers individuals but is unable to estimate and monitor their health status, except for bills paid. In countries where health insurance is not compulsory, insurance companies thus set a price equal to the average cost of insurance. This in turn leads to adverse selection, as only people with high health costs will be willing to purchase such insurance. People with health costs lower than the insurance premium, on the other hand, will not be willing to do so, as they will get a negative "return" on the insurance for themselves. This is circumvented in the case of statutory health insurance by making it compulsory or state-run healthcare. As a result, healthy people co-finance unhealthy ones. If being "unhealthy" is due to fateful genetic risks, this follows our value principle of a solidarity community. In principle, two financial incentives would be conceivable to encourage behaviour that is conducive to good health: bonus or malus.[16] A malus system seems difficult to enforce, unlike a bonus system, especially since it already exists in some countries. Bonuses would be conceivable, for example, simply for releasing your data. For your measures to maintain a healthy lifestyle, for example, attending sports courses or participating in smoking cessation and regular health checks, many health insurance companies offer benefits in kind or even bonus payments of up to several hundred euros a year. At present, however, all the lifestyle measures promoted are still too sweeping, i.e. *one-size-fits-all*, or everyone is recommended everything. As soon as enough of your data and that of many other insured persons is available and has been analysed, such subsidies or bonuses can be awarded in a much more targeted manner. Then you will no longer be recommended (and subsidized) every possible health measure that is possible, but only those that fit your risk profile. For example, you will receive a bonus if your body mass index and blood pressure are within the normal range despite your risk of diabetes and heart attack. On the other hand, those who do not release their data or lead an unhealthy lifestyle and fall ill through their own fault and despite intensive coaching would at least be excluded from bonuses. In this way, our established solidarity principle would be retained, but adapted.

Certainly, there will be a need for discussion on individual lifestyle and expectations to be still fully covered by a solidaric healthcare system. In this context, it is a frequent misconception or "excuse" that those who live unhealthily, e.g. smoke, die earlier and cost the health system less. However, smoking causes far greater economic damage than many assume. For example, the direct costs for treatment, care, and rehabilitation as well as indirect costs for lost production due to sick leave, incapacity to work, or reduced earning capacity amount to 34 billion euros annually.[17] Another example, two insured people have the same healthy lifestyle, but one of them engages in high-risk sports. Or what about someone who lives in the city and not in the country, or who drives a car all the time and never rides a bike, or who lives as a single person? Or what about someone who refused to get vaccinated against COVID-19 and ends up for several weeks in intensive care? Of course, no one should be denied health benefits, but missing out on bonuses due to an unhealthy lifestyle could provide a strong monetary incentive to both share one's data and live healthier with targeted measures.

---

[16] Perloff RM (2016) The Dynamics of Persuasion: Communication and Attitudes in the Twenty-First Century, Routledge, New York, 648 p., https://doi.org/10.4324/9781315657714, eBook ISBN 9781315657714

[17] Adams M & Effertz T (2009) The cost of smoking for health care and the national economy in Germany, dkfz, https://www.zahnarzt-dr-jochum.de/pdf/Die_Kosten_des_Rauchens.pdf

Well, this is a discussion for the future, has no "right or wrong", and highly depends on a country's society and its desire for solidarity versus "each on his own".

Nevertheless, you will or should decide whether you generate your "ome" data and once you have it whether you share this data and with whom, e.g. with your health insurance for possible bonuses. But apart from bonuses, the key question is how do you get from all this data to something tangible that will be useful to you, and over your whole life span? How can conclusions be drawn from your data and that of millions of users that then become relevant to you personally in a tailored way? One thing is for sure, no doctor could ever pull that off for even one patient, let alone all the patients cared for. No human could do this, but ...

16

Big Data Medicine

Every minute of the day, approximately 3 petabytes (in bytes, that would be a number with 15 zeros!) of internet data are generated. Considering the exposome, many of them can be declared as health-related data in a narrower or broader sense.[1] Only computers provide a solution for the analysis of these gigantic amounts of data for the purpose of individual diagnoses.

The classic term for this is artificial intelligence and was introduced in 1956 by John McCarthy at a legendary conference at Dartmouth College, New Hampshire, USA. Artificial Intelligence means that machines simulate learning as well as other features of human intelligence. Logic Theorist was the first artificial intelligence programme capable of proving dozens of mathematical theorems. However, the foundation for this was laid 20 years earlier by the British mathematician Alan Turing, who proved that a computing machine programme can execute learning processes broken down into individual steps. Technically more correct than the term artificial intelligence is therefore the term machine learning, since we are not dealing with intelligence in a human sense, but mathematics and statistics. Machine learning has already demonstrated amazing abilities in pattern recognition in huge datasets and perfectly solves text-, language-, or image-based classification and clustering problems. The algorithms excel especially at a previously well-defined single task, for example, playing chess, even though the actual IQ is zero.

Many of us have been using machine learning in our everyday lives with voice assistants such as Apple's "Siri", Microsoft's "Cortana" software, and Amazon's Echo with the "Alexa" voice service, e-mail spam filters, when we are

---

[1] Data Never Sleeps 7.0 (2019) DOMO, https://www.domo.com/learn/data-never-sleeps-7

© The Author(s), under exclusive license to Springer Nature Switzerland AG 2022
H. H. H. W. Schmidt, *The end of medicine as we know it - and why your health has a future*,
https://doi.org/10.1007/978-3-030-95293-8_16

presented with purchase recommendations or music tracks on the Internet, or when using face recognition in our photo software or on Facebook. The process of creating these programmes is basically always the same. As in school, the first step is a (machine) learning process for a problem or a class of problems, based on which computational processes or rules of action (so-called algorithms) are developed and, in a second step, validated to ensure the programme can solve new problems of the same kind. Intelligent behaviour is thus only simulated. When combining human intelligence and machine learning, so-called augmented intelligence is formed, where algorithms focus on a support role and are intended to enhance, not replace, human processing, perception, and work.

Very early on, in the early 1970s, such a machine learning programme reached medical application. The computer-aided expert system MYCIN helped doctors to treat patients with infections by pooling current expertise through formulas, rules, and a knowledge base.[2] Presently, there are more than 300,000 health apps in different app stores available, with more than 200 added daily.[3] There appears to be at least one app for every possible health problem or question. Mostly these are still more like wellness apps, although the number of apps for health management and genuine patient care is growing rapidly and now accounts for 40% of all health-related apps. All machine learning-based technologies and apps registered by the US Food and Drug Administration since 2016 have been registered on an open-access, continuously updated database since 2020.[4] But how do they work?

How Does Machine Learning Work?

Machine learning gives computers a general ability to learn without being specifically programmed for a task.[5] If one wants to write a programme that can recognize cats in photographs, machine learning is ideal, because how should one design rules by which such a programme should operate? How can you recognize a cat in a photo? You might think, "Well, two ears, two eyes,

[2] Shortliffe E (1976) Computer-Based Medical Consultations: MYCIN, Elsevier, 264 p., eBook ISBN: 9780444601735.

[3] Aitken M et al. (2017) The growing value of digital health: evidence and impact on human health and the healthcare system. IQVIA Institute for Human Data Science, https://www.iqvia.com/institute/reports/the-growing-value-of-digital-health

[4] https://medicalfuturist.com/fda-approved-ai-based-algorithms/

[5] Samuel AL (2000) Some studies in machine learning using the game of checkers. IBM J Res Dev 44:206–226

four legs and so on", but how should you define those uniquely? What is an "ear" to a computer programme that only "sees" thousands of pixels in a photo? A machine learning algorithm is just fed image after image, some of which show cats, and preferably these images are manually annotated by humans to ensure that the images the programme knows and learns from contain cats. The more such annotated images the algorithm sees, the better it will get at recognizing cats even in new images. It won't understand what a cat even is, but it will certainly recognize what we think are cats in photos. Machine learning has many subtypes and combined methods. The three main subtypes are supervised learning, unsupervised learning, and learning by reinforcement. In addition, there is a fourth, extremely advanced method, deep learning. To better understand the differences, let's imagine a situation of teacher (developer) and student (programme).

In supervised learning, teachers know what they want to teach the student, provide the expected answer, and the child learns to accomplish the task. It is used when we can precisely define the task and we want the algorithm to learn, based on data we already have. For example, the programme learns using a dataset of medical records of group A patients with family history, lab values, and other details along with diagnosis. In another set, the same data is from group B patients but without their diagnosis. A supervised model now learns from the patients in group A to also assign the correct diagnosis to the patients in group B.

In unsupervised learning, the teacher does not influence how the child learns, but observes the conclusions the student draws from solving the task. It is ultimately like learning without a teacher. We take from the above example the group B of patients with different datasets but without their diagnoses. The model now attempts to group (cluster) the patients based on similar attributes, such as symptoms, lab values, age, and gender. As a result, we might have new associations that we did not notice or consider before. For example, one example is the disease clusters from the *diseasome* that we talked about in Chap. 10. Thus, because of, for example, common risk genes, diseases that make symptoms in different organs and are treated by different specialists belong together, so we couldn't see their underlying commonalities before. So, at the beginning, we just make few rules and let the algorithm learn by itself and do not change the algorithm based on the results.

In reinforcing learning, teachers know what they want to teach the child but do not give step-by-step instructions on how the student should learn. Instead, the teacher only provides feedback after the task has been completed and asks the student to develop his or her own strategy based on the results that the teacher has rewarded. For example, the model starts by performing the task knowing only some basic rules, and after successfully or unsuccessfully completing the task, the teacher intervenes to get it to use the successful strategy more. In this way, the programme can build its own experience as it performs the task more and more independently. It is like how we train dogs. When the dog is performing or trying to perform a task, we only give it a treat when it has performed it well.

Finally, in Deep Learning, it is possible to analyse much more complex datasets from images and videos to the point of a kind of human reasoning. While having similar functions to machine learning, these programmes have a special structure of multiple layers of artificial neural networks, inspired by the network of the human brain. The advantage is that they can learn more complex tasks but need more data and more time to train. Then, however, they can process images, sound, and other high-dimensional data. In doing so, they create their own rules and strategies without any human help ahead of time. A machine learning programme can turn on the light when we say the word "dark"; a deep learning model would learn over time to do so, even if we say, "I can't see" or "It's dark here". Even its developers don't understand how deep learning concludes or what strategy it uses to solve a task. In the case of medical decisions, however, you might want to understand the decision-making processes or at least know on what basis a decision was made. In the case of these advanced algorithms, it seems that this won't be either very likely nor necessary if the predictions are correct. The most famous example of this method is how AlphaZero learned to become the best chess player or winner in any 2-player game within hours by playing millions of games against itself. Just the basic rules were entered, and the developers let the algorithm know when a game had been won.

For all these models, the larger the dataset on which the model learned, that is, the more images, texts, or other sources it has, the more accurate is the prediction of the algorithm. Thus, the problem of large "ome" datasets that we must deal with is also the solution or a necessity for machine learning. Tasks that are highly repetitive and involve quantifiable data benefit the most from machine learning in this regard. Some examples:

Babylon Health has launched an app that provides medical advice. It uses the patient's medical history and general medical knowledge. Patients provide their symptoms, which the app uses voice recognition to check against a database of diseases and suggest a course of action.[6] The medical start-up Sense.ly

---

[6] Lunden I (2020) Babylon Health is building an integrated, AI-based health app to serve a city of 300 K in England. Techcrunch, https://techcrunch.com/2020/01/22/babylon-health-is-building-an-integrated-ai-based-health-app-to-serve-a-city-of-300k-in-england

programmed Molly, a virtual nurse with a smiling face and pleasant voice. She helps patients monitor their health or manage illness between doctor visits.[7] In cardiology, apps are used to detect arrhythmias. In diabetology, apps support the management of blood glucose levels, and in ophthalmology, the early detection of diabetic damage to the retina. Other algorithms can detect as wide a range of diseases as medical specialists thus speeding up diagnoses, shortening waiting times, and optimizing drug therapy.[8] Emergency algorithms focus on acute care for patients with suspected head, spine, wrist, and chest injuries. During disasters or hospital overloads, such as in some countries during the Corona pandemic, triage programmes that can predict how serious or promising a patient's health condition is can identify those patients who are vulnerable and at high risk versus those who have no chance of survival.[9] Moreover, they are just like machines, i.e. always focused, never tired, they work around the clock and constantly use accumulated experience to improve themselves. The top two medical specialties with machine learning-based medical innovations are radiology and cardiology, with 72% and 14% of all devices and algorithms, respectively. Let's have a look at these trendsetters as they give us a glimpse into the future of AI in medicine.

Trendsetters Radiology and Oncology

In radiology, where diagnosing diseases is based on imaging techniques, machine learning algorithms already perform as well as or slightly better than physicians.[10] For example, in the USA, early low-dose radiological lung cancer screening is recommended as it reduces mortality from bronchial carcinoma.[11] If a suspicious observation is made, the diagnosis is clarified with a lung biopsy. Screening is controversial, however, because even experienced radiologists can err in their interpretation of the images, leading to a high number of false-positive findings. This not only worries patients unnecessarily and incurs

[7] Ricci M (2017) Sensely and Mayo Clinic take virtual nurse one step further. Pharmaphorum, https://pharmaphorum.com/news/sensely-mayo-clinic-develop-virtual-doctor

[8] Benjamens S et al. (2020) The state of artificial intelligence-based FDA-approved medical devices and algorithms: an online database. Npj Digit Med 3:118, https://doi.org/10.1038/s41746-020-00324-0

[9] Kang DY et al. (2020) Artificial intelligence algorithm to predict the need for critical care in prehospital emergency medical services. Scand J Trauma Resusc Emerg Med 28:17

[10] Liu X et al. (2019) A comparison of deep learning performance against healthcare professionals in detecting diseases from medical imaging: a systematic review and meta-analysis. Lancet Digital Health 1:e271–97, https://doi.org/10.1016/S2589-7500(19)30123-2

[11] Ardila D et al. (2019) End-to-end lung cancer screening with three-dimensional deep learning on low-dose chest computed tomography. Nat Med 25:954–961, https://doi.org/10.1038/s41591-019-0447-x

high costs but is dangerous to the patient as a lung biopsy is an extremely risky procedure. A Deep Learning algorithm developed by Google was therefore trained on 42,290 X-ray images of 14,851 smokers including 578, i.e. one in 25, who had a suspected lung cancer confirmed by biopsy. While the radiologist can only switch between about 100 two-dimensional slice images, the software can also generate and check the three-dimensional space, pixel by pixel. As always with machine learning, the software was first trained on a random sample, then "*tuned*" on a second independent sample, and finally came the acid test of diagnostic reliability in a third set, which the software had not yet seen. Surprisingly, the software scored a sensitivity of 95 and a specificity of 81%, whereas six experienced radiologists scored only 90% and 70%, respectively. This means that the software detects 5% more cases of lung cancer and gives 12% fewer false positives, prompting fewer unnecessary, dangerous lung biopsies. Such software is therefore ideally suited for screening and decision-making for or against a biopsy and a physician only needs to focus on the difficult cases. However, this and most other AI studies only analysed data retrospectively. It remains to be seen whether this new "deep learning plus doctor" approach also offers advantages in a forward-looking randomized study compared with the previous "doctor only" procedure and extends lifespan, as this is ultimately what matters for the smokers.

Another example is breast cancer, the most common cancer in women. Mammography is used for early detection, which is not only unpleasant, but also extremely strenuous for the radiologist, and thus errors can easily occur. Google Health has therefore developed a machine-learning algorithm that detects breast cancer more reliably than six experienced radiologists combined, reducing both false positives and false negatives.[12] It could reduce the radiologists' workload by 88%. After a learning phase, the software developed its own strategies for diagnosis and reviewed them regularly. 29,000 women were tested. Both the number of false-positive and false-negative findings were lower than those made by doctors, meaning Google Health detects breast cancers more timely and lowers the number of unnecessary biopsies and worrying women. Also, the software was eight times faster, so women don't have to wait as long for results. Of note, the software still has downside. It only tells that it has detected something, but not where—yet.

Imaging AI has also moved from macroscopy to microscopy where blood smears are stained and microscopically categorized to diagnose blood cancer (leukaemia). Specialist staff look for precursor forms of the white blood cells,

---

[12] McKinney SM et al. (2020) International evaluation of an AI system for breast cancer screening. Nature 577:89–94, https://doi.org/10.1038/s41586-019-1799-6

which are normally only found in bone marrow but not in blood. A deep-learning neural network trained with nearly 20,000 frames was able to do this independently on blood smears from 100 patients and did it at least as well as the professionals.[13] Another increasingly common blood test is called "liquid biopsy". It detects in the blood thousands of proteins, which can be used to predict 11 common health disorders,[14] or DNA that stems from decaying cancer cells.[15] Forma Grail spectacularly announced a blood test that could detect 20 cancers early and with a very low false-positive rate (specificity 99%), which is still the problem with many other tests. When a cancer was detected, the test also correctly identified where the cancer was in the body (i.e. the tissue of origin) in 97% of the cases. The test was most accurate for 12 particularly deadly cancers: anal, bladder, colon, oesophagus, head and neck, liver and bile duct, lung, lymphoma, ovarian, pancreatic, plasma cell, and stomach.[16]

Machine Learning Pervades all of Medicine

Although radiology and oncology have been the trendsetters in testing and using machine learning, machine learning is gradually permeating all of medicine, dermatology, cardiology, ophthalmology, and paediatrics. In dermatology, an overlooked black skin cancer (melanoma) can mean death for a patient. Software has now learned to distinguish between an atypical but benign mole and a melanoma. The software was trained on 2169 confirmed melanomas and 18,566 moles, and then competed with 157 dermatologists from 12 university skin clinics.[17] Physicians and the software were each presented with 100 images, including 20 melanomas and 80 moles, to decide whether to perform a biopsy because of suspected melanoma. The dermatologists achieved a mean sensitivity of 74% and a specificity of 60%; the software,

[13] Matek C et al. (2019) Human-level recognition of blast cells in acute myeloid leukaemia with convolutional neural networks. Nat Mach Intell 1:538–544, https://doi.org/10.1038/s42256-019-0101-9

[14] Williams SA et al. (2019) Plasma protein patterns as comprehensive indicators of health. Nat Med 25:1851–1857, https://doi.org/10.1038/s41591-019-0665-2

[15] Liu MC et al. (2020) Sensitive and specific multi-cancer detection and localization using methylation signatures in cell-free DNA. Annals of Oncology 31:745–759, https://doi.org/10.1016/j.annonc.2020.02.011

[16] Ofman JJ (2020) GRAIL and the quest for earlier multi-cancer detection. Nature, https://media.nature.com/original/magazine-assets/d42473-020-00079-y/d42473-020-00079-y.pdf

[17] Brinker TJ et al. (2019) Deep learning outperformed 136 of 157 dermatologists in a head-to-head dermoscopic melanoma image classification task. Eur J of Cancer 113:47–54, https://doi.org/10.1016/j.ejca.2019.04.001

the same sensitivity and higher specificity of 87% and would thus avoid many false-positive results, i.e. moles being unnecessarily biopsied. Only six dermatologists were superior to the software, 14 were equal, and the remaining 137 were inferior. Of course, the app cannot—yet—replace a dermatology specialist, who must be able to distinguish—apart from melanoma—also between more than 100 possible other diagnoses during a physical exam, some of them very rare, some barely discernible in an image. Nevertheless, in the specific question of whether a biopsy should be performed for a suspicious skin change, such software will obviously play a role in the future. However, for 26 common skin, hair, and nail conditions, Google recently announced its entry into this market with an AI-based tool that helps people to diagnose themselves or non-dermatologist physicians to diagnose more accurately just as a dermatologist.[18]

The risk of cardiovascular disease is currently determined according to the guidelines of cardiological societies,[19] which, however, are limited to only a few simple factors, age, cholesterol levels, lipids, blood pressure, smoking, diabetes, and heart attack in the family. Alternatively, four different algorithms were trained on data from nearly 700 family practices in the UK. Risk prediction was learned on 295,267 patients and tested on 82,989 others. All four algorithms were superior to the *American Heart Association* and *American College of Cardiology* score. A neural network achieved the best result: it correctly predicted 8% more cardiovascular events while reducing the number of false alarms by 2%. That would have treated 355 more patients who had otherwise gone untreated. How the algorithms arrived at their decisions, however, is unclear, but methods to identify the decisive data and values are developed.[20]

In ophthalmology, the diagnosis of corneal diseases needs to occur in time to prevent the need for corneal transplants. Currently, the cells in cornea are counted from microscopic images, a time-consuming procedure as the boundaries between cells are difficult to detect, which only a few experts can do.

---

[18] Liu Y et al. (2020) A deep learning system for differential diagnosis of skin diseases. Nat Med 26, 900–908, https://doi.org/10.1038/s41591-020-0842-3; Jain A et al. (2021) Development and Assessment of an Artificial Intelligence–Based Tool for Skin Condition Diagnosis by Primary Care Physicians and Nurse Practitioners in Teledermatology Practices. JAMA Netw Open 4:e217249, https://doi.org/10.1001/jamanetworkopen.2021.7249

[19] Assmann G et al. (2002) Simple scoring scheme for calculating the risk of acute coronary events based on the 10-year follow-up of the prospective cardiovascular Münster (PROCAM) study. Circulation. 105:310–315, https://doi.org/10.1161/hc0302.102575, Erratum (2002) Circulation 105:900, PMID: 11804985, PROCAM score calculator: http://www.scores.bnk.de/procam.html

[20] Weng SF et al. (2017) Can machine-learning improve cardiovascular risk prediction using routine clinical data? PLOS One, 12:e0174944, https://doi.org/10.1371/journal.pone.0174944

Now, a self-learning neural network software can take over this task.[21] The results matched measurements counted "by hand" but the software did so within a few seconds. Almost all images that could not be evaluated were marked as such. A more advanced diagnostic programme that can diagnose about 50 ophthalmological conditions is being developed by DeepMind, a British subsidiary of Google, with a prototype already having approval in the USA to scan retinas of diabetics.[22]

Equally far into the field of expertise of an entire specialist is a machine learning programme that can diagnose a range of diseases in children and outperformed junior paediatricians. The software learned from the electronic medical records of 567,498 paediatric patients with over a hundred million different pieces of information.[23] By comparison, a paediatrician might have contact with a few thousand patients over the course of his or her entire professional life. At first, the programme was only supposed to determine which organ systems were affected, such as gastrointestinal, pulmonary, nervous, and so on, and then make specific diagnoses, such as asthma, mononucleosis, three-day fever, influenza, and chicken pox. How it did that remained unclear. The software then went into competition with paediatricians, those with less than 8 years of experience, and more experienced colleagues to diagnose 11,926 patients. Among junior doctors, the software was more accurate, both for common conditions such as influenza but also for dangerous or life-threatening conditions such as an acute asthma attack or meningitis.

Apple Watch and Smartphone

With respect to self-monitoring, the Apple Watch has become a lighthouse project and induced a conceptual transition of a fitness monitor to a serious medical device that detects health risks and initiates further testing and treatment. The *Apple Heart Study*[24] focused on atrial fibrillation, a serious risk for

[21] Daniel MC et al. (2019) Automated segmentation of the corneal endothelium in a large set of 'real-world' specular microscopy images using the U-Net architecture. Sci Rep 9:4752, https://doi.org/10.1038/s41598-019-41034-2

[22] De Fauw J et al. (2018) Clinically applicable deep learning for diagnosis and referral in retinal disease. Nat Med 24:1342–1350, https://doi.org/10.1038/s41591-018-0107-6; Arcadu F et al. (2019) Deep learning algorithm predicts diabetic retinopathy progression in individual patients. Npj Digit Med. 2:92, https://doi.org/10.1038/s41746-019-0172-3

[23] Liang H et al. (2019) Evaluation and accurate diagnoses of pediatric diseases using artificial intelligence. Nat Med 25:433–438, https://doi.org/10.1038/s41591-018-0335-9

[24] Perez MV et al. (2019) Large-Scale Assessment of a Smartwatch to Identify Atrial Fibrillation. N Engl J Med 381:1909–1917, https://doi.org/10.1056/NEJMoa1901183

heart failure, heart attack, and stroke.[25] Initially, many patients have only intermittent atrial fibrillation. Thus, a standard ten-second ECG at the doctor's office with 12 leads is likely to miss atrial fibrillation if it was not occurring at that moment. Undetected atrial fibrillation is therefore common, and the few alternative effective continuous screening methods are time and resource intensive.[26] The Apple Watch has enabled wearable ECG technology to detect heart rhythm and aid in the detection of atrial fibrillation.[27] Irregular rhythms are first identified by the watch's optical sensor and interpreted by an algorithm. In 419,000 participants who owned an iPhone and an Apple Watch, rhythm patterns suggestive of atrial fibrillation were detected in 0.5% of participants, leading to more conventional monitoring with a mailed ECG patch.[28] In those who returned the patch, atrial fibrillation was documented in just over one-third of the participants. Most of the participants were younger than 40, and only 6% were 65 or older. Not exactly the ideal age profile for a study of atrial fibrillation and in the true age group at risk, the prevalence may be higher than the 0.1–0.2%.

Another serious cardiovascular risk is elevated blood pressure. This can occur permanently, but also only under stress, e.g. in the presence of a doctor (white-coat hypertension), or only at night and not when tested at a doctor's office and is thus missed. To not overdiagnose or underdiagnose hypertension, it would be ideal to be able to seamlessly measure blood pressure every now and then in between. But almost no one will have a blood pressure monitor with them all the time. However, with the OptiBP smartphone app, this seems to be possible in the future.[29] It was tested in comparison with the gold standard, the blood pressure measurement at the doctor's office with a stethoscope. By using the smartphone's optics, the pulse wave was analysed in the fingertip and predicted blood pressure with high precision. Both studies represent breakthroughs in simple, broad medical screening, and we will see more and more wearable, implantable, and even ingestible devices to detect,

[25] Chugh SS et al. (2014) Worldwide epidemiology of atrial fibrillation: a Global Burden of Disease 2010 Study. Circulation 129:837–47; Gallagher C et al. (2019) Increasing trends in hospitalisations due to atrial fibrillation in Australia from 1993 to 2013. Heart 105:1358–1363, https://doi.org/10.1136/heartjnl-2018-314471

[26] Sanna T et al. (2014) Cryptogenic stroke and underlying atrial fibrillation. N Engl J Med 370:2478–86

[27] Dorr M et al. (2019) The WATCH AF trial: smartwatches for detection of atrial fibrillation. JACC Clin Electrophysiol 5:199–208; Kotecha D et al. (2018) European Society of Cardiology smartphone and tablet applications for patients with atrial fibrillation and their healthcare providers. Europace 20:225–33

[28] Vivalink, https://www.vivalnk.com/products/medical-wearable-sensors/continuous-ecg-monitor

[29] Schoettker P et al. (2020) Blood pressure measurements with the OptiBP smartphone app validated against reference auscultatory measurements. Sci Rep 10:17827, https://doi.org/10.1038/s41598-020-74955-4

monitor, and treat disease.[30] Furthermore, the *Apple Heart Study* stands out as an example of reverse development, i.e. no longer linear from basic science to preclinical research to step-wise clinical trials and then to the patient or consumer, but starting right away with the consumer or patient as the direct and central interaction partner in all phases of research and development. And let's think one step further: iPhone, iPad, and Mac users know when something doesn't work on their device, they make an appointment at an Apple Store to get it fixed. If a new pilot programme from Apple in the USA, codenamed "Casper", comes to fruition, one will soon be able to make appointments for whatever health needs in company-owned clinics treated by Apple-employed doctors. But even if not, this new method will be generally available and thus potentially enable mobile health diagnostics (mHealth) at a global level in a highly affordable manner, overcoming the wealth gap in health.

Machine Learning Overcomes Wealth Gap

Examples of how machine learning can overcome the health-wealth gap are the early detection of cancer and tuberculosis. Cervical cancer has increased in the last 30 years and is the fourth most common cancer in women. Here, early screening is crucial as it may prevent invasive carcinoma stages or their precursors. However, in countries with poorer early detection options procedures such as cell-based microscopic screening are conducted less frequently. If the technology or expertise is not available locally, the cervix can be photographed, even by a non-physician, and these images are submitted to a physician for interpretation. Now, a study conducted in Costa Rica showed that digitized images can be automatically analysed my machine learning software to detect pre-cancerous lesions with a precision that outperformed a doctor and was also better than the microscopic examination of a cell smear.[31] For countries with lower screening standards, machine learning assisted screening offers the advantage of low training requirements and the use of only a mobile phone or a simple camera.

Every year, about 1.4 million people die from tuberculosis. Detecting tuberculosis on a chest X-ray is difficult even for experienced radiologists. Countries with a high incidence of tuberculosis, such as India, Indonesia, the Philippines, and Pakistan, often lack trained radiologists. To overcome this

[30] Sim I (2019) Mobile devices and health. N Engl J Med, 381:956–68, doi: 10.1056/NEJMe1913980

[31] Hu L et al. (2019) An Observational Study of Deep Learning and Automated Evaluation of Cervical Images for Cancer Screening. Journal of the National Cancer Institute, 111:923–932, https://doi.org/10.1093/jnci/djy225

gap, Google developed and trained two neural networks, both variants of classical machine learning. When both algorithms were combined, their sensitivity to detect tuberculosis was high, and in only just under 10% of cases their results did not match. Only in those cases, an experienced radiologist was needed to resolve these disputes and make the correct diagnosis. This hybrid diagnostic strategy, in which first the two artificial neural networks clarify 90% of the cases and then a radiologist needs to evaluate only the remaining 10% of disputed images, ensures a near-perfect result. But also, radiologists in industrialized countries benefit from being assisted by the software, as tuberculosis has become a very rare diagnosis in those countries and radiologists consequently lack the experience to detect it. Obviously, such software can also be adapted to other X-ray diagnoses. These two examples, early detection of cervix cancer and high throughput, precision tuberculosis detection with a tenth of human input shows that the use of machine learning can help overcome the impact of wealth disparities in healthcare. However, if 90% of the diagnosis is done by an algorithm, how will this affect the doctor-patient relationship?

The New Doctor-Patient Relationship

The shift from doctors making decisions on their own to machine algorithms as the first instance affects not only every doctor in terms of diagnosis and decision-making, but also your role as patient, your relationship with healthcare providers, and the healthcare system. Will digitization and machine learning algorithms give doctors superpowers or make them partially redundant? In between. It will have massive impacts and change a lot of the current procedures—to your benefit as a patient. Whereas in 2021 you still had to rely exclusively on the individual competence and experience of your doctor treating you, in 2031 you will be supported by your electronic health or patient record, your digital twin, and a massive medical database of all digital twins inquired by different machine learning algorithms for different medical questions. You will thus already be pre-diagnosed when seeing your doctor. The diagnosis, your treatment, and the outcome are in turn registered in your digital twin but also in the same mega medical database from which you initially benefited. Thereby your patient record helps to refine subsequent diagnoses and therapeutic decisions and so forth; one big self-improving medical evidence and knowledge cloud.

Ultimately, digitization will make our healthcare system more efficient and faster, safer by reduce human error, and achieve better overall outcomes for patients, no matter where they are treated or by whom. That means even in countries or remote locations that don't have the resources of a high-end university hospital, such as a rural clinic or a less experienced doctor or even a non-trained first responder. Whether medical algorithms or robots will one day operate independently, i.e. even without a medical doctor interfering, I cannot yet imagine for the near future. However, already today, we ride in a suburban train without a driver. On the other hand, would you fly in an airplane without a human pilot? Would you drive in a taxi without a human driver? Probably not yet. That means that there will still be limits, but they will continue to be shifted. Your biggest concern will be "What if the AI makes a mistake?" What if an AI misses a diagnosis or an autonomous surgical robot injures a patient? Would parents accept a computer rather than a doctor deciding on their child's treatment? Who will be held liable if a robot or a machine algorithm errs? But how about the alternative, the doctor?

Algorithms Make Mistakes, So Do Doctors

Doctors make mistakes too, e.g. both with respect to diagnosis and prescriptions. Each year, just in the USA about 12 million patients are affected by medical diagnostic errors. About half of those errors could be "potentially harmful", and up to 80,000 people die annually from complications resulting from wrong diagnoses.[32] Prescription writing is another common source of medical error. Each year, in the UK more than 237 million medication errors occur[33] claiming—conservatively calculated—at least 1700 lives. Worst-case estimates, however, assume up to 22,303 lost human lives per year. In countries such as Germany prescriptions are still issued on paper, which prevents digital post hoc analysis and tracking, but there is nothing to suggest that the figures would be any different. With respect to the distribution of the severity of the cases, the outpatient sector is the main problem, rather than inpatients. The two most frequently mis-prescribed groups of drugs are anti-inflammatory painkillers such as acetylsalicylic acid and the so-called blood thinners, both of which can cause fatal gastrointestinal bleeding. Other drugs where mistakes are frequently made are those used to treat epilepsy, diuretics, asthma sprays

---

[32] Singh H et al. (2014) The frequency of diagnostic errors in outpatient care: estimations from three large observational studies involving US adult populations BMJ Quality & Safety 23:727–731; Saber Tehrani AS et al. (2013) 25-Year summary of US malpractice claims for diagnostic errors 1986–2010: an analysis from the National Practitioner Data Bank BMJ Quality & Safety 22:672–680.

[33] Elliott RA et al. (2019) Economic analysis of the prevalence and clinical and economic burden of medication error in England. BMJ Quality & Safety 010206, https://doi.org/10.1136/bmjqs-2019-010206

containing cortisone, and drugs against cardiac arrhythmia. However, the current consensus is that a medical professional can be held liable, but this is only the case if the doctor uses an intervention wrongly or outside of its approval (*off-label*) or despite substantial professional doubt about its validity. In all other cases, liability falls on the creators and the companies behind the technology. Despite knowing that medical doctors make many mistakes too and liability is limited, we will need a lot of time to trust medical algorithms. Similarly, we will trust an autonomous car only after we have convinced ourselves of how it reacts in situations, we are familiar with or that it makes similar decisions to us in an emergency. It will take at least that much time for patients and medical professionals to trust machine algorithms making medical diagnoses and decisions.

Where Are the Hurdles?

To be used in healthcare, it will take longer for machine learning than in other industries because of the risks. If Amazon tries a new algorithm that doesn't work, the company could lose money. In medicine, people could die. Amazon views AI in healthcare as a frontier worth exploring and launched HealthLake a year after releasing Transcribe Medical, a service designed to transcribe medical speech for clinical staff in primary care settings compliant with the Health Insurance Portability and Accountability Act to ingest, store, query, and analyse health data. HealthLake leverages machine learning to extract medical information from unstructured data and organizes, indexes, and stores that information in chronological order as part of Amazon Web Services. The service intelligently enriches these data with standardized labels for medications, conditions, and diagnoses.

One potential barrier to adoption by medical professionals is the fear that AI will replace them. Indeed, highly repetitive and data-driven tasks are likely to be heavily impacted by automation. Moreover, routine tasks such as documentation, filling out forms, scheduling appointments, asking standard questions when a patient is admitted, and making routine diagnoses will be eliminated. Thus, AI makes time for other medical tasks that have taken a backseat in the caseload-driven years to come more to the forefront: face-to-face contact time, empathy, and compassionate care. Thus, those medical professionals who use AI will replace those who do not. So, the debate should not be about whether machine learning takes away the art of medicine, but what we gain through this synergy by allowing doctors to spend more time with patients, more than ever before. No doubt, in some cases, workers will need to be redeployed and retrained, a potentially difficult task when there is a mismatch between new technologies and their requirements and skillsets.

Another barrier is the global heterogeneity in disease prevalence. For example, the paediatric machine algorithm that has been developed in China is based on disease prevalence, e.g. hand-foot-and-mouth disease, and basic parameters, e.g. skin colour, eye shape, and hair colour, that differ from Europe. The Chinese software therefore needs to be re-trained and validated on national datasets. In doing so, the non-uniform and often not yet digital patient records would make this attempt a failure. Thus, the entire process would need to be re-done from scratch. Alternatively, algorithms that will prevail in the long term are those that can easily adapt to new regional and administrative environments, as well as different disease prevalence.

Another barrier is understanding. Many algorithms can do things better than humans, but we don't understand the decision-making criteria. Do we need a different medical school to train doctors in this, or a different health professional altogether? If a machine does things that a human can't, what exactly is the machine supposed to show for us to understand? How should a dog, which can smell much better than we can, explain to a human how or what it smells? We simply don't have that ability. Instead of waiting until algorithms can explain themselves and fully, we should remember our present inaccuracies, errors, and inefficiencies in medicine. That's why Part I of this book was so important. Most machine algorithms have a precision of 90% or more, meaning 9 out of 10 patients got the right diagnosis or therapy. Remember the hypertension example with a NNT of 100, which meant that only one patient out of every 100 treated had a benefit from their blood pressure medication, i.e. prevented heart attack or stroke. This represents a precision of 1% versus 90% by algorithm. So where is the greater risk or the greater need to understand?

Another barrier is our grotesquely non-digital in healthcare. Therefore, machine learning helped us so little in the COVID-19 pandemic. Think of how restaurants asked people to write their names, faxes from health departments to national health institutions, the many months it took to design Corona apps that were useful for pretty much nothing because everything that could have been used to track infected people was turned off for data security reasons. In idle mode of our smart phones, Google queries instead 40 of our data per hour. In active use, it's even more than 90. Fourteen of those 40 queries per hour are explicitly for location.[34] Moreover, regulation of these

---

[34] https://www.basicthinking.de/blog/2018/08/29/daten-pro-stunde-google/

technologies is lagging their exponential growth as agencies lack the highly qualified staff to be able set standards on the fly.

A final potential barrier is data transparency and data security. Here, an evolved form of machine learning is federated learning[35] emphasizing the use of decentralized data obviating the need to centralize sensitive data in the cloud in centres one cannot be sure about. Instead, the data always remain with the medical practices, hospitals, or your personal devices. Despite this decentralization, one can still work with the aggregated datasets. The security of the data remains—as it does now—your responsibility or that of your doctor or hospital. You also determine via blockchain keys who may use your data, and this in a way that can be revoked at any time. Thus:

- Accepting that we do not fully understand AI.
- Embracement of AI by medical professionals without fear of being replaced.
- Commitment of patients to comprehensive digitalization, i.e. their digital twin.
- Global adaptability and tailored AI solutions.
- A high degree of data safety technology.

are all essential ingredients to finally start using Big Data, our "omes", and Systems Medicine to their fullest potential and begin healing instead of just treating chronically. After decades of "Trust me, I'm a doctor", it's now also "Trust me, I'm an AI".

---

[35] McMahan HB et al. (2017) Proceedings of the 20th International Conference on Artificial Intelligence and Statistics (AISTATS) Fort Lauderdale, Florida, USA. JMLR: W&CP 54, http://proceedings.mlr.press/v54/mcmahan17a/mcmahan17a.pdf

17

Healed

Let's go back to my earlier car-in-the-workshop example. What was it again, back in the day? Suddenly, your car's engine wasn't pulling right. Once you even stalled on a hill. And now you were at your regular little garage. They had fixed something, replaced a few parts, but tell you when you pick it up that you'll have to come back every 3 months from now on to check on it and probably fix something again. And so, it was. You were in the shop quite a bit, and your car never really ran that great since. It was kind of chronically "sick".

But now—with Systems Medicine and Big Data—everything is different. Your car is driving perfectly fine, causing no problems whatsoever. Suddenly a warning light comes on and your smartphone app beeps, your exhaust system is about to be damaged. Your car still isn't having any problems, but you trust the Data. So, a few days later you drive to your now fully digitalized garage, their analysis computer is hooked up, and wham, the answer is there: the catalytic converter has a manufacturing problem that shows up after a while in all catalytic converters with that serial number, effectively a "catalytic converter mutant". By the way, your smartphone had informed the garage beforehand, so the new correct catalytic converter (without "mutation") is already ready, immediately replaced, and on it goes. Your car has not just been treated. More has been done than just a repair, but like a faulty gene, a faulty component has been completely replaced.

It is the same with severe monogenetic diseases, i.e. diseases caused by the defect of a single gene. Just as with the catalytic converter with manufacturing defect being replaced, your in-built flaw, i.e. the genetic variant causing problems, is completely gone from your body. In both cases, you and your car have been "cured", not just "treated".

© The Author(s), under exclusive license to Springer Nature Switzerland AG 2022
H. H. H. W. Schmidt, *The end of medicine as we know it - and why your health has a future,*
https://doi.org/10.1007/978-3-030-95293-8_17

For more complex diseases, where not only one prominent gene but several genes are involved and none of these is important on its own or more detrimental than another, this type of gene therapy is less likely to be feasible. Repairing two or three genes may become an option, but more than three? I doubt it. These more complex diseases will also be cured rather than treated, but differently. Not by gene therapy. Here, numerous components of your car have minor manufacturing flaws that make the entire car overall not running so well. It may accelerate too hard, corner too extremely, or is more susceptible to rust. The solution here will then not be to replace all these slightly defective parts—that could easily be half the car—but to identify this risk in good time and then to act accordingly in terms of your driving style (lifestyle) and to always prevent the noticeable occurrence of problems by means of minor maintenance or care measures (e.g. a medicine). By knowing exactly where the weak points are and what behaviour could lead to damage to the car, you and your workshop can carry out maintenance and care in a targeted and preventive manner, so that the latent threat of damage to the car (our body) never occurs (never symptoms). This is also a kind of apparent healing instead of treating: because symptoms never occur, even if it is not possible to carry out a complete healing due to the many affected components (or genes).

How to Cure Complex Diseases

Some of today's "scourges of humanity" are complex diseases such as type 2 diabetes mellitus (a real pandemic), high blood pressure (the deadliest risk factor of all), and cancer will disappear or become controllable. However, they are far from being totally genetically defined. There is a large lifestyle component. Diabetes is the practical role model to explain this.

The incidence of diabetes, for example, is currently at a shocking level of 8–9% of the population. In the 1950s, type 2 diabetes was called adult-onset diabetes and affected about 1% of the population. Now teenagers have this form of diabetes, which required it to be renamed to type 2. Just for completeness, type 1 diabetes is different, poorly understood, probably an autoimmune disease and with respect to prevalence constant (although also at a slight increase). The difference between the 1% of type 2 diabetes in the 1950s and 8–9% today did not result from a massive population-wide increase in new gene variants, but solely from our behaviour and sometimes from not knowing about what healthy eating and lifestyle mean and how to easily apply them. Ignorance still costs too many years of life today. Once effective prevention is implemented in a new healthcare system, type 2 diabetes will drop back to 1% (the prevalence in the 1950s) simply through lifestyle coaching alone.[1] The current diabetes "pandemic" will then be forgotten. But what about the adult-onset diabetics, who will then remain. Most likely they do carry a genetic risk for diabetes even without pro-diabetic diet faults. However, within the next 10 years, these genetic risks will be known,[2] so that patients can be closely monitored from adulthood onwards and curative or preventive therapy initiated in time so that they will not experience their diabetes. The therapy will most likely involve highly specific, i.e. mechanism-based, drugs with few side effects—different drugs than used today, which merely lower blood glucose. Their risk will then be under control, and they will have a normal life expectancy.

In addition, unhealthy foods and additives such as sugar will be taxed as heavily as cigarettes, so they will be bought or used much less. And if they are still bought or used, those taxes will go to health care. Your smartwatch, your smartphone, and even your toilet will measure whether your lifestyle changes are bearing fruit. Your health insurance company (we won't call it health insurance anymore) will give you a bonus and a voucher for a gym as a reward. That's money better spent than investing tenfold later in treating your diabetic kidney failure, years of dialysis treatment, or a kidney transplant. In general, contributions for health insurance will have become less and will hardly be a factor in non-wage costs.

Similarly, high blood pressure as a disease will have largely, or totally, disappeared. There will be no threshold above which a person will be automatically treated, not even with lifestyle measures. We do not all have the same height or hair colour and differ from each other in many other measurements without judging it as being sick. Why should a blood pressure of 130/80 be a disease and 129/79 not? In 10 years, we will know the various reasons why blood pressure can be higher than average in some people. We will know the genes responsible for this. Some of these gene variants will indeed not only induce higher blood pressure but also carry the risk of also suffering from a stroke or heart attack. Other people will just have a genetically defined tendency for a higher blood pressure, but without any risk of stroke or heart attack. Both types of patients may be able to lower their blood pressure and—if applicable—their risk for stroke and heart attack by lifestyle change. Only a small per centage of patients at risk will remain that needs drug therapy. But

[1] Kelly J et al. (2020) Type 2 Diabetes Remission and Lifestyle Medicine: A Position Statement From the American College of Lifestyle Medicine. American Journal of Lifestyle Medicine. 14:406–419, https://doi.org/10.1177/1559827620930962

[2] Li L et al. (2014) Defects in β-cell Ca2+ dynamics in age-induced diabetes. Diabetes 63:4100–4114, https://doi.org/10.2337/db13-1855

they will be different drugs compared to those used today. Not just drugs that dilate blood vessels and take away the symptom, but drugs that target the common cause of elevated blood pressure and the higher risk for stroke or heart attack. The fact that blood pressure will be lowered is almost nothing but side effect. The actual goal of the therapy is to inhibit the mechanism that can lead to stroke or heart attack. The lowered blood pressure is only a bio-marker, or sign that the therapy is apparently working.

You may be surprised, but cancer will also fit into this kind of relatively normal drug therapy. Gone will be the days when untargeted anti-cancer drugs were toxic or generally inhibited cell growth in the hope that the cancer cells would die or disappear faster than normal body cells. Not only cancer cells divide quickly, but also hair cells, immune cells, and intestinal cells. When these were also hit by anti-cancer drugs, the hair just faded out, the immune system collapsed, and severe gastrointestinal problems occurred. This was still better than having no cancer therapy, but this could not be the last word in treating cancer. Several Cancer Research Decades have been declared, most recently the European Plan to Fight Cancer in February 2020. In 2021, most cancers are incurable, and the life extension achieved is minimal and often associated with severe side effects. In 10 years, we will be able to treat almost any cancer like any other disease, with drugs that have only few if any side effects, roughly comparable to how we treat infections, and without a significantly shorter life expectancy. The basis for this will be a different view on cancer. Defective cancerous cells are constantly being produced in our bodies. Such stressed cells are usually killed by so-called natural killer cells, a type of immune cell, in a similar manner to the elimination of bacteria or viruses during an infection. The risk of such cell degeneration is increased by mutations in our genes; these mutations can be inherited and then in princi-ple endanger all body cells to form a cancer, or they can be triggered by life-style (smoking, red meat, little fibre in the diet) and environment (nitrogen oxides or fine dust in the air) and then mainly affect those organs that met the cancer-causing substances (lungs, intestines). However, not all mutations are cancer-causing. Some are of no consequence, others increase the risk of other diseases, and then there are those that cause a cell to grow out of control, e.g. by an increased rate of cell divisions, or cells leaving their organ of origin, migrating into blood vessels, and neighbouring organs and becoming par-tially independent of the oxygen supply. However, the possible mechanisms for misregulation are not endless but limited. Several mutations must accu-mulate in one of the above cellular functions, cell division, growth, etc., such that a cell starts growing in an uncontrolled manner. If this is overlooked by the immune system or if the sheer multitude of cells cannot be eliminated, cancer develops. So, the key is to know the exact mechanisms that misregulate the specific cancer cell of a patient. The organ in which the cancer is detected is irrelevant. In 10 years, no cancer (or any other disease) will be labelled by its location in the body or organ. That is, diagnoses such as "breast cancer", "lung cancer", "brain tumour", etc. will no longer exist. Instead, the whole genome from a tumour will be sequenced so that it is clear which signalling pathways are disrupted. Then drugs will be selected that normalize these signalling pathways and thereby reduce growth and give the immune system the upper hand again. This is similar to bacteriostatic antibiotics, where bacterial growth is inhibited so that the immune system can quickly eliminate them. Nonspecific and toxic drugs will seldom be used anymore, or not at all. Drugs that specifically inhibit cancer cells but do not kill them are the crucial untapped resource.[3] The side effects of this new cancer therapy, and cancer itself, will lose their terror. Cancer will not and cannot be eliminated because this is not possible. Every day we form cancer cells. But cancer will be made controllable. Hardly anyone will die "from" cancer, but "with" cancer.

Thus, curing complex diseases instead of chronically treating their symptoms will have different facets: on the one hand, a tailored healthy lifestyle and microbiome and exposome intervention will in many cases prevent a genetic risk to manifest. In those cases where the risk pressure is so high, that even the healthiest lifestyle, microbiome, and exposome cannot prevent disease symptoms, we will know the underlying molecular cause and assist therapy with precision drug therapy. Most likely this will have to be permanent, but the drugs given will be completely different from those given today. Their *Number Needed To Treat* will be 1 and the success rate 100% or very close to it. This means that every patient will benefit from their drug.

On the other hand, non-complex diseases originate typically from a single—yet important—gene, i.e. monogenetic diseases. They are also typically rare. Here, more and more gene therapy will be considered as a primary option with the potential of providing a once-off, permanent cure. However, the fact that a disease is rare imposes new challenges compared to those of complex diseases.

---

[3] Ruscetti M et al. (2018) NK cell-mediated cytotoxicity contributes to tumor control by a cytostatic drug combination. Science 362:1416–1422, https://doi.org/10.1126/science.aas9090

The Special Case of Monogenic, Rare Diseases

In Europe, a disease is defined as "rare" if it does not occur more frequently than in one in 2000 EU citizens. Due to the severity of the diseases, the medical need is also usually so great that the regulatory authorities often approve both *fast track* and *orphan drug status* for gene therapy drugs. Consequently, approval is reviewed particularly quickly due to the high unmet medical need. We all watched this procedure closely during the approval of the genetically engineered COVID-19 vaccine. Some countries such as England and the USA had even granted emergency approval, i.e. approval even before the review was completed. *Orphan drug status* due to the rarity of a disease has two advantages: First, it means that the benefit of the drug is, by definition, considered proven. Secondly, irrespective of patent protection, a 10-year period of market exclusivity is granted. All these advantages are intended to provide companies with an incentive to invest in these—at least initially—not always economically rewarding diseases. There are rare diseases that are so rare that it is difficult to even find enough patients for a clinical trial, or if you have recruited enough patients, there are hardly any patients left afterwards to whom the drug can be prescribed because most of them have already been part of the trial. In addition, the technological development effort for gene therapy—at least now in the founding years—is enormous, since a completely new form of therapy must be researched and safety-checked. Prices for these therapies have exploded in some cases, which is why the original reason of regulators to offer an incentive is gradually becoming obsolete. Instead, many pharmaceutical companies now enter into so-called value-based agreements with health insurance funds. These are individual contracts that apply per drug, per disease, and per health insurance company. According to these agreements, it is no longer the drug per se *that is* reimbursed by the health insurance company, but only the jointly defined therapeutic success. If the drug does not work, no money goes to the company. In itself very sensible, and I would like to see this for all other drugs in view of the high *Numbers Needed To Treat*. One criticism of these contracts, however, is that the criteria for what constitutes efficacy are essentially defined by the health insurance funds, but not, or hardly at all, by the patients themselves. But how does gene therapy work?

Principles of Gene Therapy

First, there is not "the" gene therapy, but several possibilities with pros and cons. To understand these therapies, it helps to remember what genes are and do: Genes encode the construction plans for all proteins in our cells, i.e. the players. The code is written in DNA but sits in the nucleus of a cell. However, proteins are made outside the nucleus. Thus, a copy is written from the DNA that tells the protein synthesis machinery which protein to make and how— the RNA. Based on this RNA, the protein is then built. If the gene is missing, the RNA and protein are missing as well. If the gene has a defect, the RNA and protein have it as well. If the protein is essential for the cell and the defect severe, the cell will be "sick" and lead to disease symptoms. The therapeutic reversal or cure of such a scenario is analogous and can occur at every step (Fig. 17.1):

- The gene product, the protein, is replaced.

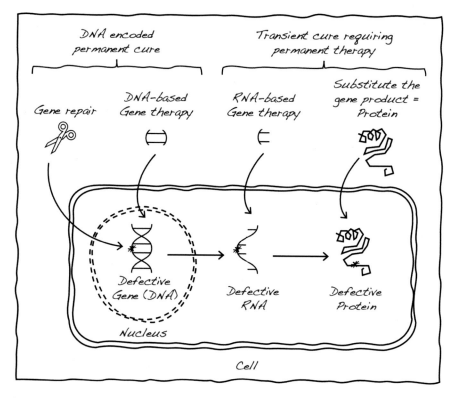

Fig. 17.1 Gene therapy options. From left to right: Permanent correction of a gene defect or an entire gene at the DNA level in the cell nucleus, temporary correction at the RNA level, or by substituting the protein encoded by the gene

- RNA is used as drug to either provide the entire genetic information for the cell to synthesize the protein or to modulate the endogenous RNA function.
- The whole gene is replaced as DNA in the nucleus.
- The endogenous gene defect is repaired with so-called genetic scissors.

Of note, the last two approaches induce a permanent cure. Once the missing or defective gene is inserted or repaired, the disease is gone. No further therapy is needed. The first two approaches require repetitive substitution or application of RNA or protein. Probably the intervals are much longer than a daily drug dose, e.g. every 3 months or so, but still these two therapies offer only transient cure and need to be regularly repeated.

Substituting the Gene Product, the Protein

The simplest form of "gene" therapy, replacing the "gene product", i.e. the protein, is the oldest. One example that you will have heard of is insulin replacement in type 1 (and increasingly also in type 2) diabetes, which was first done as early as 1922. In diabetes, the gene is in fact intact, but the insulin producing cells have been destroyed. Another example is the supplementation of clotting factors, e.g. factor VIII for the therapy of haemophilia, which in the late 1960s were purified from the plasma from thousands of humans. This source was later discovered to be transmitting potentially deadly bloodborne viruses, including hepatitis viruses and HIV, which is why factor VIII is now synthesized by genetic engineering. More recently, other rarer diseases have also been increasingly treated in this way. For example, Lumizyme replaces the enzyme acid alpha glucosidase, which is missing in patients with Pompe disease, which can lead to muscle weakness, respiratory paralysis, and death. Costs are US$626,400 per year. Cerliponase alfa is used to treat a metabolic disease with only 20 cases per year, a so-called ultra-rare disease, with costs of US$702,000 per year. Similar recent examples include Biomarin's Naglazyme for the treatment of patients with the rare disease mucopolysaccharidosis VI. Only a few dozen people a year are diagnosed and treated with this therapy, and the cost of the drug adds up to more than US$485,000 a year. Recordati's drug Carbaglu helps correct a deficiency in N-acetylglutamate synthase (NAGS), a genetic disorder that limits or blocks the body's ability to break down excess ammonia. High levels of ammonia in the blood can lead to brain damage or even death. Since only a few people are affected by this genetic defect, the treatment is also very expensive at over US$585,000 a year.

Not only must these proteins be replaced repeatedly for a lifetime, but proteins would also be destroyed in the acidic stomach or by the digestive enzymes in our intestines. Thus, they cannot be administered as tablets like other drugs, but must be injected either into a muscle from where they pass into the blood, or directly into a blood vessel, and thus bypassing the gastrointestinal tract.

Gene therapy in the narrower sense, however, is only the replacement or repair of a disease-causing gene at the DNA (permanent) or RNA (transient) level. Moreover, from the route of administration, the easier and most accessible form was to harvest the affected cells in a patient, treat them outside the body in a laboratory, and reintroduce the engineered, healthy cells back. Much more challenging and riskier was the treatment of the entire body, e.g. by injecting a gene therapeutic agent.

Gene Therapy Stage 1, outside the Body

Gene therapy at the DNA level, i.e. on our chromosomes located in the nucleus, can in principle be carried out in two ways: by inserting the entire healthy gene or by the so-called gene scissors (CRISPR-Cas9). To transport the components required for this into the cell nucleus, helper viruses are usually used. Since COVID-19, the word "virus" has signalled danger to many of us rather than something we want to be injected with. But viruses, like bacteria and fungi, are part of our microbiome, so they are not dangerous per se. The two biggest possible risks they potentially pose are that the therapeutic DNA they carry into the nucleus will insert itself into an inappropriate place within the patient's genome, impairing the function of other previously intact genes, or that helper viruses can trigger an immune response or, in too high a dose, damage the liver.[4] Conversely, in too low a dosage, the effect may not last long enough. All these risks can now be minimized by selecting suitable helper viruses and adapting the virus dose to the patient. Non-viral transfer techniques are now also being tested for the use of gene scissors, so that this risk could one day be eliminated.[5]

---

[4] Stolberg SG (1999) The biotech death of Jesse Gelsinger. N Y Times Mag. 136:49–50, https://www.nytimes.com/1999/11/28/magazine/the-biotech-death-of-jesse-gelsinger.html; Editor (2020) High-dose AAV gene therapy deaths. Nat Biotechnol 38:910, https://doi.org/10.1038/s41587-020-0642-9

[5] Finn JD et al. (2018) A Single Administration of CRISPR/Cas9 Lipid Nanoparticles Achieves Robust and Persistent In Vivo Genome Editing. Cell Rep 22:2227–2235, https://doi.org/10.1016/j.celrep.2018.02.014; Cheng Q et al. (2020) Selective organ targeting (SORT) nanoparticles for tissue-specific mRNA delivery and CRISPR-Cas gene editing. Nat Nanotechnol 15:313–320, https://doi.org/10.1038/s41565-020-0669-6

To hunt down cancer cells, lymph cells originating from the thymus, or T-cells for short, can be harvested from a patient, genetically reprogrammed and reinjected. This has started a revolution in the immunotherapy of tumours. The procedure involves inserting a gene (CAR) into immune T-cells that recognizes a surface protein of a cancer cell. When these CAR T-cells are reinfused into the patient, they bind to the cancer cells and kill them. This has led to long remissions in leukaemia and lymphoma. The treatment has fewer complications than feared. The trick is the highly individual nature, i.e. choosing the right therapy for the right patient at the right time.

Another gene therapy on immune cells concerns patients with chronic immune deficiency caused by the X-chromosome.[6] In this case, important immune cells for the rapid fight against bacteria and fungi are defective and can no longer produce oxygen radicals. The patients suffer from severe infections which encapsulate in various organs to form granulomas, hence the name granulomatosis for the disease. The patients are dependent on constant antibacterial and antifungal prophylaxis throughout their lives. After gene therapy was performed for the first time, almost all patients were able to avoid antibiotics. The gene therapy was again performed outside the body on stem cells of the patients and corresponds to a conventional stem cell therapy: The old blood-forming bone marrow is destroyed by chemotherapy and then replaced by a new bone marrow after infusion of the stem cells. In contrast to normal stem cell therapy, however, the patients receive their own stem cells back—only genetically modified. A donor is therefore not needed.

No less spectacular is another gene therapy outside the body that has cured a Parkinson's patient.[7] In this disease, nerve cells in the brain that produce the neurotransmitter dopamine perish. Dopamine causes fine-tuning of muscle movements through the interplay of contraction and relaxation. Without dopamine this is disturbed. So-called stem cells were taken from a skin sample of the patient. These are a kind of reserve cell that does not yet have a function of its own, but which can still transform into many other cell types. In the laboratory, these cells were "reprogrammed" to produce dopamine and then transplanted into the brain of the Parkinson's patient. Even after 2 years, the muscle function was still significantly improved.

The skin is also predestined for relatively simple gene therapy. A spectacular example is the dramatic disease, epidermolysis bullosa. As a result of at least 18 different genetic defects, the skin tends to blister over large areas, even with

[6] Kohn DB et al. (2020) Lentiviral gene therapy for X-linked chronic granulomatous disease. Nat Med 26:200–206, https://doi.org/10.1038/s41591-019-0735-5

[7] Schweitzer JS et al. (2020) Personalized iPSC-derived dopamine progenitor cells for Parkinson's disease. N Engl J Med. 382:1926–1932, https://doi.org/10.1056/NEJMoa1915872

slight injuries, mere contact or even spontaneously, and severe infections can set in. After gene therapy of skin cells in the laboratory of a severely affected seven-year-old boy who only had skin on 20 per cent of his body surface and was in a life-threatening condition, he had his own skin on more than 80 per cent of his body surface after 2 years of treatment. During this procedure 20 times small pieces of skin were gene-therapeutically treated, multiplied in cell cultures and re-transplanted as cell lawns. Afterwards, the boy was able to leave the hospital, attended school again shortly afterwards, and now leads a largely normal life.[8] Anyone looking at the shocking pictures of the boy before and after treatment would believe in a miracle. Larger clinical trials on correcting the skin gene collagen COL7A1 have started.

However, most other monogenic diseases are not treatable outside our body by harvesting and altering a few cells. The whole body needs to be treated.

Whole-Body Gene Therapy

By 2021, worldwide approximately 250 patients with monogenic diseases for which there were previously no treatment options have successfully received whole-body gene therapy either at the RNA (transient) or DNA (whole gene or gene editing) level. These are still many fewer patients than the thousands who have received treatments with cells that have been genetically modified outside the body (see above), but the potential is high. However, the first steps in gene therapy were dramatic and tragic. In 1999, an 18-year-old boy died from a new experimental gene treatment. He suffered from the rare metabolic disorder, ornithine transcarbamylase deficiency (OTCD), syndrome, in which ammonia builds up in the body to lethal levels leading to coma soon after birth, brain damage, and death within a month. This patient had a milder version controllable with a low-protein diet but still needed to take close to 50 pills per day. He volunteered in a study testing an adenovirus, a type of cold virus, altered to be harmless and carrying the ornithine transcarbamylase gene that he was missing. The virus was supposed to infect his liver cells and integrate this gene into his DNA. Previous patients in the trial had experienced maximally flu-like symptoms, but this boy had intense inflammation damaging his liver (causing jaundice and blood-clotting disorder), kidney, and lung.

---

[8] Hirsch T et al. (2017) Regeneration of the entire human epidermis using transgenic stem cells. Nature 551:327–332, https://doi.org/10.1038/nature24487; Fox M (2017) Gene Therapy Skin Grafts Save Boy With Rare Disease. NBC News, https://www.nbcnews.com/health/health-news/gene-engineered-skin-grafts-save-boy-rare-disease-n818936

After 4 days he died.[9] Only a few years later, in 2003, several people treated for immunodeficiency developed leukaemia because the virus had randomly inserted its cargo DNA into regions of the patient's genome that promote cancer.[10] These two catastrophic failures sent a shock wave through the field for more than 10 years. However, science evolved, and the following improvements and discoveries were made:

- Improved adeno-associated virus, whose DNA cargo remains within the cell as separate, free-floating elements rather than stably integrating into the patient cell's genome, thereby eliminating cancer gene activation.
- Lentiviruses that insert DNA into regions with minimal cancer risk and longer-lasting benefits than adeno-associated virus.
- The Nobel Prize-winning DNA scissors, CRISPR/Cas-9.
- RNA-based therapies, transient but without cancer risk.

The latter was applied in amyloidosis, cholesterol lowering, and a severe muscle disease. About 50,000 patients worldwide have lost their mobility due to amyloidosis, diseases in which protein deposits occur in cells, and are soon thereafter confined to a wheelchair or even bedridden. The average survival time is 10–15 years; if the heart is also affected, it is only 2–5 years. Previous treatment options have included liver transplantation or the administration of stabilizers that slow down the deposition of the protein somewhat. However, none of these treatments stopped the long-term progression of the disease. Patisiran (Onpattro®) prevents the formation of an amyloid protein at the RNA level and reverses the disease process. The cost of therapy is substantial at US$450,000 per year but justified through a so-called value-based arrangement with health insurers where the cost of the drug is only reimbursed if it has worked.

RNA-based therapy has even expanded into cardiovascular disease. In patients with a familial hypercholesterolaemia, therapy with the most prescribed cholesterol-lowering drugs, statins, is not sufficient. Inclisiran (Leqvio®) binds to the PCSK9 RNA and prevents the formation of the protein of the same name. PCSK9 normally breaks down a protein that removes cholesterol from the blood. Inclisiran prevents this and more cholesterol is removed from the blood, which lowers cholesterol levels by up to 50 per cent. It only needs to be injected under the skin twice a year.

[9] Rinde MR (2019) The Death of Jesse Gelsinger, 20 Years Later. Science History Institute; https://www.sciencehistory.org/distillations/the-death-of-jesse-gelsinger-20-years-later

[10] Hacein-Bey-Abina S et al. (2008) Insertional oncogenesis in 4 patients after retrovirus-mediated gene therapy of SCID-X1. J Clin Invest 118:3132–3142, https://doi.org/10.1172/JCI35700

Spinal muscular atrophy is a rare hereditary disease that occurs in one in 10,000 new-borns caused by a defect in the *survival motor neuron gene* (SMN1) essential for maintaining the nerve cells in the spinal cord. If these cells perish, nerve impulses are no longer transmitted to the muscles resulting in paralysis and muscle degradation. If cranial nerve cells are affected, even swallowing, chewing, and speaking can be impaired. RNA technology introduced the first ever therapy spinal muscular atrophy, nusinersen (Spinraza®). This RNA drug cannot not replace the defective gene at the DNA level but corrects the subsequent reading process from RNA to protein. The result is a healthy protein. Some of the infants treated in this way can subsequently hold their heads upright, grasp, stand, and even walk. However, this does not mean a real cure, as the gene remains defective and the RNA needs to be reapplied in regular intervals. The cost per patient is US$750,000 in the first year and $375,000 in each subsequent year. Due to obvious cost discussions, approval of nusinersen was delayed in some countries, leading to protests from distraught parents. Concerns about cost continued after approval and vary from country to country and sometimes from health insurance company to health insurance company. This tragically leads to sick people not having access to treatment due to economic factors. Two children's fates went through the press. One of them was few months old Samuel. He was treated with nusinersen but his condition deteriorated dramatically. He had to be artificially fed through a tube and continuously breathed through a mask.

Then came the turnaround, innovative DNA-based gene replacement technologies that are safe overcoming the dramatic set-backs of the late 1990s and 2000s. Through a hardship programme, Samuel was awarded a new DNA-based gene therapy with onasemnogene abeparvovec (Zolgensma®), another innovation for spinal muscular atrophy, which inserts a functional SMN1 gene and therefore only needs to be given once. The price for this one dose is around two million US dollars, making it one of the most expensive drugs in the world. But this one dose cures, potentially saves a life, and avoids expensive follow-up treatments. The manufacturer Novartis announced that it would give away 100 treatments, which patient associations and health ministers criticized as unethical.[11] Samuel was one of those kids treated for free. Only a few months later it was clear that it had worked. Probably, the boy is cured of his severe muscle disease. One can imagine the joy of the parents, who must have experienced this treatment like a miracle. Shortly afterwards, little Hannah from Berlin was treated, this time paid for by the health

---

[11] Dyer O (2020) Health ministers condemn Novartis lottery for Zolgensma, the world's most expensive drug. BMJ 368:m580, https://doi.org/10.1136/bmj.m580

insurance. She was already older, just under 2 years, could not crawl, could not move her legs, and could only sit upright with help. Again, a success. Shortly after the treatment, she made daily progress, became more mobile, and started walking with the support of her parents.

For patients with haemophilia, lacking factor VIII (see above), injecting the artificially produced clotting factor protein reduced the risk of bleeding so drastically that patients could lead an almost normal life. In the 1980s the treatment of haemophiliacs accounted for 2 per cent of the total cost of pharmaceuticals. Even today, this treatment is one of the most expensive therapies worldwide. However, now a one-time gene therapy with valoctocogene roxaparvovec (Walton®) corrects this defect, once and for all. The haemophiliac patient is cured.[12] The cost, however, ranges between 2 and 3 million US dollars, which then displaces Zolgensma® from the number one spot as the most expensive drug in the world.

The miracle of DNA-based therapy goes further. The drug voretigene neparvovec (Luxturna®) is the first cure of retinitis pigmentosa, an early childhood form of blindness. Patients have a mutation of the RPE65 gene on both chromosomes, the maternal and paternal. As a result the retina degenerates and patients lose the perception of light; the visual field shrinks and shrinks. In 2018, a 13-year-old boy was the first patient treated,[13] followed by eight-year-old Sam from Canada. The treatment brought sight back to both. Sam was quoted around the world as saying, "I've never seen the stars". Sam used to be unable to see the sky on a cloudy day and could not make out shapes in the dark. He always had to have lights on and had trouble seeing his shoes or objects on the ground. And the disease was progressive, meaning it would have gotten worse as he got older. A single injection in each eye is enough to introduce a correct version of the RPE65 gene into the retina of the eyes, stopping the deterioration of the tissue and restoring vision, at least partially. The earlier the gene is inserted, the more vision is saved. Costs amount to US$850,000. What a breakthrough in ophthalmology, not just for these two patients, but conceptually. Most advances in medicine tend to be incremental. Occasionally, maybe once in a generation, something revolutionary like this comes along that radically changes the course of medicine. The eye is easily accessible and virtually predestined for gene therapy, and so it is likely that many more developments in this direction will follow.

---

[12] Pasi KJ et al. (2020) Multiyear follow-up of AAV5-hFVIII-SQ Gene Therapy for Hemophilia A. N Engl J Med 382:29–40, https://doi.org/10.1056/NEJMoa1908490

[13] STAT (2018) 'That's $425,000 right there'—the anxious launch of a gene therapy with a record sticker price

Finally, in 2020 the Nobel Prize in chemistry was awarded for the most elegant method of repairing a genetic defect using the CRISPR/Cas-9 gene scissors.[14] In that year, the application of this invention was successful in nine boys aged 6–12 who had been living with Duchenne's muscular dystrophy since birth, a genetic disease that causes progressive degeneration and weakening of the muscles. It is caused by mutations in the gene that makes the protein molecule dystrophin. Dystrophin is used to build and strengthen muscle fibres in skeletal and cardiac muscles. Since the gene is located on the X chromosome, the disease mainly affects boys because they have only one X chromosome and girls usually have a healthy second X chromosome that can compensate for this defect. Many patients with Duchenne muscular dystrophy end up in a wheelchair, on ventilators, or both. Until now, there has been no cure for the disease, which is why life expectancy has been only a little over 30 years, despite advances in cardiology and pulmonology. CRISPR/Cas-9 replaced the defective dystrophin gene. One year after treatment, 7 of the 9 boys showed significant improvement in muscle strength and function. Before treatment, a nine-year-old could not walk up more than four flights of stairs without having to stop. Within 3 weeks of treatment, he was able to walk up the entire flight of stairs. "I can walk faster. I can stand better. And I can walk [...] more than 2 miles, and I couldn't do that before", he was quoted as saying. Something like this is the most wonderful thing that can happen to a biomedical scientist, and I'm hugely happy for everyone involved in this success, which can't be celebrated highly enough. Although the already lost muscle cells do not grow back, the treatment seems to restore the normal function of the protein, which is to fix the muscle fibres and help them grow so that no further degeneration takes place.

The results are a milestone in gene therapy and encourage not only patients with muscular dystrophy, but also many patients with other genetic diseases for whom similar treatments may soon be developed. So far, this approach is only considered for monogenetic diseases, but I would not rule out the possibility that in a few years' time, when gene therapy has become increasingly unspectacular and almost routine, we will also venture into diseases caused by two, three, and more gene variants. Based on the safety and successes of these recent interventions another discussion has gained momentum: Currently, we gene-treat only the bodily cells of a patient, not his or her germline cells. Thus, even if cured, a male or female would still transmit a genetically

---

[14] The Royal Swedish Academy of Sciences (2020) Scientific Background on the Nobel Prize in Chemistry 2020. A Tool For Genome Editing, https://www.nobelprize.org/uploads/2020/10/advanced-chemistryprize2020.pdf

dominant disease to their children, and the child would need to be treated again. Why not treat the germ cells and eliminate this way the disease for all children, and grandchildren, and…

Germline Gene Therapy?

A major current ethical restriction is that gene therapy may only be carried out in the body's cells, but not in the so-called germ line cells (i.e. sperm and egg cells) that serve reproduction purposes. All currently approved gene therapies are therefore only effective for the treated patient. The children of those treated with gene therapy may inherit the same genetic defect. In contrast, treating germline cells would mean that all offspring would be born without this genetic defect and would no longer need any therapy. In most countries, germline therapy is prohibited under Embryo Protection Acts. This is intended to prevent a gene therapy modification of the DNA from being passed on to the patient's children—virtually without their consent and thus ethically potentially problematic. In addition, there are still methodological safety concerns, since we know from experiments on plants and animals of high failure rates, i.e. there is a high per centage of embryos that, due to unintentional changes in previously healthy parts of their genetic material, show newly emerging malformations, from which they often die.

But when this methodological problem has been solved, there will, in my eyes, no longer be any reason for the still very widespread assumption that the children would subsequently reject the gene therapy transferred to them by their parents and would have preferred to decide on gene therapy themselves. But this rejectionist position is already softening. The UK has approved germline genome editing within experimental research. Japan approved research involving human embryo editing, but later recommended a ban on implanting the edited embryos.[15] Australia updated their Gene Technology Regulations requiring a licence to perform research on human embryos (though it has yet to grant such a license).[16] China has proposed to update their legislation by regulating germline editing research under civil legislation requiring all experiments to be approved through the Ministry of Health.[17]

---

[15] Cyranoski D (2018) Japan set to allow gene editing in human embryos. Nature; https://doi.org/10.1038/d41586-018-06847-7

[16] Mallapaty S (2019) Australian gene-editing rules adopt 'middle ground'. Nature; https://doi.org/10.1038/d41586-019-01282-8

[17] Cyranoski D (2019) China set to introduce gene-editing regulation following CRISPR-baby furore. Nature; https://doi.org/10.1038/d41586-019-01580-1

The German Ethics Council has taken a position on this issue and included a broad spectrum of very different points of view, ranging from parental wishes and the anticipation of the needs of future children to social concerns and the human self-image. A large majority of the Council members considered germline interventions to prevent diseases that are monogenic, i.e. determined by only one gene, to be permissible under certain conditions.[18] The USA National Academy of Sciences, Engineering, and Medicine convened the International Commission on the Clinical Use of Human Germline Genome Editing to develop a framework from pre-clinical trials to long-term monitoring of the germline-edited patients.[19] In this way, serious hereditary diseases could ultimately be eliminated. New techniques that only correct a mutation and do not introduce a gene should be safe, since only the healthy gene is restored. Given how far gene therapy has come to date, it is not presumptuous to speculate that this too will be achievable and that, over a few generations, severe genetic diseases will even be eliminated altogether, in much the same way as we have achieved this for infectious diseases such as smallpox or polio through vaccination.

However, the risks and importance of the ethical questions around germline editing became world news when a Chinese scientist announced that he had illegally used CRISPR-Cas9 to edit the genomes of two human embryos.[20] His goal was to inactivate a gene, which encodes a protein used by HIV to infect human cells. The modified embryos were implanted and carried to term, leading to the first babies born with heritable genome edits. Despite a worldwide outcry for many reasons, this did not stop a Russian scientist from planning human embryo edits, albeit with more transparency and better medical justification, i.e. congenital deafness.[21] The discussion is open and competent and global regulation is urgently needed. Just banning will apparently not work.

---

[18] German Ethics Council (2019) Ethics Council: germline interventions currently too risky, but ethically not to be ruled out in principle, https://www.ethikrat.org/mitteilungen/2019/ethikrat-keimbahneingriffe-derzeit-zu-risikoreich-aber-ethisch-nicht-grundsaetzlich-auszuschliessen/

[19] National Academies of Sciences, Medicine E et al. (2019) International commission on the clinical use of human germline genome editing. Projects & Activities; https://www8.nationalacademies.org/pa/projectview.aspx

[20] Cyranoski D (2018) First CRISPR babies: six questions that remain. Nature; https://doi.org/10.1038/d41586-018-07607-3; Regalado A2018) Exclusive: Chinese scientists are creating CRISPR babies. MIT Technology Review; https://www.technologyreview.com/2018/11/25/138962/exclusive-chinese-scientists-are-creating-crispr-babies/

[21] Cyranoski D (2019) Russian biologist plans more CRISPR-edited babies. Nature; https://www.nature.com/articles/d41586-019-01770-x; Cohen J (2019) Embattled Russian scientist sharpens plans to create gene-edited babies. Science; https://www.sciencemag.org/news/2019/10/embattled-russian-scientist-sharpens-plans-create-gene-edited-babies

Live Forever?

These are all wonderful successes that show the potential and blessing of gene therapy. And you can probably sense my enthusiasm for this as you read these lines (except for the unacceptable Chinese experiment). These therapies are costly, usually focus on dramatic, deadly diseases with few patients, and require an extreme methodological discovery effort, which at least partly explains their high price. Most often, they are applied in rather easily accessible organs, such as the blood vessels, eye, and skin, or outside the body in the laboratory followed by infusion back. One does not have to be a prophet to predict that the development of gene therapies will become more and more routine, resulting in a broader range of applications and, once all the necessary methods have been developed, a reduction in effort and cost is foreseeable. Broader application can mean that in principle all organs become accessible, but also that gene therapies can be used for diseases in which more than one gene is affected. Work is also being carried out on methods that not only lead to gene on or gene off, but also intermediate stages, i.e. gene partially off or partially on, which would correspond even better to natural gene regulation. From a certain number of affected genes onwards, we will have to decide whether to use gene therapy or whether to treat the disease with classical drugs. However, the essential difference to today will remain: to heal instead of just treating symptoms.

At this point, at the latest, you might be asking yourself, "What are we going to die of now, or are we not?" In fact, Google's chief futurist Ray Kurzweil believes we will be able to live forever starting in 2029. This, of course, fits with Google's vision of eliminating age-related diseases. Treating it sounds feasible, but eliminating them altogether? No, that won't work. I don't believe in that kind of prediction. That's not what curing is about. We will remain mortal. Our goal should be to age healthily for as long as possible, i.e. not to suffer from dramatic illnesses such as strokes or cancer that can disable us for years, but to fall asleep gently at some point in old age—ideally.

Many ageing processes will be known and can be delayed for a long time, but our organs are complex structures in which many biochemical reactions and physical processes take place. Healing instead of treating will therefore mean that in 10 years' time the life expectancy of new-born babies will be 110 or more years. The oldest woman in the world so far documented, Jeanne Calment from France, lived from 1875 to 1997 to 122 years. According to Jan Vijg of *Albert Einstein College of Medicine* in New York, the upper limit for human age is 125 years. Chaim Cohen of Bar Ilan University and biologist

Siegfried Hekimi of McGill University in Montreal believe that humans may even exceed this limit and live up to 140 years. Probably most relevant to absolute life expectancy is our lung. When we breathe in, it is actively stretched by the diaphragm muscle, which separates the chest from the abdomen, so that air flows in. The process of exhalation, on the other hand, is passive. The lungs are elastic and simply contract again, allowing air to escape. So, you can think of the lungs as an elastic rubber balloon. At some point, the elasticity of any rubber balloon, and also of the lungs, wears off. Biophysical estimates assume that this is the case after about 130 years. The number of air bubbles in the lung and adjacent small blood vessels for oxygen uptake also decrease. As a result, less oxygen reaches the blood and our physical capacity decreases. The field of tissue engineering claims to be able to artificially produce human organs in the future. I can imagine this for individual cells, but not for tissue. I remain of the view that, at some point, we're going to have to die. But let's wait and see, maybe I'm wrong about this. Anyway, living longer also enables us to fill the longer life with meaning.

Having read all these exciting developments, you will realize that, wherever you live, your current health care systems do not really seem to fit in with all of this—Big Data, systems medicine, prevention, etc. Thus for the final implementation step of part 2 of my book and the new medicine, a completely new health care system is emerging that really deserves the term "health" in it. Our current disease system elements still have a place in there, but only a very minor one.

18

Well-Tech

Before we get started on the new health care system, let's pause for a moment to consider all that we have and need: How far have we come since Part I of the book? Diseases were recognized too late. When symptoms appeared, their cause was not known, and only the symptom could be treated. Since diseases could neither be prevented nor cured, many diseases became chronic. However, few patients benefited from their chronic medication. Men lived shorter than women, less educated/lower income men shorter than well-educated/higher income men. Medicine and biomedical sciences which both focused on one organ had come to a dead end. Moreover, biomedical research was often unreproducible, of poor quality, and not patient-centred. Even Big Pharma giants seemed to be heading towards their demise. The increase in life expectancy stagnated or even declined in some countries, even as the cost of health steadily increased.

But then in Part II everything changed. I hope I have been able to show that there must, and will, be a huge push for innovation and a new kind of medicine. Now, research and practice will be done in interdisciplinary medicine teams, both with massive support from machine learning algorithms. These algorithms increasingly help us to understand the exact molecular causes of disease, as well as possible triggers or enhancers in the microbiome and exposome. This will allow us to detect diseases earlier, even before symptoms appear, and prevent symptoms from ever occurring. As a result, there will be no chronic diseases, only chronic risks that are kept in check or—with gene therapy—even cured so that diseases disappear from our body. You as a patient can be sure to benefit from every preventive measure or therapy as they will be precise and tailored to your individual needs. Biomedical research

H. H. H. W. Schmidt, *The end of medicine as we know it - and why your health has a future*, https://doi.org/10.1007/978-3-030-95293-8_18

will be reproducible, of excellent quality and patient-focused, and essentially achieve its goals in terms of disease and health, i.e. they are understood. Our life expectancy will increase and gradually reach the humanly possible maximum of about 125 years. Men will have the same life expectancy as women, and everyone will be sufficiently educated, individually coached, and resourced so that lack of education or income is no longer a disadvantage in terms of life expectancy.

Our healthcare systems, whatever they are now, cannot remain unaffected by all these changes. They will also be changing, but it will not be incremental. It will be like moving from a candle to an electric light bulb; it will be a revolution, something completely new. Current and new healthcare providers will need to find their niche, always and primarily, however, for the benefit of the people (not patients, ideally). People will move from their current rather peripheral role of occasional users of health services to the centre. Everything will revolve around them. Constantly, i.e. not only when there are symptoms. And with it, numerous business models and questions of reimbursement and financing of health and health maintenance will also change.

Pharmaceutical giants as we once knew them will disappear. For a few years, they will fill the remaining gaps in classical drugs; then they will develop or optimize gene and cell therapeutics until they become an off-the-shelf methodology; eventually, they will become manufacturing companies that produce and distribute mostly off-patent generics cheaply and in different places worldwide. At the same time this will end the dependence on single production companies and the frequent supply problems associated with this. Sometimes, they will optimize a drug a little more, e.g. to increase its half-life, stability, or make it 2D- or 3D-printing compatible. But there will not only be companies that have massively changed or disappeared; there will also be entirely new companies and industries. In fact a whole new sector of the economy is already emerging driving the next big socioeconomic revolution.

New Health Companies

Prime drivers and, of course, also economic profiteers of this new medicine are completely new health companies and business areas. I have already mentioned Alphabet and Google, Amazon, and Apple several times. But also, other platform companies, which belong to the top 10 worldwide, show increasing engagement in the health sector: Microsoft with its Microsoft *Cloud for Healthcare* and e-health solutions such as Azure Service Health; Alibaba with Alibaba Health Information Technology; Facebook with the

Preventive Health tool; or Tencent with Tencent Health, a service platform on WeChat. Walmart has opened 30+ healthcare centres offering primary care, urgent care, labs, counselling, and other services. Ninety percent of Americans live within 10 miles of a Walmart store demonstrating the potential. Walmart also partnered with Medicare Advantage insurer Clover Health on its first health insurance plans. Thus, none of the leading platform giants is not active in health, some earlier and more intensively, others later and less intensively, but all of them are there and this is just the beginning.

With the boom in gene and cell therapy and the mere production of low-cost, off-patent generics, will anything exciting happen to medicines as we know them today? Oh yes, a lot. This time, it's not Google, Apple, Amazon, but a German tech start-up leading the way. Forget everything you knew about tablets and capsules. Digital Health Systems GmbH (DiHeSys) is developing two- and three-dimensional printed medicines for you personally. You might ask yourself: "Okay, everything is 3D printed now. Now also pharmaceuticals. Where is the innovation, please?"

The innovation is huge. Every person is unique—but medical treatments tend not to be. Body weight, gender, and metabolism are just some of the factors that influence therapies. One example of the common "one size fits all" approach is tablets and capsules. They are currently mass-produced industrially, and only in fixed dosages. This does not allow individual therapy. Let's take an example: drug A is available in pharmacies in strengths of 10, 20, and 50 mg per tablet. But what if 34 milligrams would be ideal for you? Well, you could take one tablet with 10 mg and one with 20 mg or two 20 mg tablets. In the first case you would be slightly underdosed, in the second case slightly overdosed. In the first case, you might not have quite the full desired effect, in the second you might have side effects that you would have been spared with 34 mg. Or perhaps you would prefer to take only 5 mg. That low dosage is not available at all. Then many patients use imprecise methods like dividing the tablets in half or four quarters. This is what DiHeSys overcomes which allow you as a patient to order your exact 34 mg tablet printed in a pharmacy using an App to which both your doctor and your pharmacist have access. You will no longer need to work with a pre-package from the pharmacy, i.e. fixed strength, and in many countries also fixed quantity, of tablets. Instead you will have the exact number of tablets you need per month printed out and individualized in the strength and combination with other drugs that is necessary for you. To stay with the example above, with 34 mg you would then have the full effect with minimal side effects.

Looking at the development of miniaturization and cost-reduction of 3D printers, in the next stage of development, if you must take a medicine over a long time or permanently you would have a 2- or 3D tablet printer at home. This would even allow you to adjust the strength of your tablet day by day or piece by piece. Then you would no longer pick up tablets at the pharmacy, but a printer cartridge with its medicine. Does this sound too unrealistic too you? Not at all. Think of diabetic patients, for example. They are also prescribed an injectable solution with insulin but inject themselves three times a day with the dose of insulin that they determine to exactly match their physical activities (calorie consumption) and food intake (calorie intake). Or, the diabetic patient may use a so-called closed-loop system insulin pump, which automatically injects insulin based on the measured blood glucose values.[1] No doctor could prescribe the daily insulin doses in advance. In the same way, you as a patient will be able to individually dose your medicine every day based on the desired effect size or side effects. Possibly, in some cases, the range in which you are permitted to adjust the doses or the new dose itself may need to be pre-approved by your doctor or pharmacist. But these are just procedures and could run in the background or even by AI. Thus, personalized dosing even for highly potent medications is absolutely feasible.

Consider another scenario where this printing technology is clearly the future. For example, you would have to take medicines A, B, and C in the morning, medicines B, D, and E at lunchtime, and medicines A and B in the evening. It is easy to imagine that you would get mixed up, which is currently prevented by pill boxes or, in elderly homes, by blistering the individual tablets into small sachets or plastic pockets. Personally, I already forget tablets when I must take an antibiotic for 7 days because I am simply not used to it. Imagine if you would presently have to take six different medicines in the right combination three times a day every day. In the future instead, you go to the pharmacy and have single tablets printed for your medicines; one for the morning (green with an "M" printed on), one for lunch (yellow with an "L" on), and one for dinner (blue with a "D" on). This would result in fewer mistakes in taking the tablets. The extreme variant would be even one single tablet for the entire day that also has the time distribution of the drug release imprinted, a so-called 4D tablet. It really couldn't be any simpler or safer for you.

Technically, printers are digitally controlled devices that print the drug and excipients in layered patterns. The most used techniques include inkjet printing and fusion processes, which required the development and

---

[1]TauschmannM et al. (2018) Closed-loop insulin delivery in suboptimally controlled type 1 diabetes: a multicentre, 12-week randomised trial. Lancet 392:1321–1329, https://doi.org/10.1016/S0140-6736(18)31947-0

optimization of new plastics such as polylactic acid. Small quantities can be printed two-dimensionally on a kind of filter paper. They are placed on your tongue, dissolve in seconds and the drug can be easily swallowed, ideal for people with swallowing difficulties and children. Only for larger quantities three-dimensional tablets are needed. However, they are often smaller than conventional ones because fewer excipients are needed. This also makes them easier to swallow. In addition, the tablets can be coded by colour and shape (see above). Of course, you wouldn't do this for an ordinary aspirin tablet or ibuprofen, where precise dosing by milligrams is not that important, but you would do it for highly potent drugs with potentially severe side effects, or if you need to take more than four drugs at a time during the day.

This new type of tablet has another advantage, at least on those countries where pre-packaged products are prescribed. Here, many medicines are thrown away unused and, in the worst case, end up in drinking water. The main sources of human drugs in surface water are indeed patient excretions, but at least 10% are also improperly disposed of via toilet and sink.[2] Around 60% of the total consumption of diclofenac, for example, ends up in wastewater, where to date it cannot be removed in sewage treatment plants. With 2D and 3D printing, only the exact quantities of tablets that would be safely taken would be printed. The rest would remain in the cartridge.

Additional problems often occur in patients with impaired organ function, for example, kidney or liver. Drugs are either broken down and excreted via the kidneys (in the urine) or the liver (metabolized). If the liver or kidney are impaired, then this will obviously affect the blood levels of the drugs. Two patients taking the same dose but with different kidney or liver function will experience different blood levels, effects, and side effects as a result. This is particularly problematic with drugs where there is a fine line between the dose for effect and the dose for side effect. Doctors are then completely flexible in their prescriptions and choose the dose that enables the optimal effect profile for you. These data for each medication and the individual medication plan are processed on an IT platform, to identify also unwanted drug-drug interactions, and transmitted directly to the printer, either to the pharmacy or directly to your home. This also reduces errors in the transmission of the prescription. Pure dreams of the future? Pilot project are already underway. 2D and 3D printed tablets are coming. All of this were classical medicine

---

[2] Zylka-Menhorn V (2018) Pharmaceutical residues in water: prevention and elimination. Dtsch Arztebl 115:A-1054, https://www.aerzteblatt.de/archiv/198237/Arzneimittelrueckstaende-im-Wasser-Vermeidung-und-Elimination

themes, however, just covered by new additional players in a slightly different format. What about all the innovations in Part II of this book that they cannot cover?

Health beyond Medicine

Many chronic or complex diseases have a genetic predisposition but are ultimately very much influenced by wrong lifestyle or preventable by an optimal lifestyle. Education and coaching have been proven to be effective ways of knowing and implementing the individually tailored lifestyle changes that are needed. However, doctors as traditional health care providers are not really trained and obviously not sufficient for this purpose. Moreover, offers with the prefix "health" usually have a connotation of renunciation, duty, precaution, and not "fun". Not exactly motivating for most of us.

Wellness and wellbeing, on the other hand, sound seductively like holidays and leisure. To make prevention attractive and effective, many new health service providers are currently strategically reshaping themselves into a wellness or well-being industry. This has an estimated worldwide market volume of four trillion, or 4000 billion US dollars. Classical medicine is also part of it, but only a small part, because prevention covers the entire rest of our life, beyond medicine.

The crucial point is that you as a patient are not an occasional consumer, but permanently at the centre of the action. Everything is built around you. Of course, it's a business, but so is the current healthcare system, and that is more concerned with your illnesses. Well-Tech, on the other hand, is primarily focused on your health. Of course in the beginning, there will be also some ineffective offerings. It is only in the scientific evidence of all the elements that the wheat will gradually be separated from the chaff. We have already discussed the potential of another risk of such a Well-Tech industry in the first iteration: if the focus is too much on health and self-optimization and maximum relief.

This core industry includes technology offerings, sports and fitness clothing and accessories, apps, wearables, telemedicine and tele fitness, insurance and mobility, all the way to vacations and leisure planning, but also a health-promoting workplace design. Whereas now our healthcare system exists for itself and you as a patient dock in from the outside for a short or longer period, use the services briefly and then—preferably as quickly as possible—leave it again, in the new Well-Tech system you are the king customer and permanent central hub. From a medical point of view, this also makes sense.

If you want prevention, then it must be permanent; it must become a habit. Everything revolves around you. Ideally, you remain a customer and never become a patient. In other words, a real health system, but one that prefers to call itself a wellness-wellbeing system for marketing reasons. This is the fundamental difference to our current system, which is precisely not a health system but a disease system. As someone who is still healthy, you are not interesting for the current system; in the new system, you are always of interest.

For an industrialized country, the USA is particularly challenged. Thirty-eight per cent of the population belong to ethnic minorities with higher rates of chronic disease and premature death than the white population. Here Community Health Workers come into place. They build trust with patients, often seeing them as a family member. They connect because they have shared life experiences and can provide culturally competent care—healthcare that meets the social, cultural, and linguistic needs of patients—who might be otherwise out of sight or marginalized by mainstream healthcare providers. Thus in 2010, Community Health Workers were included as a health profession in the USA Patient Protection and Affordable Care Act, distinct from social workers or case managers at the medical clinic or at the hospital. The Copenhagen Institute for Futures Studies describes this as Transformative Resilience, i.e. not to bounce back in response to difficulties, but to thrive in the face of challenges, and thus achieve a healthy lifestyle, leaving no one behind but also asking everyone to contribute by self-cultivation. Your health and well-being will no longer be something that you delegate.[3] Nevertheless technology will be key and the major facilitator.

Well-being by Well-Tech

The terms wellness and wellbeing are often used interchangeably, although they don't quite mean the same thing. Wellness is the older term and rather subsumes feel-good consumption that one treats oneself to on vacation, such as spas, baths, massage, aromatherapies, and so on. Wellbeing goes further and has a clear health reference and combines wellness and other components to a lifestyle coaching. One wants to get away from terms like healthy living and healthy eating, which contain a touch of strenuousness and renunciation, respectively. The wellbeing industry comes very much from the motivational level and tries to make offers with an individual goal in mind—and in the

---

[3] The Copenhagen Institute for Futures Studies (2019) Nordic Health 2030; http://nordichealth2030. org.linux14.dandomainserver.dk/wp-content/uploads/2019/11/nordic-health-2030-magazine.pdf

most pleasant way. Here Amazon, among others, reappears with *Amazon fresh*, restaurants and *meal kits as far as* food is concerned, Amazon Fashion as far as sports and functional clothing is concerned, and more recently *Amazon Pharmacy* and numerous medical internet services. Ultimately, the goal—as is already the case in the USA—is not to have to leave the "Amazon world" about health.

Wellbeing encompasses more than just physical health. It considers the whole person, both body and mind, and not just the "absence of disease". Its approach to "health" includes the presence of positive mental states, emotions, and moods, and identifies the condition to achieve a fulfilling, self-determined life. Wellbeing does not heal, and wellness certainly does not heal. However, both create the necessary conditions for physical, mental, and social health, help us cope with adversity, and trigger and maintain behavioural changes for greater balance, harmony, and social wellbeing. It is about the eight behavioural or lifestyle mistakes (see Chap. 4) that can trigger disease....

Technology plays an important role in all of this, which is why I think rather the term Well-Tech is appropriate and the correct description. This way, well-being will also become measurable, which will open the door for serious, evidence-based Well-Tech offerings (*Wellbeing-as-a-Service*, WaaS) and thereby enable the merging of at least parts of the current wellness and health industry into one homogeneous market, the Well-Tech industry. For without evidence, none of the current payers or individuals will agree to pay for the offerings in the long run, unless entirely new types of insurance—health as opposed to health insurance—and entirely new payment streams are added. This would be possible if traditional health insurance and its concept of "healing instead of treating" were to become less important.

Well-Tech is an ecosystem of technologies that are interconnected to assist in all areas of life and life goals. Digitization is transforming wellness and is not just for so-called *digital natives*, fitness enthusiasts, or the wealthy. Inexpensive devices, apps, and sophisticated machine learning algorithms will democratize the Well-Tech market more and more. This will become a global phenomenon that helps fulfil primal human needs for a good life. And this global movement has already begun. Our society has taken a turn. People are more concerned than ever about their physical, mental, and spiritual health. Some call it work-life balance, but it's always about the same thing: being happy and healthy is becoming a top priority.

The King of Bhutan exchanged gross national product for gross national happiness as early as 1972. France, Great Britain, and New Zealand, the OECD, and the UN followed suit by defining wellbeing as a goal. Finland set up an economic development programme for the Well-Tech industry. And since 2020, the *Frontiers Next Wellbeing World Congress* has been held.[4]

Measuring wellbeing will become increasingly relevant because it is the best indicator of the health of a community, country, company, or business. Many HR departments of large companies are shifting their focus to employee satisfaction and including wellbeing in their profit and loss indicators. Well-Tech will surround us everywhere, redefining our spaces at work, at home and in our city, developing our communities, stimulating our minds, and supporting our bodies.

But well tech is of course also a real business, a growing market with the expectation of exponential growth based on the phenomenon of exponential growth of the experience economy. It's an area in which many different companies therefore see a huge opportunity and want to be a part of. People are no longer consuming products and services for their mere need satisfaction, but to improve their quality of life, to live their lives in a better way. So, people are asking businesses to help them achieve what they want. And, after all, there can be no greater economic value that a company can create than to help someone achieve their goals. This high ethical standard and its fulfilment will determine the success of a Well-Tech company. Ninety-six per cent of people see a direct correlation between well-being, performance, and success in life. Companies with highly satisfied, engaged employees saw a 41% decrease in absenteeism and a 17% increase in productivity.[5] In addition, as mentioned earlier, healthcare is moving towards greater human- or customer-centricity, including shared decision-making. Technological innovations, particularly machine learning again, will be able to assess frustration, pleasure, anxiety, safety, and other emotional elements such as depression with increasing reliability. Wellbeing will thus become a product or service to subscribe to, with different brands offering different methods and pathways. And again, at this point, we should refer to the first interjection that health may be the product, but not the person. Amid all these offers, the individual must not seek maximum relief or be seduced to do so, but merely supported on a self-determined path. If necessary, as in our current health care system, regulatory authorities must grant licenses to reputable providers or deny them to dubious ones.

---

[4] Frontiers Next Wellbeing, Milan, Italy, https://www.frontiersconferences.com/our-conferences/frontiers-next

[5] Sorenson S (2013) How Employee Engagement Drives Growth. Gallup Workplace, https://www.gallup.com/workplace/236927/employee-engagement-drives-growth.aspx

Beware Self-Optimization

On the user side, the strongest drivers of the Well-Tech movement will be the Millennials (Generation Y, born 1981–1996) and Centennials (Gen Z, iGen, born since 1997). They have always been confronted with a world that is completely different from that of previous generations. Technological advances have dramatically lowered the prices of some goods and created others that are entirely new. Consumer goods—especially technology—have steadily declined in price (you remember Moore's Law in Chap. 12). Necessities like housing and food, however, have risen in price, justified by rising wages, even though most of that income increase has gone to the already wealthy. At the same time, the cost of health care continues to rise, and depending on the system, it is either borne by society's solidarity community or individually. Millennials perceive this as a threat, as their high stress levels and typically smaller support networks have led to more and more frequent health problems than previous generations. They are also more prone or at risk to self-optimization that is no longer meaningful, excessive, and especially not specifically focused on personally relevant health goals.[6] The goal is not to create an optimal, Instagram-ready one-size-fits-all human being, but to set only those health or well-being goals that are relevant based on one's risk profile. Moreover, the mental and physical reserves of millions of people from all walks of life seem to be depleted. At $200 billion a year in health care costs, the phenomenon of burnout is becoming too expensive to ignore. Burnout is the exact opposite of wellbeing, a state of emotional, physical, and mental exhaustion caused by excessive and prolonged stress. It occurs when one feels overwhelmed and emotionally drained, unable to cope with constant demands.

And as if burnout wasn't enough, mental health issues are skyrocketing among Millennials and Centennials. The access that technological innovation provides to all kinds of information and facts that are increasingly difficult for laypeople to evaluate for their level of truth has them scared, and in many cases, they have no idea how to deal with it.[7] British market and opinion

---

[6] Beaton C (2016) Never Good Enough: Why Millennials Are Obsessed With Self-Improvement. Forbes, https://www.forbes.com/sites/carolinebeaton/2016/02/25/never-good-enough-why-millennials-are-obsessed-with-self-improvement/; Petersen AH (2019) How Millennials Became The Burnout Generation. BuzzFeed, https://www.buzzfeednews.com/article/annehelenpetersen/millennials-burnout-generation-debt-work

[7] Hoffower H & Akhtar A (2019) Lonely, burned out, and depressed: The state of millennials' mental health in 2019. Business Insider, https://www.businessinsider.de/international/millennials-mental-health-burnout-lonely-depressed-money-stress-2/#if-youre-struggling-with-depression-get-help-14

research firm YouGov sees Millennials as the loneliest generation. Thirty per cent of Millennials say they always or often feel lonely, compared with 20 per cent of Generation X (the age group born around 1965 to 1975) and 15% of Boomers (those born between 1955 and 1969). Millennials were also more likely than others to report having no acquaintances, friends, close friends, or best friends. At the same time, this generation has internalized inclusion, sustainability, ethics, and safety, including emotional security, as high values, which in turn are necessary conditions for a strong pursuit of well-being. Thus, this generation is aware that there is a causal relationship between nutrition and health (physical and mental). Millennials are also willing to change their diet towards organic, sustainable food. On the flip side, this also leads to a fear of processed foods and a thirst for knowledge about food quality and processing transparency, which is difficult for laypeople to answer objectively through Google searches. The youngest generation also seems ill-prepared for the massive upcoming job restructuring, personal development and challenges, as they tend to expect solutions that are presented to them or that they can buy.

This is not meant to be an assessment; it is merely meant to realistically outline the tension between positive and negative factors in the high demand for solutions to improve wellbeing. Wellbeing—at least in the richer industrialized nations—is often achieved too much by "having" than by "being". Caution is warranted when new apps—which can be useful if used purposefully—supposedly balance this need, but ultimately also just lead to unthinking "having". Users are already paying hundreds of millions of dollars for digital Well-Tech and the more than 318,000 health-related apps. For example, there are apps for sleep, weight loss, anxiety, anger, depression, trauma care, breathing, meditation, and more. According to Google Trends, in 2019 there was a doubling of searches for virtual fitness solutions, breathing apps, wellness resorts, and healthy eating, and a tripling of searches for holistic healing.

Airbnb now offers Airbnb Animal Experiences, which responds to the growing demand for a solution to reduce anxiety and stress through contact with animals. Similarly, Pravassa or Good Escapes offer *Transformative Travels.* Apple increased its presence in the personal health and wellness space with new sensors for breath tracking and new health app features for menstrual cycle and environmental noise levels. Google acquired Fitbit for $2.1 billion. Talkspace and MoodPath are online therapy apps that use human speech to detect sleepiness, fatigue, and depression. Bayer invested in OneDrop, a behavioural recommendation company. Kaia Health is a smartphone-based app to manage chronic conditions like back pain and gives users real-time feedback on their exercise performance via their smartphone camera. Elovee focuses on providing solutions for seniors with dementia, their families, and caregivers. In addition, new start-ups are emerging almost daily to provide workplace wellness solutions such as dieting, fitness, mindfulness, mental health, heart disease and diabetes programmes, and a variety of family planning and financial security programmes. A big part of the mindfulness movement revolves around identifying the things in life that you can influence and limiting the challenges that come from the things you can't change. There will be no way around solutions that help us deal with adversity, preserve soul and body, improve our lives, and practice new habits that lead to greater balance, harmony, and social wellbeing. However, it will be extremely important that these are quality checked and not consumed indiscriminately but used specifically to suit one's "risk" profile. Good competent coaching will be essential here; otherwise there is a risk of a gigantic pseudo-scientific bubble from which nothing would be gained.

So, we now know the scientific basis of why our medicine is in crisis and how it will be integrated into a Well-Tech industry and a great need for wellbeing through Big Data, completely new definitions of disease, curing instead of treating and even better through prevention. Was that it? Are we at the end of Part II? No, not quite yet. How is the traditional health care system and its sectors changing within these changes?

A New Health System

It's impossible that the entire health universe will change, while the islands of "classical" hospitals and doctor's offices will remain unchanged. These will also have to adapt. It may well be the final mile of change since medicine is a very conservative profession with a high degree of self-value and persistence on the part of all those involved. Mind you, Systems Medicine suggests abolishing almost all organ-based disciplines, which will mean closing departments and retraining senior doctors. This will not go down easily. Therefore, this last mile is likely to be the hardest within each country to implement. It is where the most resistance can be expected. Without political guidance and decisions, it will not work, or take an extremely long time. It is obvious that the changes will come; when this will happen, depends on readers like You: how much You personally get involved with Big Data (some tips on this follow in Part 3) and how proactively You question the "offers" of the current health care system with all the information you have gained so far (and can continue to learn via my podcast with the same name as this book), and You demand changes.

While most of the Well-Tech market is ultimately business, hospitals and doctors' surgeries—at least as far as their financing by compulsory insurance and the solidarity community is concerned—have a public mandate within the framework of services of general interest. Certainly, the described wrong ways of profit maximization of the present "illness system" must be turned back, without creating new wrong ways of profit maximization of the new Well-Tech system. To avoid jumping from the frying pan into the fire, we all must agree on what are reasonable individual health claims and costs that should be borne by society, and from where on is a claim unjustified and should no longer be covered. This includes aspects such as: How close does a full-fledged hospital have to be to where I live? Am I allowed to go straight to the emergency room of a hospital if I think it is an emergency, or should someone check before? How often and how soon do I really need a doctor appointment? When do I need to see a GP; and when a specialist (as long as they still exist)? To what extent am I responsible for my own health and to what extent does the community have to finance the consequences of my health-related misconduct (keyword: lifestyle, anti-vaxxers)?

Before we set out to reform ourselves and our "disease system" into a "health care system", let's recap where we currently stand. Currently, the public health care system is a kind of market, which would never work in a free economy: Services of different quality and efficacy are reimbursed the same, as no one measures quality and efficacy. It's all about quantity, so preferably a lot is done and fast. Practically all health care providers receive false quantitative, but not qualitative incentives, which have ultimately been perverted to maximize profits and do not, or at least not always, exclusively serve the patient's well-being. But these misaligned incentives are again only symptoms of the actual and even more important cause, that in no country has there been a broad societal discussion and consensus among all citizens about how to define optimal and economically defensible patient wellbeing and how to set the incentives to achieve it. This is essential, however, if we are to implement innovation in medicine, since more precise, curative medicine has quality as its sole objective and this must be defined, and resources are, of course, limited. Avoiding pointless interventions from which the patient has no benefit naturally reduces the number and costs but cannot be the primary goal. The hypothesis is that early investment in targeted prevention will result in less treatment and illness costs later and still result in a better quality of life and healthy ageing.

In hospital care, the balance between basic care in the countryside and specialization in a few centres must be achieved. Hospital planning must be carried out according to uniform nationwide criteria that guarantee three levels of care in different densities: Primary, Specialty, and Maximum Care. Public hospitals must receive a lump-sum guarantee for their maintenance costs, on the one hand, and for their personnel costs, on the other hand, which are reimbursed according to need and performance, i.e. according to quality. This eliminates any incentive for hospitals to collect flat rates per case and maximize profits by cutting personnel costs. Reimbursement according to need means that operations currently performed unnecessarily due to misguided incentives will not be reimbursed, at least not by the health insurance and certainly not funds. Only a small fraction of patients in the emergency room must become inpatients (European average of 22–33 per cent). Denmark has carried out a hospital reform as proposed here. There, the interventional care of heart attack patients was reduced to only 21 hospitals for a population of six million, with the result that only 4% die compared to 8% in Germany with its many but not very experienced interventional cardiology units. A relative risk reduction of 50%, i.e. almost half the number of deaths. Denmark is thus in second place internationally in managing heart attacks, Germany in the lower twenties. Even small hospitals must be stopped from having cardiac catheter laboratories. This leads to fewer cases arriving at the large centres and to a drop in the quality of training because the doctors lack practice.

Administratively, all hospitals must undergo a massive, coordinated digitization push. With paperwork and paper forms medicine will not be able to benefit from Big Data and machine learning. This must begin at the point of admission, as with the check-in at an airport. The referring doctor or the patients at home should have already digitally uploaded all the necessary documents, filled out forms, and signed them. They can then go straight to their room. All important information is already available on the ward: previous medical history, medication, meals, and planned measures. With this data on all patients, all internal processes can be efficiently controlled: logistics, staffing, operating room schedules, and so on. The patient also knows when rounds and examinations are scheduled. Uniformly structured data make it possible to integrate machine learning and algorithms into hospital processes, enabling doctors and nurses to make optimal decisions quickly. External consultation with colleagues is also possible at any time. In the event of an emergency, the emergency doctor and ambulance are already digitally connected to the clinic before arrival. All vital data, blood group, and diagnosis are transmitted in real time, so that all important steps for further treatment are already prepared during transport. The operation plan is updated, and any resulting postponements of planned operations are visible in real time to all involved, including the patients concerned. Specialists are connected directly to the ambulance via video during the journey and are virtually at the side of their colleagues, who are usually more generalists than specialists.

When hospital care is planned on a larger scale, the focus should be on the wellbeing of the patients, not the hospitals. As a result, some hospitals will either close due to local overuse, be supported by specialists in private practice as general practitioners, or, as in the Netherlands, for example, be given an outpatient care mandate in the form of medical care centres with attached emergency outpatient departments, which makes more sense than a clinic with all-round care. Regional care and rehabilitation facilities should cooperate with both hospitals and local specialists.

However, most patients have their most frequent contacts with the current health care system not with hospitals, but in outpatient care provided by general practitioners and specialists in private practice. These must not continue to operate side by side, quasi in competition and with partly antagonistic goals, but must be integrated into a holistic, joint care concept. No sector (not even rehabilitation and nursing as a third sector) may systematically have advantages at the expense of another sector. Of course, the outpatient sector as well as rehabilitation and care need the same, technically compatible digitization push as hospitals. This is the only way to ensure that data transfer between all sectors functions smoothly and for the benefit of the patient. And only then can the power of Big Data be harnessed in these sectors too, not only for the benefit of the patient, but also to increase efficiency, so that doctors have time for more important things than filling out forms and channelling as many patients as possible through the practice per hour doing useless routine check-ups. Instead, physicians should be allowed to gain time to focus on those tasks where the most benefit can be achieved, i.e. in personal emphatic interaction with a patient, prevention through lifestyle counselling and risk factor reduction. However, the usual 5 or 7 min that Austrian or German doctors currently spend with patients are not enough for this. Also the 9 min in the UK are not much better. The USA is relatively good in this respect with 27 min per patient; Australia (15 min) and Canada (16 min) in the middle. China with an astonishing 2 min at the low end.[8] The so-called talking medicine cannot have any effect in so little time. Topics such as insufficient sleep, too much stress or lack of ability to avoid or deal

---

[8] Winnat C (2017) German doctors take around seven minutes per patient. Ärztezeitung, https://www.aerztezeitung.de/Wirtschaft/Deutsche-Aerzte-nehmen-sich-rund-sieben-Minuten-Zeit-pro-Patient-298572.html; Irving G et al. (2017) International variations in primary care physician consultation time: a systematic review of 67 countries. BMJ Open 7:e017902; https://doi.org/10.1136/bmjopen-2017-017902

with stress, too little physical fitness (endurance, musculature, and mobility), unhealthy diet (too many calories, too little vegetable, too much red meat, too much sugar), excessive alcohol consumption, and smoking can thus not be sufficiently addressed and treated. The question generally arises as to whether a doctor can cover all these aspects with a 5-year degree plus specialization. Nutritional sciences alone are a complete bachelor's degree programme. Probably a sports scientist (personal coach) or physiotherapist (in many countries also a Bachelor and Master) can better advise on topics such as endurance, musculature, and mobility more competently and individually than a doctor. Probably a psychologist can advise more competently, better, or just as well on topics such as stress management, stress avoidance, and sleep. And as for the clinic, sometimes a nurse or caregiver may know better what to do or advise. In general, with the introduction of machine learning and machine diagnosis systems, there will be a redefinition of the medical profession both in terms of function and training. The role of nursing will become more and more central and must become an academic subject of study in every country with corresponding status and payment. Many professions that we may currently consider to be outside of medicine will become just as important as a doctor for a true "health care system". You may still have a GP as your primary contact in the future, but after that they should have a team of peers behind them to coach you effectively, and you may not even come to the doctor after that, but the psychologist, personal coach, or nutritionist will take over. Doctors cannot possibly still be the sole knowers in the broad of a systemic, preventive medicine, nor should they be the sole decision-maker.

This means that, for reasons of both competence and quality, we will have to say goodbye to the small, romantic family doctor's practice and increasingly move towards medical care centres in which the disciplines just mentioned and other specialists and, of course, IT specialists all work together under one roof like a large team. Up to the size of a small town, such a medical care centre is no problem. In the countryside, however, there is already a shortage of doctors, and this will remain the case. Although more and more doctors are studying medicine, only a few young doctors and their families subsequently move to a place where there is no school and no cultural offerings. This distribution problem is not a problem of medicine, but a problem of sparsely populated unattractive areas. Consequently, it cannot be solved with higher fees. So completely new care concepts must be implemented. Nurses, for example, can take on simpler tasks such as follow-up checks or changing dressings. Mobile practices are being introduced instead of fixed practices. Then, for example, the doctor comes to the location once a week for a fixed appointment. Telemedicine is even more efficient. For those with statutory health insurance, the cost of this will be covered. Google wants to offer telemedicine all over the world and will work together with the largest telemedicine provider Amwell. While Amwell mainly offers video consultations via internet browser or app, Google wants to use machine learning algorithms to support admission, diagnosis, forwarding to the best-qualified service provider and automatic language translation services. Additionally, sophisticated data analytics tools will help with remote home health monitoring. The goal so far is to help poorly served seniors and patients with chronic conditions in new ways without compromising quality of care or user trust. In other words, wherever reforms are initiated in the current healthcare system, they must be based solely on whether they make sense and are of high quality. But how do you measure quality?

Quality Instead of Quantity

In most healthcare systems, nobody is seriously interested in transparent assessment and publication of quality and outcomes by different providers. They operate mainly in an input reimbursement manner, a closed system. However, when (a) doctors in the outpatient sector—for reasons of quality—will want to spend more than a few minutes with you in order to achieve prevention goals, when (b) nursing staff positions that have been rationalized away in hospitals, rehabilitation clinics, and nursing homes are re-established and paid more, when (c) new players focused on prevention rather than sick care will want to enter the system, then the current healthcare system will either collapse financially, or the share for health in the gross domestic product will have to be increased further probably to an unsustainable level. The example of the USA already shows, however, that simply putting more money into a health care system without reforming it does not improve results at all, on the contrary.

Instead, if quality and best patient-relevant outcomes shall be the main goal or measure, then the entire system must reorder itself around these parameters rather than the current volume-based structure. Only quality must be rewarded, not the input. Thus, in future competition between healthcare providers and concepts, only those who deliver the highest quality will prevail, and those who do not will be paid less or not at all. Quality measurement, however, requires transparency, and transparency means complete and ideally a priori openness. Openness, however, is one of the most unpopular words in the health care system, which currently makes it so susceptible to evidence-free service expansions for private liquidation. Our current health-care system requires an extremely expensive *post-hoc* control and regulatory effort on the part of the legislator, the Associations of Statutory Health Insurance Physicians, Medical Services, health insurance funds, etc.

But how do we want to measure quality in healthcare in the future? Certainly not with parameters like length of stay in the hospital, etc. Even though you are hopefully not in hospital longer than you must, simply the fastest possible discharge and a high number of cases cannot be a goal per se, certainly not for You. It would make instead much more sense to use so-called *patient-reported outcome measures* (PROMs) as a remuneration system. These are questionnaires that you fill out about your health and quality of life. The information collected from these PROMs helps to monitor your health progress, to facilitate communication between professionals and you, and to measure and, if necessary, improve the quality of health care services. Furthermore, quality of care can be measured by recurrence rates (describe the frequency of recurrence of a condition after temporarily successful treatment), complication rates, and mortality from surgery. It must become obvious in medical practice if doctors prescribe outdated or suboptimal drugs, or if their treatment methods have shortcomings. If a doctor disproportionately performs certain diagnoses or imaging procedures—because he or she has purchased expensive imaging equipment, for example—it must become obvious. Of course, this requires data, and this needs to be nationwide or, better, uniform across different countries, so that national phenomena (such as the disproportionately frequent surgeries in Germany or poor healthcare for minorities in the USA) can also be easily identified. The digital platform needed for this is your personal so-called digital patient file, a lifelong bundling of all diagnoses and therapies. For a long time cloud-based solutions were favoured for this. However, for reasons of data security a decentralized storage under your exclusive control or that of your doctor or hospital, respectively, may make more sense and generate more trust. This way, you can always control what health data you share and with whom. Via blockchain technology, data sharing could also retroactively be revoked at any time. Right now, national governments, almost every health insurance company on its own, and private providers are building their individual—and probably incompatible with each other—digital patient records in a completely unco-ordinated way. Without the fastest possible introduction of binding, uniform standards that still leave room for flexibility and individual offerings, such an approach obviously makes no sense at all. Thus, Apple and Google with their Health and Fit apps, respectively (plus their additional research apps), are years ahead of these first national digital walking attempts. Cooperation would therefore make much more sense, as we should ultimately be aiming for international harmonized solutions, but not necessarily in the hands of global companies.

The next step then is, once the quality of treatment is known and possibly insufficient, to ask how can it be improved? Where is the new incentive? The remuneration of physicians and clinics should be therefore results-oriented. *Pay for Performance* (P4P) pursues the goal of linking physician remuneration closely to the achievement of qualitatively or quantitatively measurable goals. However, this requires not only complete transparency but also scientific analysis with valid data and methods, presumably AI-supported. If health insurance companies paid better for better services, e.g. because there were fewer follow-up costs after a surgery (and not the surgery itself), hospital administrations would have a quality incentive and would also be proud to publish their data. Other centres may no longer perform certain procedures if they continue to deliver lower quality outcomes, at least they would not get reimbursed for them. This would concentrate excellent resources, especially personnel, and use them thus more efficiently. And you as a patient?

You as a patient would be guided accordingly where to go, and where not. I strongly recommend that You inform yourself and no longer simply go to the nearest hospital or general practitioner, but to the one that has been proven to provide the best care and the best results. To do this, you should demand access to valid transparent data to enable you to make this decision. Such a *public reporting/public disclosure* system should publish all measured indicators and parameters that allow statements about performance and quality of, for example, a hospital or a doctor's office. By the way, every health insurance company, especially the big ones, could already produce such rankings. Publication can either be restricted to a limited group of addressees, for example, comparable facilities in a region, or it can take place without restriction via the Internet. And let us think even further: why should you—for an ultra-rare disease or a very complicated surgery—not be treated by a doctor in a neighbouring country via telemedicine if he or she is the absolute expert worldwide. Why should every country, small as it is, must have its own "expert" for every disease? Even for operations, it is now possible via robotics to have them performed by a doctor in another country.[9]

You see, we are now slowly entering practical applications of Part II of my book. I will provide you with even more hands-on tips. But, before we enter, let's also be realistic about some risks based on some very clever concerns of

---

[9] Kottasová I (2019) Doctor uses 5G to direct surgery live from a stage at Mobile World Congress. CNN Business, https://edition.cnn.com/2019/02/27/tech/5g-surgery-mobile-world-congress/index.html

two very clever persons, Yuval Noah Harari and Stephen Hawking. Is everything positive about this new medicine? Does artificial intelligence and gene editing also harbour dangers? Knowing about these will help to prevent abuse and increase overall acceptance.

19

Interjection 2: Superhumans

With all my euphoria about a new desirable epoch—or sixth wave—for medicine or better health, and before I give you some very concrete tips on how you can become part of the future right now, it is worth pausing for a moment and taking a bird's eye view, moving away from the details a little, gaining more of an overview. Maybe we will discover new or different things from up here and interpret what has been said, so far, a little differently.

Two core elements of the end of medicine as we know it are, firstly, the gigantic variety and depth of data that, thanks to machine learning, are not only becoming controllable but are leading to completely new insights into our bodies and our diseases and are being harnessed for new cures, and secondly, the ability to modify our genome with high precision in such a way that the most serious diseases disappear from our bodies almost miraculously. Two recent books spontaneously came to mind here: Yuval Noah Harari's book *Homo Deus*[1] and Stephen Hawking's last publication before his death, the essay collection *Short Answers to Big Questions*.[2]

What I like about Harari's book is already the title, because it provides a perfect reference to Hawking's essays. It even may have been a suitable alternative title for this essay. Harari is primarily concerned with the concept of "artificial intelligence". His specific fear is the end of humanism. This would be replaced by informatism, in which everything that happens in the world is seen as a flow of information. Harari, as a philosopher and non-expert, is fascinated by technology and believes it is limitless. Specifically, he fears that

---

[1] Harari YN (2020) Homo Deus. A history of tomorrow, 653 p., 12th edition, C. H. Beck, Munich
[2] Hawking S (2020) Short answers to big questions. 253 p., first edition, Klett-Cotta, Stuttgart

people act according to algorithms and ultimately become algorithms. But here I feel he seems have succumbed to the frequent misinterpretation of the word "artificial intelligence". As already explained in detail in Part 2 of my book, algorithms are just a set of mathematical instructions, even if they can be self-learning. They have no intelligence whatsoever. The same thing existed before, when nineteenth-century philosophers saw machines and those of the twentieth century saw computers as human substitutes. Harari believes that humans slavishly follow what algorithms and artificial intelligence tell them, thereby abandoning their human nature, i.e. humanism in general. The title of the book stems from his vision that there will be a few fabulously wealthy god-like humans (Homo Deus) who will develop and manipulate these algorithms, while the rest of us will have no jobs, no opportunities, or no purpose. Honestly, I don't think so. He's going too far on that one. There are and will be—unfortunately and probably unpreventably—super-rich people who barely pay taxes, but they won't rule us through algorithms. Algorithms are too unintelligent for that. But, *Homo Deus* fits perfectly with Stephen Hawking's fear, which to me highlights a real danger.

For Stephen Hawking, there is another threat to humanity besides climate change or a nuclear catastrophe—the emergence of "superhumans". They no longer evolve by Darwinian evolution, making us more intelligent and benign over thousands or millions of years, but by self-designed evolution beyond the elimination of disease, i.e. changing and improving our DNA and thus ourselves. And on that, I'm afraid I'd agree with Hawking. I've said before that I don't think germline gene therapy is unethical if it could prevent a serious disease from occurring in the children of someone with the disease. The risk, however, is that once serious, genetically defined diseases have been elucidated and eliminated (or at least kept in check), research—public and private—will turn to normal human traits, such as intelligence, strong physique, muscular strength, longevity, beauty, creativity, musicality, leadership, emotional intelligence, and so on. If these genes are known, then the temptation is great, especially for those who can afford it, to optimize themselves and their offspring gradually genetically into "superhumans". Every technology bears the danger of misuse, as Alfred Nobel, the inventor of dynamite, had to learn. There will be increasing problems between supermen with improved DNA and "ordinary" people. Superhumans will be so superior that ordinary people will eventually become extinct or irrelevant. And this is where the term Homo Deus fits very well, evolving independently from us who are all *Homo sapiens* into a new human race. You remember that we can all be traced back to a single woman in Africa. That is how resoundingly successful a few genetic changes can be.

There may even be a race between self-designing beings constantly improving themselves: Chinese versus Americans versus Russians. I am getting a little sad as I write this because it drags the brilliant scientific achievement of genetic scissors into the diabolical, virtually into the mud, and the risk is unfortunately undeniable. Perhaps that's how Julius Robert Oppenheimer, one of the fathers of the American atomic bomb, felt when he warned about the devastating technology after World War II and was similarly sceptical about building the hydrogen bomb. As a result, Oppenheimer was suspected of spying for the Soviet Union. And as we all know and experience: If this technology falls into the wrong hands of inhumane, dictatorial regimes, as in Iran or North Korea, it becomes a global risk. Stephen Hawking must have felt similarly with his warning, his final message to humanity. Hawking noted that attempts would be made to prevent such genetic manipulation through genetic engineering laws. However, it is just as likely that some people will not be able to resist the temptation to optimize themselves.

Part III

The Future Has Begun...

20

Self-Diagnosis

I don't want to end this book with a futuristic outlook into a wonderful new world of health, so that you can then put the book down—better prepared for what's coming, of course—but still just waiting for what may come. I would like You to:

Start today with the future,

with those innovations that you can already use and apply now. Let's start with a revolutionary way to diagnose yourself.

Through the Internet, many "inform" themselves about symptoms and possible diseases or best therapies. Two out of three patients inform themselves about health topics on the Internet before or after their visit to the doctor.[1] About the same number, 60%, also see themselves on an equal footing with their doctors, questioning and discussing medical findings and recommendations. But Dr. Google and his search engines don't really help us. The COVID-19 pandemic was the perfect example for this, where antivaxxers and those questioning that there is a virus or suspecting a world conspiration ended up in self-fulfilling bubbles. Using the same search terms, everyone will get different answers from "Dr. Google", and even if correct they only represent a fraction of all the information necessary for an educated decision. Maybe the first 100 search results are completely irrelevant to you, but the 101st would have been, but you'll miss it. So, such searches are more

---

[1] vitabook (2018) Dr. Google urges doctors and patients to work as a team, https://www.vitabook.de/presse/dr-google-fordert-aerzte-und-patienten-zur-teamarbeit-auf/

likely to contribute to uncertainty or misinformation. To get a reliable statement or the state of the art in science, one would have to, as in science, firstly, perform a so-called Systematic Review, a systematic search with elaborately defined and sophisticated search criteria, which ensure that no single piece of information is overlooked, and secondly, perform a so-called Meta-Analysis of all the data extracted from this. This is the only exact, but very time-consuming method to get useful results. The total number of results usually does not stop at number 100 but goes into thousands of entries. Then all the relevant search results must be evaluated, preferably quantitatively, because you can hardly give the same importance to a study on ten patients as to a similar study on 1000 patients. All this takes weeks to months if you want reliable results. You certainly don't want to do this work for yourself.

But if you don't do this, you will always get only random results, which will then be distorted by your personal expectations or preferences—or those that Google has determined for you. So, if Google knows that you are constantly searching for naturopathic topics, you will get naturopathic answers to your health searches. COVID-19 was the first exception when social media and Google provided you with evidence no matter what you searched before or seem to believe. But this was really the only case ever. Getting again and again naturopathic results will, of course, reinforce your impression that for your particular questions, the answer can only come from naturopathy. Someone else who exclusively researches registered drugs will get registered drug results for the same search question. Naturopathy was not a topic for them before and their research confirms this. Both can be wrong, because perhaps the optimal answer would have been a lifestyle change, but neither is really interested in that, so Google doesn't bother them. If you don't click, Google makes no money. Google knows, both the naturopath and the registered drug fan rather prefer the quick *fix*, the quick solution without much effort, either with "something natural" or a "real medicine", but no lifestyle change, please. Google already knows this about you and doesn't offer you the right solutions at all, because Google doesn't make its business by offering you right solutions, but by the fact that you click further, e.g. in the first case, on the advertisements for naturopathic remedies that appear on the right, left, above, or below, or, in the second case, on the advertisements of a mail-order pharmacy. With those clicks, Google has taken a few additional cents. Your health doesn't really interest Google, at least not their search engine. It's estimated that Google's health-related searches total about 70,000 per minute. But Google returns the wrong results two-thirds of the time.

If you want to read good meta-analyses, there is, conveniently, only one site you need to remember: Cochrane (cochrane.org), an international research network that creates the evidence base for health decisions through systematic reviews and meta-analysis. However, I don't think you want to do this work for every little question, and it may also be very likely that your current topic, "my left metacarpophalangeal joint suddenly hurts so much" or "I have such a stabbing pain in my right upper abdomen, could it be the appendix?" is not the content covered by international Cochrane reviews and meta-analyses. There you can get evidence-based information about the optimal therapy once your diagnosis is crystal clear. But how to get there, even yourself?

There is an option, and this is my tip #1, a tool that you can ask these exact questions about your thumb or abdominal pain and get a usable answer: Symptom checkers. These are chat-enabled machine algorithms that draw on internal symptom databases of varying sizes. Sooner or later, they will become every patient's first port of call to track down simpler conditions themselves and only see a doctor if they are likely to have more serious problems. In parallel, doctors will use similar diagnostic tools, since of all the approximately 20,000 diseases, a single doctor can only manage about 400 on their own, but what if a patient sits in front of them with one of the other 19,600 diseases? So, it's a mutual win-win situation: symptom checkers relieve doctors of trivia and offer you, the user, quick help without long and error-laden googling on the Internet. The best symptom checkers are now so sophisticated that I can recommend them as a part of eHealth for you to use them as of now. They are easy to use, either as an app or online website, and many are free. Since most don't require registration or sync your electronic health record that you may have, these symptom checkers don't have any medical history on you. So, you can interact anonymously, but they may need to ask in turn 30 or more questions to proceed carefully.

However, not all symptom checkers are equal. For example, an Australian study found that English-language symptom checkers are accurate only about one-third of the time.[2] Of 36 international smartphone- or web-based symptom checkers, the correct diagnosis was among the top symptom checker suggestions only 36% of the time, and among the top three 52% of the time. That means if you're not using the right app, you're still missing the right diagnosis half the time. The advice for seeking medical help for emergencies was appropriate in about 60% of cases, but not for non-emergencies. Here, the advice was correct only 30–40% of the time. In general, though, the symptom checker erred more toward the side of caution, which is reassuring in some ways, but can lead people to go to an emergency room or doctor

---

[2] Hill MG et al. (2020) The quality of diagnosis and triage advice provided by free online symptom checkers and apps in Australia. Med J Aust 212:514-519, https://doi.org/10.5694/mja2.50600

when they don't really need to. That said many of these symptom checkers are unreliable at best and can be dangerous at worst if not pointed to a doctor's visit when it is needed.

The Medical Futurist website also offers a quality check of English-language symptom checkers. The rating is based on a not entirely transparent point system, according to which Your.MD, Symptomate (symptomate.com), and Ada Health (ada.com) achieved 4 out of 5 points, but WebMD and Mayo Clinic only 3 and 2.5, respectively.[3] When two physicians independently processed 16 internal medicine case reports by entering the recorded symptoms into the Ada Health app and compared the app's diagnostic and differential results with the "gold standard" textbook, the average completion time per case was 4 min, during which an average of just over 30 questions were asked. In at least 13 cases, the correct diagnosis was among the options given, and in at least 11 cases it was the option favoured by the app. That's an 80% accuracy rate.[4] You must put these 20% in relation to doctor's diagnoses, which have a margin of error of at least 5%.[5] Difficulties arise when symptoms of two diseases are entered at the same time. However, unlike a textbook, Ada Health was able to list these possible additional diagnoses that should be clarified. In conclusion, it was confirmed that Ada Health has a high diagnostic accuracy qualitatively superior to unstructured "Googling" and provides relevant results for laypersons.

A third study compared several symptom checkers limited to ear, nose, and throat cases. In addition to Ada Health, Symptoma, FindZebra, Isabel, Mediktor, and Babylon were also tested. All symptom checkers had diagnostic accuracy rates within the previously determined range. One surprise was Symptoma, which had the correct diagnosis in the initial diagnosis 82% of the time and in the top three diagnostic suggestions 100% of the time and was a clear exception.[6] Symptoma (symptoma.com) thus reached a new level of quality—at least in this indication group—in terms of precision. Further studies need to validate these results of course in other indications as well.

---

[3] Editor (2019) Feeling sick? There's an app for that! - The Big Symptom Checker Review. Medical Futurist, https://medicalfuturist.com/the-big-symptom-checker-review/

[4] Kuhn S et al. (2018) Artificial intelligence for physicians and patients: "Googling" was yesterday. Dtsch Arztebl 115:A-1262, https://www.aerzteblatt.de/archiv/198854/Kuenstliche-Intelligenz-fuer-Aerzte-und-Patienten-Googeln-war-gestern; Pottgießer T & Ophoven S (2015) The 50 most important cases of internal medicine (third edition), Urban & Fischer, Munich.

[5] Singh H et al. (2014) The frequency of diagnostic errors in outpatient care: estimations from three large observational studies involving US adult populations. BMJ Qual Saf 23:727-731, https://doi.org/10.1016/S0140-6736(18)32819-8

[6] Nateqi J et al. (2019) From symptom to diagnosis - fitness for purpose of symptom checkers: update from an ENT perspective. HNO 67:334-342, https://doi.org/10.1007/s00106-019-0666-y

This makes Symptoma and Ada Health two of the top-rated symptom checkers. Both also provided highly accurate stand-alone solutions for the rapid differential diagnosis of COVID-19 in comparison with other infections as a special service, and the city of Vienna used this as an official chat bot.[7] Symptoma also analyses the spatial and temporal data of their symptom checker, which is equally available in many other languages, and correlates this data with the number of newly confirmed COVID-19 cases. Indeed, in many countries, the percentage of Symptoma users who were at high risk of SARS-CoV-2 infection according to the algorithm correlated with official infectivity, that is, in countries where a high proportion of the population was confirmed to be infected with SARS-CoV-2, the algorithm also predicted this for many users, more so than in other countries. For most countries, Symptoma's COVID-19 symptom checker had a predictive power of 5 days for new Corona hotspots, predestining the app to detect such hotspots early, making it another tool in the fight against this and future pandemics.[8] Not surprisingly, the Symptoma app, based on 14 years of research by doctors and data scientists, is the most used symptom checker worldwide, both by patients and doctors with millions of users and searches per month. Its founder, Dr. Jama Nateqi, was named "Austrian of the Year" in research. Symptoma cites one of its strengths as being the diagnosis of rare diseases that are often misdiagnosed or not recognized. The story of three-year-old Isac is such an example of a misdiagnosis. Isac suddenly began grunting and screaming for hours as if he were in pain. When he wasn't screaming, he would stare blankly into space. At the age of five, he became depressed and suicidal with horrible thoughts. Whenever the word "death" crossed his mind, he would bang his head full force against windows and walls to stop those thoughts. He could no longer go to the bathroom by himself because of the voices he heard in his head and the things he saw. His fears were extreme and debilitating. Over the course of 4 years, about a hundred doctor visits, and a multitude of misdiagnoses and mistreatments, his parents tried to come to terms with the idea that their son might never be normal again. Through luck and chance alone, his parents stumbled upon a crucial piece of information via the Symptoma app that no doctor could have so easily figured out for them: namely, that his

---

[7] Ada Health COVID-19 Screener https://ada.com/de/covid-19-screener/; Symptoma COVID-19 https://www.symptoma.de/de/info/covid-19#test

[8] Zobel M et al. (2020) Predicting Global Trends in COVID-19 Cases Via Online Symptom Checkers Self-Assessments Social Science Research Network, https://ssrn.com/abstract=3729913 or https://doi.org/10.2139/ssrn.3729913; Munsch N et al. (2020) Diagnostic Accuracy of Web-Based COVID-19 Symptom Checkers: Comparison Study. J Med Internet Res 22:e21299, https://doi.org/10.2196/21299; Martin A et al. (2020) An artificial intelligence-based first-line defense against COVID-19: digitally screening citizens for risks via a chatbot. Sci Rep 10:19012, https://doi.org/10.1038/s41598-020-75912-x

symptoms fit a condition called PANDAS (*Pediatric Autoimmune Neuropsychiatric Disorder Associated with* Streptococcal *Infections*), a rare autoimmune disorder associated with infection by streptococcal bacteria. The treatment was a simple antibiotic. The results were dramatic. His anxiety disappeared overnight, and he smiled for the first time in nearly 4 years. Within a few weeks, all other symptoms disappeared as well.

So, my tip #1 is to use Symptoma (symptoma.com) and/or Ada Health (ada.com) for occasional self-diagnosis and deciding whether you need to see a doctor or not. Your doctor uses algorithms like this too.

21

Self-Therapy

Most of our genetically defined disease risks will involve so many genes that it will be unrealistic to erase them from our body by gene therapy. They will thus remain a chronic risk or weakness. However, whether they materialize into symptoms will often be preventable by a lifestyle adapted to your personal risk profile. At least the severity of symptoms can be greatly reduced. And this is not your doctor's job or of any other healthcare provider, but eventually you can and should take charge of yourself. Once this is laid out to you in a precise and targeted manner, this will be more motivating than the current generic approach. Therefore, do not be fobbed off with general tips that are recommended to the entire population as a uniform healthy lifestyle. Much of it won't apply to you and will only distract you from focusing on what's important for you. However, if a human geneticist proves to you with hard facts that you personally have an extremely high genetic risk of developing, for example, Alzheimer's disease[1] and in particular that your sleeping problems[2] and lack of exercise[3] together with increased blood pressure[4] and

[1] National Institute of Aging (2019) Alzheimer's Disease Genetics Fact Sheet. Health Information, https://www.nia.nih.gov/health/alzheimers-disease-genetics-fact-sheet

[2] Brzecka A et al. (2018). Sleep Disorders Associated With Alzheimer's Disease: A Perspective. Frontiers in neuroscience 12:330, https://doi.org/10.3389/fnins.2018.00330

[3] Meng Q et al. (2020) Relationship Between Exercise and Alzheimer's Disease: A Narrative Literature Review. Frontiers in neuroscience 14:131, https://doi.org/10.3389/fnins.2020.00131

[4] Ding J et al. (2019) Antihypertensive medications and risk for incident dementia and Alzheimer's disease: a meta-analysis of individual participant data from prospective cohort studies. Lancet Neurology, pii:S1474–4422(19)30393-X, https://doi.org/10.1016/S1474-4422(19)30393-X

© The Author(s), under exclusive license to Springer Nature Switzerland AG 2022
H. H. H. W. Schmidt, *The end of medicine as we know it - and why your health has a future*,
https://doi.org/10.1007/978-3-030-95293-8_21

manifestation of your latent diabetes[5] will make you highly likely to develop dementia in 25 years, then this will trigger a tremendous motivation in you to change precisely these specific lifestyle parameters.

Unfortunately, this insight and impulse alone will not be enough. Lifestyle changes are lengthy re-learning processes. What we've been doing for 40 years, we don't just change in 2 weeks. And your lifestyle coach, personal trainer, psychologist, or nutritionist is not standing next to you every day and certainly not next to your bed, desk, or TV when it's time to wind-down for your essential sleeping needs. In this phase of translating insight and motivation into action, digital health apps will become essential therapeutic companions for you, companions for self-therapy. You will be treating yourself! Some of these apps will even be prescribed to you and paid by your health insurance, just like a drug or physiotherapy.

Even when we have the knowledge and conviction to change our behaviour, we often fail, or we do not always behave rationally. The problem is that we humans are not purely rational beings. We are precisely not just algorithms, as Harari is afraid of. Even a smoker who wants to quit smoking usually doesn't succeed. Everyone knows the importance of vaccinations, but in adulthood—when Mum and the paediatrician no longer take care of us—vaccination appointments are often missed. We and many others, the vast majority, have a positive attitude towards organ donation, but only just over 39% have an organ donor card. Or, as another example, prescribed medications are forgotten, not taken, or taken infrequently so that they don't work or at least not to their full potential. For doctors, coaches, and counsellors to encourage patients to take meaningful action, the findings of behavioural science are helpful. But why not learn directly from this ourselves?

In medicine as well as in public health care, it has been assumed that people make their decisions in an objective, rational manner, and that they only need facts to decide in favour of them. However, this was disproved decades ago by decision psychology. We make most decisions automatically and subconsciously or by rules of thumb. The psychologist Daniel Hahnemann identified two types of thinking: fast, instinctive, and emotional thinking (System 1) and slow, reasoned, and logical thinking (System 2).[6] System 2 quickly becomes lazy, overworked, and exhausted, and then promotes unrealistic

---

[5] Vieira MN et al. (2018) Connecting Alzheimer's disease to diabetes: underlying mechanisms and potential therapeutic targets. Neuropharmacology 136:160–171, https://doi.org/10.1016/j.neuropharm.2017.11.014; Rosales-Corral S et al. (2015) Diabetes and Alzheimer's disease, two overlapping pathologies with the same background: oxidative stress. Oxidative Medicine and Cellular Longevity 985,845, https://doi.org/10.1155/2015/985845

[6] Kahneman D (2012) Fast thinking, slow thinking. Siedler Verlag, Munich, ISBN 978–3–88,680-886-1

ways of thinking. It is very difficult for the brain to think statistically correctly from large, meaningful sets of numbers. So it prefers to simplify to single observations and generalize. Thus, based on incomplete or incorrect information, the brain can quickly jump to conclusions, also called the halo effect: "What I see is all there is". Questions that are difficult to answer are often simplified by rules of thumb (heuristics). We all met examples of this during the COVID-19 crisis, when the existence of the virus, the risk of being infected, and the usefulness of masks and vaccination were denied based on single observations or even without facts. Even if these were extreme cases, let's not trick ourselves into complacency and ignoring the facts about our true lifestyle status. Dear reader, from my own experience I know that adherence to lifestyle changes or a long-term therapy is difficult. We haven't done something for a long time, or we've never done it before, and now suddenly, it's supposed to become a habit? To master this, let yourself be tricked by so-called nudging.

Nudging

A well-intentioned nudge to behave sensibly can be just enough to do the right and important thing. Personally, for example, I am lucky that my wife reminds me every Sunday and reminds me again and again to go jogging and to stretch afterwards—which I hate. Twice a week it's time for the gym in the evening. I don't always feel like it either, but then I go anyway. And all this, although I really should know and have written in dozens of places here in the book that there is virtually no risk of illness for which fitness would not be an advantage. For a long time, I had a worsening sleep problem: going to bed late, waking up in the night, sleeping badly, feeling tired in the morning, getting tired during the day but not getting tired in time in the evening, and I experimented a bit with melatonin pills from a drug store. Melatonin regulates the day-night cycle. That didn't help. All of this went so far that I then attributed a disease to myself, namely, that I had too long a biorhythm and simply couldn't cope with the 24-hour rhythm on planet Earth and that nothing could be done about it except to live on another planet with a 28-hour day. Then I came across a study about an online therapy for sleep disorders, but more about that in a moment.

Lifestyle interventions preferentially target System 1 thinking. Commercial advertising does this perfectly and could be a model. Advertising for a car is hardly about Your System 2 or any of the specs of the car. It's all about you and your family on a weekend trip, or you and someone attractive and fun to be with sitting next to you while cruising in a new cabrio… Why don't health ministers run elaborate and well-done advertising campaigns aimed at promoting health? In fact, national communications on the COVID-19 pandemic were negative examples of how it shouldn't be done. It was all about facts and fear. Not what System 1 likes. The magic word, instead, is motivational nudging.[7] Information needs to be conveyed in a simple and understandable way, especially not just in words, but through visualization and repeatedly graphical representation of—if need be—numerical facts. I have tried to implement a bit of this through the very simple (but hopefully clear) graphs in this book. These are meant to stick in the mind, as a picture is often worth a thousand words. Good examples are typical billboard or newspaper ads. Incentives like payback cards or gamification make health notices more appealing. Overweight patients can use an app to find a "buddy" with whom they each agree on a goal and must donate something if one doesn't meet the goal, for example. As for exercise, yes there are pedometers, or your smartphone registers your steps and shares them with you, praising you for what you have achieved and trying to encourage you to keep it up. An app that reminds you of health screening and vaccination appointments ideally engages in nudging. A company doctor could give out small rewards such as meal vouchers for SMART goals achieved. Ideally, your goals should always be SMART, i.e.:

- Specific – Not general goals such as "I do more for my fitness", but "I jog every Sunday, and afterwards stretch" or "I build my muscles twice a week".
- Measurable – When losing weight, commit to an exact number of kilograms, or when doing interval fasting, define how long it shall be, every day.
- Achievable – Is it realistic, otherwise it is better to go initially for a little less, but then achieve it.
- Relevant – Think carefully about what would really motivate you: an abstract number of kilograms on your scale while losing weight, or fitting back into your old jeans or leather jacket—for your System 1, something emotional is better than something rational.
- Timed – Set a deadline, not sometime this year or as soon as possible, but set a date by which you want to have achieved the goal, ideally the date should not be arbitrary, but make really sense, e.g. getting your beach body back by June (or by December for my Australian readers).

---

[7] #nudge2021 online conference, https://www.laeuft.eu/konferenz-nudging-und-gesundheit/

And: Celebrate your successes! Both with nudging and celebrating, health apps become increasingly popular and useful so that some of them are already prescribed by doctors and covered by health insurances.

Apps on Prescription

If health apps are prescribed and paid for by health insurance, nearly 60% of all insured persons would use them. However, only 6% would pay for a medical app themselves. In 2020, the German Digital Health Care Act gave doctors for the first time official permission to prescribe apps to patients. Surprisingly, this made Germany—otherwise a digitalization snail—the first country to allow this. Each app must be reviewed by the Federal Institute for Drugs and Medical Devices and approved as a digital health app (diga.bfarm.de). After inclusion in the German directory, prices are then negotiated with health insurance companies and vary from 117 euros for a tinnitus app to 476 euros for a therapy programme against anxiety disorders. In the USA, The Food and Drug Administration (FDA)'s Center for Devices and Radiological Health (CDRH) has established the Digital Health Center of Excellence which seeks to empower digital health stakeholders to advance health care. Different laws can in principle apply, FDA, Federal Trade Commission (FTC), or Office of Civil Rights (OCR). In Australia, healthdirect, a government-funded service, provides advice on quality and health-related evidence.[8] Novartis Pharma and Sandoz Germany have been awarding the Digital Health Prize since 2018,[9] e.g. to the Neolexon app, which helps people regain their speech after brain damage, such as a stroke, and the OPEN Project controlling insulin supply of patients with type 1 diabetes almost autonomously via an artificial pancreas.[10]

I can even contribute a personal experience on software-based self-therapy of sleeping problems. Sleep disorders are quite common (women being affected twice as often as men) and have both relevant short-term and long-term health consequences.[11] In the short term, they cause decreased stress

---

[8] FDA, https://www.fda.gov/medical-devices/digital-health-center-excellence/what-digital-health; healthdirect, https://www.healthdirect.gov.au/health-and-wellbeing-apps

[9] https://www.novartis.de/aktuelles/digitaler-gesundheitspreis/rueckblick

[10] O'Donnell S et al. (2019) Evidence on User-Led Innovation in Diabetes Technology (The OPEN Project): protocol for a mixed methods study. JMIR Research Protocols 8:e15368, https://doi.org/10.2196/15368

[11] Medic G et al. (2017) Short- and long-term health consequences of sleep disruption. Nature and science of sleep 9:151–161, https://doi.org/10.2147/NSS.S134864

tolerance, pain, decreased quality of life, memory and performance deficits, and increased risk behaviours; in the long term, hypertension, dyslipidaemia, cardiovascular disease, weight problems, type 2 diabetes mellitus, colon cancer, and, in men, increased mortality. Common causes of sleep disorders are, for example, poorly processed stress, alcohol (although you may fall asleep more quickly, you sleep more restlessly and wake up at night due to alcohol breakdown products), drugs for depression and Parkinson's disease, pain, nocturnal urge to urinate or hot flushes, nocturnal breathing pauses (sleep apnoea), shift work, light or the wrong room temperature, intensive sport shortly before bedtime or blue light, for example, from computer screens or smartphones.

In turn, many of these causes can be avoided or treated: Only going to bed when you are tired, ideally fixed bedtime and rising times (also on weekends), finding out your maximum and necessary sleep duration, a maximum of 18 °C in the bedroom, avoiding light (possibly through sleep glasses), no coffee or tea 6 h before sleep, no alcohol 4 h before bedtime, and at least 2 h before sleep a "wind-down" phase in which only quiet, relaxing activities such as reading or going for a walk are done, but no more sitting at the computer or mobile phone and better no more television. Develop a bedtime routine that indirectly signals to the body that sleep is about to come. In addition to brushing your teeth, this includes writing down unfinished tasks on a piece of paper and planning for the next day so that these things don't occur to you during the night. If you ever lie awake for 2 or 3 min, don't make a problem out of it. You'll go back to sleep. Everybody wakes up in the night. But if you lie awake for 15 min or more, you should get up, go to a quiet place and do something relaxing like reading until you get tired again by yourself. Under no circumstances should you toss and turn in bed for more than 15 min; otherwise you will lose the unconscious so-called bed-sleep coupling. What this means is that if you do too many other activities in bed (reading, watching TV, eating breakfast, lying awake for a long time, and so on), your body will lose the subconscious go-to-sleep impulse. In addition, relaxation techniques such as Jacobsen progressive muscle relaxation can be useful, but not permanent sleeping pills. All this is summarized under the term "sleep hygiene", which does not mean taking a shower before going to bed but following these fixed rituals and rules that promote your sleep. This involves discipline. Whether naps during the day are good is not clearly studied. Personally, I'm not a fan of them. The day is for being awake. If you get tired during the day, it's a sign that your night sleep wasn't restful enough. The fact that you feel better after a nap doesn't say that's a desirable scenario. For example, if you can only climb two flights of stairs without taking a break, and you feel better after the break, you'd be more likely to see that as a worrisome phenomenon. It's the same with napping. Frequent habitual power napping is associated with several negative sequelae, including increased risk of hypertension, depression, diabetes, osteoporosis, increased mortality, and mental decline, not only in older adults but also in middle age and young adults.[12]

Before you treat your sleep disorder, analysis comes first. You can do so with apps like Sleep Cycle, which I have had good experiences with myself and use daily.[13] In addition to the alarm function, the app records my nightly sleep cycles (see Fig. 21.1). In addition, I can enter how my day was, what I ate and drank or otherwise did before sleeping. Over time, the app's algorithm individually calculates from these entries which factors promote my sleep and which hinder it. In my case, for example, there was a very clear dependency on the phases of the moon, which of course I didn't want to believe until I remembered that a full moon actually brings a little more light into the bedroom. Since my sleep is obviously very sensitive to light, I bought a comfortable sleeping mask and the "moon dependency" was gone, as was my poorer sleep in high summer when the sun rises early.

Most importantly, record your sleep cycles each night. An average sleep-wake cycle includes five sleep phases: Phases 1–2 are light sleep, 3–4 are deep sleep, and the fifth phase is *Rapid Eye Movement* (REM) sleep. In light sleep, you drift in and out of sleep. Your eyes move slowly, your muscle activity is low, and you are easily awakened. In deep sleep, your brain waves change to almost exclusively slow delta waves. In the fifth stage, REM sleep, your eyes are closed but move quickly from side to side due to the renewed intense brain and dream activity. Sleep Cycle uses your smartphone's built-in microphone via sound analysis—which filters out talking and snoring—and the built-in accelerometer to analyse your movements during sleep and detect sleep states.

But all these are just observations. They are not enough to treat persistent sleep disorders. This can be achieved with apps. Within a course of several weeks based on cognitive behavioural therapy, the sleep characteristics of

---

[12] Bursztyn M et al. (1999) The siesta in the elderly: risk factor for mortality? Arch Intern Med 159:1582–6; Cross N et al. (2015) Napping in older people 'at risk' of dementia: relationships with depression, cognition, medical burden and sleep quality. J Sleep Res 24:494–502; Chen G et al. (2015) Afternoon nap and nighttime sleep with risk of micro- and macrovascular disease in middle-aged and elderly population. Int J Cardiol. 187:553–5; Cao Z et al. (2014) The effects of midday nap duration on the risk of hypertension in a middle-aged and elderly Chinese population: a preliminary evidence from the Tongji-Dongfeng Cohort Study, China. J Hypertens. 32:1993–8; Mantua J & Spencer RM (2015) The interactive effects of nocturnal sleep and daytime naps in relation to serum C-reactive protein. Sleep Med. 16:1213–6.

[13] Sleep Cycle App, iTunes: https://itunes.apple.com/de/app/sleep-cycle-alarm-clock/id320606217?mt=8, Android https://play.google.com/store/apps/details?id=com.northcube.sleepcycle&hl=en

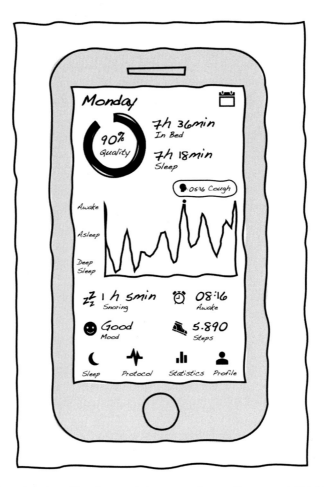

Fig. 21.1 Functional profile of a smartphone app for continuous monitoring and evaluation of one's own sleep cycles and sleep quality

patients with chronic sleep disorders are sustainably improved.[14] Sleepio has been validated on 3755 patients (www.sleepio.com). In the process, patients learn techniques such as sleep restriction (regular sleep schedules are

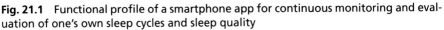

[14] Freeman D et al. (2017) The effects of improving sleep on mental health (OASIS): a randomised controlled trial with mediation analysis. Lancet Psychiatry 4:749–758, https://doi.org/10.1016/S2215-0366(17)30328-0; Espie C et al. (2012) A randomized, placebo-controlled trial of online cognitive behavioral therapy for chronic insomnia disorder delivered via an automated media-rich web application. Sleep 35:769–781, https://doi.org/10.5665/sleep.1872; Luik A et al. (2017) Treating depression and anxiety with digital cognitive behavioural therapy for insomnia: a real world NHS evaluation using standardized outcome measures. Behav Cogn Psychother 45:91–96, https://doi.org/10.1017/S1352465816000369

established that must be adhered to) and stimulus control (avoid sleep-preventing activities such as smartphone use in the bedroom and learn sleep-promoting ones that have been shown to increase sleep quality). The human therapist is replaced by a machine algorithm that effectively simulates a therapist. Before the consultation begins, the patient answers questions about his or her sleep behaviour and begins to analyse it (e.g. with Sleep Cycle). This information and the data from the sleep diary then form the basis for an in-depth analysis and individual consultation, during which the various problems are worked through. In addition to my light sensitivity, I thereby ironed out some bad habits, i.e. irregular sleep and awake times, no wind-down in the evening, late-night alcohol and food, and in the beginning lying awake in bed for more than 15 min. Now my sleep is perfect 9 out 10 nights and I feel much more refreshed.

These are just a few examples of how you can nudge yourself towards a healthier lifestyle that suits you, using validated and simple methods that can even be a bit fun and quite entertaining. Give it a try but educate yourself on which apps are truly science- and evidence-based. You can assume so for pre-scription and Digital Health Award winners. Also, feel free to listen in on my podcast. I'll be featuring validated new apps there every now and then.

So, my tip #2 for you for now: Use Sleep Cycle to monitor your sleep and Sleepio to correct less than optimal sleep. If you're 40 now, when you're 65, you'll thank yourself.

22

Your Digital Twin

Go digital! Create your digital twin! Have your genome sequenced now, determine your microbiome (or its metabolites), and use an electronic health record. The term electronic "health" record is more attractive and important than the more commonly used term electronic "patient" record. The latter suggests that this tool only becomes relevant to you when you are sick, i.e. become a patient. This does not do justice to the much greater potential of digitalization in the prevention and avoidance of illness. Electronic health record expresses this goal much better and collects much more data than when you are sick. Ideally, it integrates your genome, microbiome, exposome data, and so on, i.e. it generates a digital alter ego of you, your digital twin. Only when your health risk and status is digital will you be able to benefit from the Big Data revolution in medicine. Algorithms will not be able to analyse dispersed paper files. Algorithms need numeric data to work with. What you need to be able to stay in charge, however, is who can access your data and for what purpose. To enable you to decide who has access to your individual documents and who does not, there will be a rights management system. Blockchain technology would be ideal, as it allows access rights to be revoked at any time—even after the data has been downloaded.

Therefore, the next question that arises is, of course, where to store your health data: centralized on a government or provider server, or remotely wherever the data were generated in the first place, i.e. on your doctor's PC, in the hospital system, or on your smartphone. Centralized storage has the problem that if there is a successful hacking attack, all the data is lost or stolen. With decentralized storage, each part of the network only has a subset of your data. An attacker has no obvious target to focus on when searching for your data and, if they have accidentally found some, where to search for the rest. However, this solution is not completely risk-free either. In the case of decentralized storage, people who are not professionally trained in data security are responsible for storing data and maintaining the software. In addition, in an emergency, the medical staff must be able to access your data quickly, wherever it is, e.g. about any life-threatening allergies and pre-existing conditions. The ideal case is probably a hybrid between the two, some essentials centralized and others decentralized.

In addition to networking of data and service providers in the health care system, one goal referring to you is to encourage you, dear reader, to start dealing with your health data yourself in a sovereign manner. In this way, you are involved and do not passively consume health services but take care of your health at a new level. To maximize usability, electronic patient records should be uniform between different healthcare providers and insurance companies and clear in terms of content. Typically, they are divided into individual so-called medical information objects. Examples of these documents are an electronic medication plan, an emergency data record, the dental status booklet, the *International Patient Summary*—an English-language patient summary (even in non-English-speaking countries) that can be used internationally—nursing documents, hospital discharge letters, laboratory findings, and an electronic vaccination certificate. Through the latter unnecessary repeat vaccinations, such as tetanus, may be prevented in situations where the patient does not remember whether they have been vaccinated. One major advantage of an electronic patient record for every patient will be an improvement in drug safety.

Drug Safety

Currently, personal drug safety is in most countries non-existent due to a lack of transparency and networking between the various sectors of the healthcare system. This particularly affects patients who take four or more medications at the same time. With such polypharmacy, drug-drug interactions and drug-related side effects are increasingly likely. This affects about 40% of those over 80 years of age and one-third of those between 65 and 79 years of age. Seventy-one per cent of patients lack a QR coded medication plan; 17% do not have even a list of their medications; half of the patients have at least a medication plan, albeit without a QR code. However, most medication plans are usually incomplete because the patients were previously treated by several doctors. The loss of information between the outpatient and inpatient sectors jeopardizes patient safety. The fault does not necessarily lie with the individual doctors, but in the system. In most countries, the supply of medicines is poorly organized, non-transparent, and not digital enough. Every second patient admitted to hospital is an emergency. Here the information situation is even worse than for planned hospital admissions. When patients are discharged from hospital and transferred to the outpatient sector, the information breakdown is repeated. More than 40% of hospital patients receive at least one new drug during their treatment, but no new medication plan. Drugs that were only intended for short-term use often continue to be prescribed in this way. But there are also communication problems in long-term treatment by general practitioners and specialists. On top of that, the documentation of self-medication is often completely missing, but may be the source of serious drug-drug interactions and side effects. A first step is of course to move from the medication plan on a piece of paper to a digital medication plan in which the most competent body in the provision of medicines, the pharmacy, ideally plays the leading role. Moreover, the act of prescribing a medicine should become electronic (e-prescription) in every country to improve processes in the supply of medicines, avoid typing errors, or imprecise information.

With this, information on medication treatment can be voluntarily stored as an electronic medication plan—in short, e-medication plan—if you expressly wish this and consent to the storage. Doctors, dentists, psychotherapists, and pharmacists have access to the medication treatment and any allergies and can thus take into account possible drug interactions if you are prescribed new medicines, you buy over-the-counter medicines in the pharmacy (self-medication), the time of taking a medicine or the dose of a medicine changes, the taking of a medicine is suspended, side effects occur, or trade names of medicines change. However, it would also be important that medication plans can be viewed by you and are comprehensible to you as a patient and without any extra knowledge. Very few, mostly older, polymedication patients understand what they are taking for what or against what. Hence the Heidelberg Medication Plan has been developed[1] and is an excellent example, as it does not contain any abbreviations and explains the reason for the use of a drug, for example, the important difference between a long-term, basal asthma therapy and short-term acute asthma attack medication (see Fig. 22.1). Furthermore, the time of intake (before meals, after meals, at night) is

---

[1] Aktionsbündnis sicher Arzneimittelanwendung Rhein-Neckar-Kreis Heidelberg, Clinical Pharmacology of the University of Heidelberg, https://www.klinikum.uni-heidelberg.de/fileadmin/medizinische_klinik/Klinische_Pharmakologie/Downloads/MeinPlan_Medikationsplan.pdf

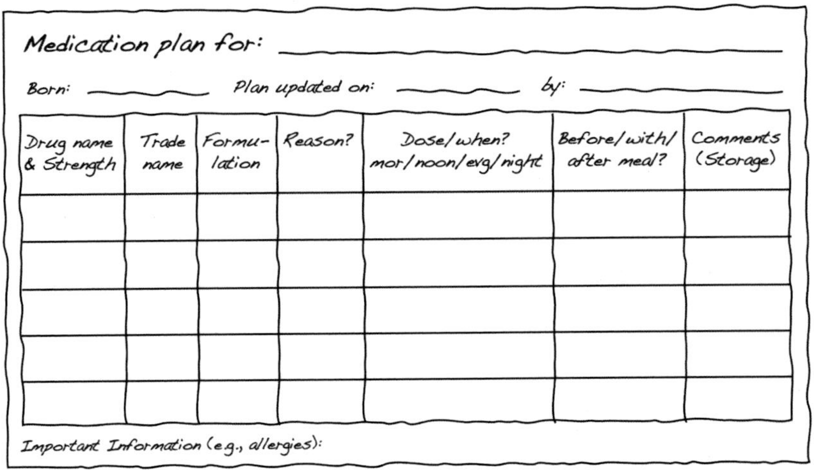

Drug name & Strength	Trade name	Formu- lation	Reason?	Dose/when? mor/noon/evg/night	Before/with/ after meal?	Comments (Storage)

Medication plan for: _____

Born: _____   Plan updated on: _____   by: _____

Important Information (e.g., allergies): _____

Fig. 22.1 Basic structure of the patient-oriented Heidelberg Medication Plan

explained, and there is space for instructions on use, such as not dividing the tablets, shaking the spray before use, and also how long eye drops, for example, can be kept after opening.

Since many medications can induce states of confusion and even drug-induced dementia, increase the risk of falls or prolong hospital treatment times, especially in older patients, and since there are practically no evidence-based guidelines for older patients, drug therapy must be individually monitored and adjusted by physicians and pharmacists. One ideal compendium for this is the *Fit fOR The Aged* (FORTA) list.[2] On the one hand, this list indicates those drugs that are unsuitable for older patients, as in a purely negative list, but it also names the drugs that have been proven to be useful, i.e. it is also a positive list. It uses four categories for this purpose: indispensable, beneficial, questionable, avoid. This allows even an elderly patient to critically question his or her therapy. The FORTA principle has been positively confirmed in several studies regarding usefulness and advantage for the patient. Its application leads to 20% fewer side effects, corresponding to a Number Needed to Treat (NNT) of five patients to prevent one adverse effect. The list can be viewed online, downloaded as a PDF, and there is also an app.

[2] Wehling M & Burkhardt H (2018) The FORTA list, https://www.medikamente-im-alter.de/medikamente-im-alter/forta-liste; Wehling M et al. (2016) VALFORTA: a randomised trial to validate the FORTA (Fit fOR The Aged) classification. Ageing 45:262–267, https://doi.org/10.1093/ageing/afv200; App: https://play.google.com/store/apps/details?id=de.sisdev.forta&hl=de

Patients like us

One element that is not taken sufficiently into account in eHealth is the networking of you with other patients having a similar condition or health-related question. You may be familiar with self-help groups networked locally or by a national organization for a particular disease. These are voluntary, mostly loose associations of people whose activities are aimed at jointly coping with an illness. Either they are affected themselves or as relatives. Their aim is to support each other, to exchange valuable tips and occasionally to raise awareness of their concerns among the public, thus bringing about socio-political action. The group helps to lift the external and internal isolation. Unlike other forms of civic engagement, the goals of self-help groups are directed primarily at their members rather than outsiders. Self-help groups are usually run by lay people rather than professionals, but with a stronger focus on the practical patient perspective than other sectors. Occasionally, national or local experts are consulted on specific issues. The common experiences of the members of a self-help group often cause them to have similar feelings, concerns, everyday problems, treatment decisions, or treatment side effects.

However, self-help groups also have risks or can have disadvantages. Effective groups generally depend very much on the moderator, who should help to avoid the conversations or written communication in online groups being dominated by complaints and negativity, confidentiality being broken, and inappropriate or not evidence-based medical advice being spread. Also, it is easy for local support groups, especially in small towns, to be too small, so that there is a lack of continuity or experience, whereas networking of many small local support groups could overcome this problem.

For this reason, online support groups have been created. The world's largest is PatientsLikeMe, which also markets itself as a data platform. It originally emerged from a self-help group for amyotrophic lateral sclerosis and now unites 830,000 people with over 2900 diseases. A special feature is that the data generated by the patients themselves are systematically collected and quantified, which has led to more than 100 publications in medical and scientific journals, but also to intensive cooperation with the pharmaceutical industry. PatientsLikeMe, for example, is now an investor-owned company that sells data with the argument that this should indirectly benefit patients in the long term by creating medicines and products that better meet their needs. The benefits of online groups include more frequent and flexible participation—when you have time, much like a social network. It may be the only option for people who don't have local support groups, and it offers a greater degree of privacy or anonymity, as well as access to more resources and information. For example, a patient in one city may have a crucial tip for a patient in another city 500 km/miles away. Normally, they would have never met. With an online patient network this may well happen. Experts are also more likely to join a single online group than dozens of small regional groups. The disadvantages or risks of online support groups include that communication is essentially written and therefore more likely to lead to misunderstanding or confusion. However, live chats would prevent this. Anonymity can lead to inappropriate or disrespectful comments or behaviour. Online communities can be particularly prone to misinformation or information overload. However, in my opinion, with good moderation, the advantages outweigh possible disadvantages of an online self-help group. Therefore, together with physician and pharmacist colleagues and patients, I founded the currently German-language platform PatientenWieWir (patientenwiewir.de), which connects patients in freely selectable groups throughout the German-speaking world, without ads and commercialization. We and other moderators suggest some topics that complement each other meaningfully in terms of content with other sources, e.g. books, blogs, and podcasts. We will expand this to many other languages in the same manner. Other countries may already have such not-for-profit networks.

Nevertheless, my tip #3 for you: Go digital! Take advantage of the many eHealth opportunities, connect, empower yourself! An individual decision to be made is whom to trust? As many countries will now ramp up their digital health momentum, it is important for governments and business leaders to satisfactorily and proactively address user-relevant privacy and security issues.[3] The "market" is still a bit confusing and not fully transparent. Apple and Google are years ahead with their services. However, the most convincing and reliable solutions will soon become apparent. And network as a patient, as another dimension, either locally or online, for example, in not-for-profit networks and organizations such as the German version, patientenwiewir.de, and their future native language spin-offs. Use a medication plan that you can understand and, as an older patient, adjust your medication according to the FORTA list, in consultation with your doctor and pharmacist, of course.

[3] Chakravorti B et al. (2021) How Digital Trust Varies Around the World. Harvard Business Reviews, https://hbr.org/2021/02/how-digital-trust-varies-around-the-world

Epilogue: Nobody is Sick Anymore

The year is 2036, and every parent can have their baby's DNA sequenced, informing about their offspring's potential risk of cancer, diabetes, or heart disease. Everyone may know what potentially harmful genetic mutations they carry, with free sequencing available through the health care system. 30 years ago, the World Wide Web had just been born, 15 years ago the first iPhone was released into stores. So, when thinking about medicine in 15–30 years, it only makes sense to think big and without boundaries. In 2052, you will be able to use a global well-tech infrastructure based on detailed, multifaceted data (genome, microbiome, exposome) from billions of people, collected over multiple life stages and going far beyond disease and health. Focused on the personal well-being of each user, this infrastructure consists of hybrid models of machine learning—including neural networks and yet-to-be-developed systems—and human empathy. Virtual and real coaches help you with your individual prevention and the optimal management of possible illnesses.

Let's visit Max from the prologue. The year is just 2037, and Max is doing fine. Twenty more years, then he will retire at 80. In 2023, he had his entire genome sequenced and his microbiome (or metabolites) determined early on when the technology became affordable although not yet covered by health insurance. As a result, he was found to have none of the known risk pathways for heart attack, but a small risk of stroke, which was dangerously amplified by his then-sluggish lifestyle of obesity and elevated blood pressure. Without further action, he was very likely to have suffered minor strokes or a major stroke by now, very likely to have suffered a second stroke thereafter, and equally likely to have suffered deficits in movement and speech thereafter. After all, when he was 40, stroke was still the third leading cause of death. Today he doesn't know anyone else who has had a stroke, and certainly no long-term consequences.

By the way, the health app on his phone not only collects all his medical data, but also measures how many steps he walks, how many floors he climbs, as well as blood pressure, pulse and blood sugar, sleep, oxygen saturation, heart rhythm, stress levels, and many environmental factors. Instead of a primary care physician, he is now seen by a health centre in his part of town; there are doctors of all disciplines, psychologists, physical therapists, pharmacists, nutritionists, and his personal trainer. He almost never goes there, though, "The team monitors my health through some AI around the clock", he is assured, "and I get a message, or a call should anything be wrong".

By the way, his risk of stroke was reduced to 0% by a highly effective drug that normalizes the causal, disturbed signal pathway for his elevated blood pressure. "I used to have to take several tablets throughout the day, but now only one a day printed for me in 3D with my name on and when to take it. I no longer get them from the pharmacy but print them out myself at home". His Well-Tech app controls with a little home test how much of the drug he should take and adjusts his daily dose at the printer accordingly. "When I run out of "ink" I get a new drug cartridge from the pharmacy, which is part of the health centre now and manages all of my medication and supplements".

Doctors are supported with all diagnoses and measures by computer algorithms. Pharmacists then select the optimal medication, if needed. On patientenwieich.de and other networks, Max and other patients, who have the same risk profile as he does, join self-help groups to exchange ideas, give tips, receive advice and sometimes a little motivation, if necessary; for example, to get enough exercise, or sometimes a delicious cooking recipe.

When Max's son was born, he naturally worried whether he was also at risk of stroke. But the health centre was able to reassure him. No risk. On the other hand, his son tends to develop asthma, but this has been prevented at an early age. Max is sure, "My son will never experience an asthma attack. Ten years ago, this probably would have happened. By the way, his life expectancy is 120 years".

It's crazy how much has changed. When Max is missing something, or otherwise the shoe pinches with a little something, he talks to his symptom checker on his smartphone. It asks and asks until the problem is circled, and Max can either help himself or is advised to go to the health centre, which gets a parallel message and, if urgent, will contact or call Max proactively. Actually, "No one" Max knows "is sick anymore". Max isn't either. "Even cancer is now detected extremely early". At the daily shower, for example, Max is scanned with an ultrasound which detects the smallest changes in his body over time and reports if something suspicious is detected. Treating cancer is like treating an infection. "No one dies from cancer anymore, only maximally with cancer". In his circle of acquaintances, he doesn't really know anyone who talks about his illness, not even the older ones. The term "chronically ill" no longer exists at all. "A few friends or their children probably had something serious once, but then they were gene-treated, and the risk was gone". Oops, here comes a message from his personal trainer", and Max must go, exercise time...

And I, dear reader, am also at the end—with this book. Thank you very much for following me this far. I hope I have been able to convince you that, although there is a huge need for change in medicine, on the other hand, the solutions are not just futuristic visions and the door to a completely new world of health and well-being and a much deeper understanding of our bodies has already been opened. All of this will be so efficient and thus cost-effective that it will be available to everyone in the world, which, of all the inequalities that exist today, will at least have eliminated the inequality in health.

So, let's do it! Let's demand change. Now!

Honesty first: Our medicine and biomedical research are by far not as successful as we doctors and scientists like to tell ourselves or as you as a patient would like to believe. I don't want to reproach anyone with this book, as I was amazed when I gradually gathered the many facts and recognized connections. But whoever still thinks after reading this book that we can continue as before, I'd accuse of ignorance. Therefore, at the end of my book, I would like to appeal to doctors, scientists, politicians and You, dear reader, with five changes that are particularly close to my heart:

- Medicine must abandon its single-organ structure of clinics and specialists and start thinking and acting systemic. Quality (healing and prevention) and not quantity (treatment) must become the essential incentive.
- Pharmaceutical companies must be judged on whether their therapies cure rather than chronically treat symptoms.
- Biomedical scientists must have the patient's well-being as their sole goal, not a perverted pursuit of printed paper in some supposedly ultimately important (high impact) journals, most of whose content is then not even reproducible. And because biomedical science is expensive, and biomedical scientists are inevitably guided by where research funding comes from, the

primary responsibility is on those who give out research funding. Please stop counting publications and impact factors, look solely at the patient benefit achieved by a research group.

- The blatant injustice that lack of education and social status, as well as male gender, reduces life expectancy by many years must become the major issues in biomedical research and health policy.
- You, the reader, please get involved with Big Data for the benefit of Your own health so that you can benefit from all the coming innovations Yourself as soon as possible. Start with the three tips from Part III of the book (use Symptoma and/or Ada Health for self-diagnosis; use Sleep Cycle and Sleepio to check and correct your sleep; go digital in the form of the electronic patient record). And: from now on, critically question everything that happens or is supposed to happen to you medically!

Here's to reading or listening again!
Stay healthy!

Appendix A: Special Page 1

Dear reader,

If you want to get to the bottom of your genetic risk profile or genome, I am pleased to announce that the following company has offered to readers of this book a discount code limited to the year 2022. It is important for me to mention that I have no personal benefit from this.

Heart Genetics

Coupon code: aks20

*The voucher includes a 20% discount on the Adding Knowledge Service (https://www.heartgenetics.com/product/addingknowledge/) and is redeemable until 31.12.2022. Cash payment is not possible. Only one voucher can be redeemed per order. The voucher is non-transferable and cannot be extended as it is a limited business discount. The voucher is valid for orders placed on www.dantelabs.com. Resale via online platforms such as amazon or ebay is excluded.

H. H. H. W. Schmidt, *The end of medicine as we know it - and why your health has a future*, https://doi.org/10.1007/978-3-030-95293-8

Appendix B: Special Page 2

Dear reader,

In such a dynamic field, about which you are now well informed, innovation does not stop, of course. After all, we are just at the beginning of the revolution. I would therefore be delighted if you would remain loyal readers and listeners until a new, completely revised edition is published:

Book website:
The End Of Medicine As We Know It
www.teomawki.online

Twitter handles:
The End Of Medicine As We Know It @teomawki
Harald Schmidt @hhhw_schmidt

Podcast:
The End Of Medicine As We Know It

YouTube channel:
The End Of Medicine As We Know It

Printed in the United States
by Baker & Taylor Publisher Services